THE INNOVATIVE UNIVERSITY

T0345241

THE INNOVATIVE UNIVERSITY

Edited by
Daniel P. Resnick and Dana S. Scott

Carnegie Mellon University Press
Pittsburgh 2004

Library of Congress Catalog Card Number 2003100704
ISBN 0–88748–376–3 Pbk.
Copyright © 2004 by Carnegie Mellon University
Book design and composition: Richard Foerster, York Beach, Maine
Printed and bound in the United States of America

10   9   8   7   6   5   4   3   2

ACKNOWLEDGMENTS

The editors would like to acknowledge the many colleagues and collaborators who made this volume possible. First, a word of thanks to our contributors, all members of the Carnegie Mellon faculty. Their essays were developed specifically for this book, in interaction with the editors. We enjoyed our conversations, an informal part of the ongoing seminar that faculty at a lively university carry on with one another. Only one chapter, drawn by Herbert Simon from his autobiography, *Models of My Life*, appeared elsewhere; we express our appreciation to The MIT Press for permission to include it here. Herb died before this volume could go to press, but he provided not only a chapter, but the focus on innovation and the title for this work.

Our second set of thanks goes to the leaders of this institution who have shown on countless occasions how much they appreciate faculty energy, initiative, staying power, and risk-taking—all key and pivotal for the university's future. Special thanks are due to Jared L. Cohon, eighth president of Carnegie Mellon, who initiated this project in conversations with leaders of the faculty, encouraged the editors to bring it to fruition, and provided the foreword.

Finally, we would like to thank those who might be less visible to our readers. First, Cynthia Lamb, Senior Editor of Carnegie Mellon University Press, for many hours of copy editing and almost endless patience; then Christina Koshzow, who at the same time that she was launching a new publishing venture with other Carnegie Mellon graduates, provided the cover and graphic interface for this volume, complete with author bios, photos, and selections for each of the chapters (click on htpp://innovativeuniversity.hss.cmu.edu); finally, three who played a critical role in bringing our chapters to print—Marcie Mastracci Hayhurst, who added her fine talents as reader and editor; Neema

< v >

Avashia, who contributed enormously to this university during her undergraduate years, and continued that practice by the assistance she provided to the editors; and Donna Konias, whose organizational talents and technical skills were well employed, from the outset of the project to its conclusion. If there are errors in execution, the editors assume responsibility; if this work pleases our readers, we are happy to share in that pleasure.

Daniel P. Resnick
Dana S. Scott

< vi >

Daniel P. Resnick is Professor of History Emeritus at Carnegie Mellon, and a winner of the Elliott Dunlap Smith Prize for Excellence in Teaching in the College of Humanities and Social Sciences. He is Special Assistant to the President for Academic Affairs. His research interests are post-revolutionary societies, literacy development in Europe and the United States, and the measurement of educational success. He has taught at Harvard University, Sarah Lawrence College, and Stanford University. He joined the Carnegie Mellon faculty in 1966.

Dana S. Scott is the Hillman University Professor of Computer Science, Philosophy, and Mathematical Logic at Carnegie Mellon. His philosophical interests are the foundations of logic, the philosophy of mathematics, and the semantical analysis of natural language. He has taught at the University of Chicago, the University of California, Berkeley, Stanford University, the University of Amsterdam, Princeton University, Oxford University, and the University of Linz, Austria. He joined the Carnegie Mellon faculty in 1981.

< vii >

Foreword

Jared L. Cohon
President, Carnegie Mellon University

Dr. Cohon earned a B.S. degree in civil engineering from the University of Pennsylvania, and M.S. and Ph.D. degrees in civil engineering from MIT. He began his teaching career at The Johns Hopkins University, where he was a faculty member in the Department of Geography and Environmental Engineering, eventually serving as Vice Provost for Research. In 1992, he became dean of the School of Forestry and Environmental Studies and professor of environmental systems analysis at Yale University. He assumed his duties as the eighth president of Carnegie Mellon University on July 1, 1997.

As a way of commemorating the centennial of this university, founded in 1900, the faculty at Carnegie Mellon, through its Senate, conceived the idea of a set of lectures about our history, culture, and collaborative style. The lectures were soon replaced by a project of chapter-length essays, designed to share our experience with colleagues at other universities, parents of college-age students, scholars who follow closely what is happening in higher education, and our own alumni.

The twenty-five faculty authors and co-authors who have contributed the twenty chapters in *The Innovative University* have worked at Carnegie Mellon for periods of time that range from

< ix >

five years to more than fifty—on average, for more than fifteen years. Although not all of our more than thirty disciplines have a place in this volume, every one of our seven colleges is represented. Readers will find that there are contributions in the fine arts and the sciences, the humanities and the social sciences, engineering and computer science, business, and public policy. The authors include department heads and former heads, university professors, division heads, directors of programs, winners of prizes for teaching, distinguished researchers—anchored all in different disciplines, but innovators in teaching, research, and real-world applications.

The stories that my colleagues tell in this volume offer insight into an unusual institution that stands out among its peers. It is a small research university, with only 5,000 undergraduate students and 4,000 graduate students. On a campus of one hundred ten acres, teaching and research are conducted in more than thirty different fields of the arts, the humanities, engineering, the sciences, social science, management, and public policy. Students and faculty in these areas are in daily contact with one another, pursuing interdisciplinary projects, re-defining fields of knowledge, pursuing their own visions of the possible, and contributing to the world around them.

Carnegie Mellon has combined its smallness and its diversity of programs and people with a collaborative and innovative culture to create a remarkable foundation for excellence. Other institutions look to us for ideas, best practices, and, in some measure, inspiration. Against other top-ranked major research universities that are older, better endowed, and larger, we compete successfully for faculty, students, research support, and philanthropy.

We are helped to excel by an unusual history, which I want to recount briefly, and a distinctive culture that is celebrated by our faculty and administration, memorialized by campus buildings and exhibits, and frequently referenced in our ceremonies and prizes. That culture is all about excellence and innovation, and bears the stamp of our founder, Andrew Carnegie. It is marked by a focus on real-world problems, collaboration across disciplines, hands-on effort, shared responsibility for students, high standards, thinking "outside the box," modest spending habits, and hard work.

Our history is as distinctive for a modern research university as our culture. We were founded as a set of technical schools and not as a center for either the liberal arts or scientific research.

< x >

It was on November 15, 1900 that Andrew Carnegie, the steel magnate and greatest philanthropist in American history, sent his now-famous letter to Pittsburgh mayor William J. Diehl. Carnegie indicated his intention to make available $1 million—the equivalent of about $20 million in today's dollars—to create a technical school if the city of Pittsburgh would make available sufficient land for the new school and its expansion.[1] Carnegie ended his letter by noting that starting a new school would be a great challenge but that "my heart is in the work"—a phrase that became a motto for the school.

And thus Carnegie Technical Schools was born. The circumstances of our birth and our early years are worth understanding, for the great university that we were to become had quite humble beginnings. Indeed, no temples of knowledge or bastions of research for Carnegie; he wanted a *technical institute*, a place where manual labor would be emphasized along with very practical educational topics. As indicated in his letter, he was inspired by the likes of Hannibal, who had been a blacksmith; Lincoln, who was a rail splitter; and Shakespeare, who had worked as a wool carder.

For our first dozen years, that's what we were: a trade school. Our current competitors were already more than 50 years old; some of them more than 200 years old. And they had started offering Ph.D. degrees 25 years before Carnegie took pen to hand. Of course, we've come a long way, but we value and have good reason to cherish this modest beginning. The commitment to addressing the needs of the world outside and the emphasis on making things, rather than just theorizing, remain distinctive characteristics of Carnegie Mellon today. Unlike other great research universities which have had to move from strength in liberal arts toward an appreciation for what the Greeks called *techne*—know-how in arts and crafts—we have moved instead from a firm grounding in the knowledge of how things work and hands-on building and design to a concern with theory, reflection, and ideas.

In 1912 we changed our name to the Carnegie Institute of Technology and received approval to grant bachelor's degrees. This was the first significant morphing of this institution, from trade school to an institute of technology, which over the next 55 years developed a strong reputation in engineering, the sciences, business, and remarkably in light of all the rest, the arts. Carnegie Tech refined the practical approach of its predecessor school and developed an emphasis on problem solving, analysis, and thinking that is a characteristic of our educational programs today.

< xi >

Under the leadership of our third president, Robert Doherty, the Carnegie Plan was created in the 1930s and implemented in the '40s. Doherty's vision was that engineers—engineering was the dominant program at Carnegie Tech at the time—must be educated in the humanities and social sciences, exposed to the arts, and trained in written and oral communication. This was a great innovation that put Carnegie Tech on the national stage for the first time—educationally, that is, as we were already well known for football. And, with natural evolution the Carnegie Plan is still with us today. We have extended it to apply to all students and to create new multidisciplinary majors and courses.

The next great change came in 1967, when Carnegie Tech merged with the Mellon Institute for Industrial Research to form Carnegie Mellon University. From that moment Carnegie Mellon's rise to the top ranks of national research universities has been nothing short of breathtaking. Today, the Mellon Institute is the home of the Mellon College of Science, a dynamic, cohesive academic community motivated by innovation and interdisciplinary collaboration. Andrew Mellon, the institute's benefactor, wanted the building to have a monumental Ionic colonnade that would embody an ageless simplicity for the practice of modern science. The site remains one of our city's landmarks.

The seeds of interdisciplinarity in the Carnegie Plan became something special in the 1970s and '80s under the brilliant leadership of our sixth president, Richard Cyert. He led the faculty in thinking strategically—choosing important problem areas and developing interdisciplinary research teams to solve them.[2] More than anything else, this style of research that derived maximum leverage from selected areas of excellence catapulted Carnegie Mellon to the top ranks of universities by the end of the 1980s. And, it was during this period and in this fashion that we created our strength in computer science, humanities and social sciences, and public policy and management, to complement our past and continuing excellence in the sciences, engineering, business, and the arts.

Carnegie Mellon now enjoys a reputation as one of the truly excellent and innovative research universities of the world. As such, it asks for recognition of the excellence of its faculty from established disciplines, but it also encourages its faculty to work across disciplines and in ways that challenge disciplinary knowledge. Faculty members of research universities are their heart and core, and they are expected to make contributions to the knowledge base and methods of the fields in which they were trained.

< xii >

Their disciplines support publication of their research in journals, offer them leadership roles in professional associations, and encourage their mentoring of younger entrants into the field. Their disciplines thus encourage them to play a conservative role; professional rewards are channeled to those who make incremental contributions to field knowledge, publish in the established journals of a field, and increase the prestige of a discipline.

Faculty here find themselves in a culture of innovation and interdisciplinary collaboration—in research *and* education. As researchers, they reformulate the questions posed by a discipline, pioneer research using novel methods, work with colleagues and students to change the boundaries of fields, conceive new applications, and redirect the work of others. Faculty routinely push outside existing disciplines and develop collaborations that did not exist before. When this happens successfully—and it does more often than not—multidisciplinary institutes and centers are created, external funding is found to support this work, tools and machines may be utilized for previously unimagined purposes, graduate students are trained in the new approaches, and different kinds of relationships with cultural institutions, industry, and government often follow. In this volume, you will see many examples of this kind of innovation at Carnegie Mellon.

Innovation can also occur in education, through curricular programs, teaching methods, course design, ways of assessing learning, use of technology, structuring of major and minor programs, and other ways of guiding students through their own learning. There are many examples of educational innovation in this volume, in engineering, drama, public policy, business, philosophy, and the wedding of humanities and the arts. No one carried this innovative bent further than our own Herb Simon, Carnegie Mellon faculty member for more than fifty years, and winner of a Nobel prize. The opening chapter of *The Innovative University* is from his autobiography, and it is the only chapter that was not written specifically for this volume. Herb, however, insisted on the title which this volume now bears, and his own contribution meshes well with those that follow.

Innovation is not easy, and pursuing it unavoidably encounters the tension between preserving knowledge and culture, and generating and sharing it in new ways. This book reveals the stress and joys of invention for our creative and generous faculty, as they navigate in both mapped channels and open seas. They are a tribute to the vision of Andrew Carnegie, and to the hard work and imagination of all who have worked in our laboratories, stu-

< xiii >

dios, libraries, and classrooms, performed on our stages, and exhibited in our galleries. These chapters tell a story, and in that story students appear as builders of bridges across programs and disciplines, collaborators on projects, challenges in the classroom, goads to invention, and achievers to celebrate.

Our students are full participants in our culture of making, showing, and performing. They freely acknowledge that they have been motivated and instructed by the example of their faculty. We, in turn, are very proud of this student body, and our internal publications and b-boards always celebrate the ways in which our young people show their excellence. The cover of this volume, which captures the exuberance of our students at Commencement, reminds us that no university, no matter how distinguished its faculty, can achieve and maintain eminence without the engagement of its student body. And working with faculty and students is a very devoted staff, supporting both in a very broad array of services.

Carnegie Mellon is a unique institution that has achieved success through innovation and interdisciplinary collaboration among its unusual mix of disciplines. I am very pleased that the faculty—the very people responsible for this success—have captured in this volume the essence of this great place. Carnegie Mellon is an important story in the history of American higher education, and this collection is important for helping to tell it.

Notes

[1] Andrew Carnegie, during his lifetime, would increase his contribution to more than $400 million in today's dollars to endow, design and build Carnegie Technical Schools, the mother institution of Carnegie Mellon. Henry Hornbostel, an architect trained in the Beaux Arts tradition, created the campus plan and designed the first buildings. Herb Simon, as his chapter in this volume indicates, admired the aesthetic vision and craftsmanship of this fine architect. See Edwin Fenton, *Carnegie Mellon 1900-2000: A Centennial History.* Pittsburgh: Carnegie Mellon Press, 2000.

[2] See George Keller, *Academic Strategy: The Management Revolution in American Higher Education,* Foreword by Richard M. Cyert (Baltimore: The Johns Hopkins University Press, 1983).

< xiv >

The Innovative University
Table of Contents

Anchoring

< xv >

OLD AND NEW FRONTIERS

ENVIRONMENT, DESIGN, AND PUBLIC POLICY

< xvi >

EXTENDING THE UNIVERSITY'S REACH

< xvii >

CONSTRUCTING A UNIVERSITY

Herbert Simon

Herb Simon (1916–2001), University Professor of Psychology, played a major role at Carnegie Mellon in the development of the Graduate School of Industrial Administration, the Department of Psychology, and the School of Computer Science. The thread of continuity through all his work was his interest in human decision-making, problem-solving processes, and social institutions. In 1978, Professor Simon won the Nobel Prize for Economics. He received his Ph.D. from the University of Chicago in 1943, and was on the faculty at Carnegie Mellon for 52 years, championing excellence and innovation.

In 1948, at Bill Cooper's invitation,[1] I visited Carnegie Institute of Technology to give a seminar for the economists. Pittsburgh had been for me, as for everyone, the Smoky City, the city where the streetlights had to burn at noon to pierce the sulfurous smog. I had seen Pittsburgh only from an overnight Pullman, which stopped there around midnight on my trips between Chicago and Washington.

Wakened by the shunting and switching of the cars, I would peer out the window of my berth as the train slowly maneuvered through the steepwalled valley of the Monongahela, the hillsides reflecting the lurid red glare of the open hearths, the coke ovens, and the blast furnaces of the great steel mills that lined the valley.

< 1 >

Intermittently, a Bessemer converter would send up a great flaming flare, turning the scene almost daylight-bright. With the smoke and flame, the blackness lit by the red fires, it was a preview of hell.

I had a curious first impression of the Carnegie campus, too. I arrived there by cab through a snow-covered Schenley Park on a bright winter morning, catching a glimpse of Henry Hornbostel's stately Palladian buildings, then sitting almost outdoors, it seemed, in Bill's many-windowed office, surrounded by snow-carpeted lawns. I lectured to the economists on disguised unemployment in agriculture in "backward" economies, a topic I had explored in the course of my studies of the economic effects of atomic energy. The economists detected a bit of a foreign accent, but were polite.

Pittsburgh was a far more pleasant city than my midnight experiences had led me to expect. I learned of the Pittsburgh Renaissance which was just then ridding the city of most of its major sources of smog and pollution: houses heated by coal (replaced by natural gas), steam locomotives (replaced by diesels), and Bessemer converters (replaced by open hearths). Technological changes had conspired at this time to make all of these polluters uneconomical, and civic action had introduced strong and successful regulations to clean the air. (Was invention—the new technology—the mother of necessity here?)

Sometime in 1948, soon after my first visit to Pittsburgh, the Carnegie Institute of Technology received a gift of $5 million in endowment and $1 million for a building for a new Graduate School of Industrial Administration (GSIA) that would provide business education for students with undergraduate degrees in science and engineering. The donor was William Larimer Mellon,[2] who had founded the Gulf Oil Company.

From his industrial experience, he had concluded that modern high-tech firms needed top executives who both were skilled in management and understood science and technology. The provost of Carnegie Tech, Elliott Dunlap Smith, had described to Mellon the newly revised undergraduate industrial management curriculum as a rough prototype for a program that would attain these goals. Mr. Mellon was impressed, and the gift followed.

At Bill's suggestion, I was asked to come to Carnegie again to discuss the plans for the new school with Provost Smith and Lee Bach, chairman of the Economics Department. An invitation to join the faculty as professor of administration and chairman of the Department of Industrial Management soon followed. I was

< 2 >

not eager to leave Illinois Tech, for I had confidence that with Don Smithburg and Victor Thompson we could build a strong public administration program there. We were also writing our textbook in public administration (published in 1950). I had sunk deep roots into IIT. I was finally convinced, however, that the financial resources of GSIA could launch, much sooner than at IIT, the program of empirical research in organization that seemed the logical sequel to Administrative Behavior. My visits to Pittsburgh showed me that it was a livable city, no dirtier than Chicago, perhaps cleaner.

Having made the decision, on a trip to Pittsburgh in April 1949, I took a long walk early one morning through much of the north part of Squirrel Hill. Just before this visit, I had drawn on a map of Pittsburgh a circle of one mile radius around the Carnegie Tech campus, for I was resolved to walk to work instead of commuting, and had checked the census tract data to discover which portions of this area were inhabited by college-educated, middle-class families. I looked in these portions for a house we could afford. In the last lap of my walk, I climbed the steep slope behind the campus to the Schenley Park Golf Course, and walked east a half-mile on a street called Northumberland. The houses were noticeably nicer than the house we had just bought in Chicago. From the corner of Northumberland and Inverness, I looked at the lawns and flowers a bit enviously, glad that I would soon be able to bring the children to a brighter and greener neighborhood.

That was more than forty years ago. We still live in the house on Northumberland Street that we bought in the summer of 1949, just a mile from the Carnegie campus, from which I have walked back and forth each day, gradually erasing the memories of commuting on Chicago streetcars. I estimate that I have walked nearly 20,000 miles on that one mile of Northumberland Street, enough to carry me around the world if I don't stick too close to the equator (but only, as a friend has pointed out, if I can walk on water). . . .

Getting Started

Life during the early years of GSIA was a three-ring circus. Lee Bach, who was appointed dean of the new school, Bill Cooper, and I played leading roles in developing its faculty and curriculum. Provost Smith, who had an industrial and academic background in personnel administration, was also very active. We had

< 3 >

almost a clean slate, but what had previously been written on it is worth mentioning.

First, we inherited the undergraduate industrial management (read "industrial engineering") curriculum, which Bach, Cooper, and Smith had revamped, and which in fact provided an excellent template for our new graduate program. Second, Lee Bach had come to Carnegie in 1947, at age thirty, with the promise that he could start a small doctoral program in economics, and had hired several economists on the strength of that promise. The first of these two inheritances gave us a good start, the second, as I shall recount, caused complications. Almost none of the founding fathers of GSIA (except Provost Smith) had extensive backgrounds in management or business education. We were social scientists who had discovered in one way or another that organizational and business environments provide a fertile source of basic research ideas, and who therefore did not regard basic and applied as antithetical terms. Accurately or not, we perceived American business education at that time as a wasteland of vocationalism that needed to be transformed into science-based professionalism, as medicine and engineering had been transformed a generation or two earlier. We were most fortunate in that we took on this task at that particular moment in history. World War II had spawned something called "operational analysis" or "operations research," the use of quantitative tools for managerial problem solving and decision making. Just after the war, a number of people were seeking to transfer these tools to peacetime industrial applications, and new tools (such as linear programming) were being discovered.

At about the same time, the behavioral sciences were flourishing and were being brought to bear on issues in organization and management. (The activities of the Political Science Department at Chicago, Barnard's The Functions of the Executive, and my Administrative Behavior were examples of these trends.) Publication of the extensive field studies carried out in the Hawthorne Works of the Western Electric Company by F. J. Roethlisberger and W. J. Dickson (1939) had begun before the war, and our field experiment in the California State Relief Administration was completed in 1941.

The postwar flowering of management science and of the behavioral approach to organization theory provided the substance of applied science we needed. The quantitative undergraduate training of our students made it possible to put that science into the curriculum. Having worked out a Master's cur-

< 4 >

riculum appropriate to these goals, we developed two major research areas: organizational behavior and quantitative management science. I assumed leadership in the former, in collaboration with Harold Guetzkow, who joined a year later. Bill Cooper took the principal initiative in the quantitative area, but I also participated heavily in that, heading one of his research teams. So during this period I was at once organization theorist, management scientist, and business school administrator—the three rings of my circus. . . .

Bill Cooper had come to Carnegie Institute of Technology in 1947, recommended to Lee Bach by someone at Chicago. He had meanwhile spent some years after graduation from college as assistant to the controller of the Tennessee Valley Authority, as a graduate student at Columbia University, as an economist in the Bureau of the Budget, and, just after World War II, as an assistant professor at the University of Chicago. He arrived in Pittsburgh in time to become one of the entrepreneurs who attracted the six million GSIA dollars to Carnegie. Bill was not only an entrepreneur but a revolutionary. His imagination and his indifference to convention were critical ingredients in the successful GSIA effort. . . .

Keeping the balance of the scientific and the professional, of the economic and the behavioral, was an arduous job. Only the complete dedication and strong leadership of Lee Bach held the venture on course. In my paper on business schools, I wrote that "organizing a professional school . . . is very much like mixing oil with water: . . . And the task is not finished when the goal has been achieved. Left to themselves, the oil and water will separate again. So also will the disciplines and the professions" (Simon 1967a, p. 16). By hard work, we managed to keep GSIA pretty well emulsified, at least until the 1960s. In my essay from which the preceding quotation comes, I explain why these problems are endemic to professional education—in medicine, engineering, and business. This law of nature, learned during my first two years at GSIA, continued to influence the development of the school.

The great thing about such controversy as we had in GSIA was that it was more about principles, issues, and policies than about personal or organizational advantage. I see Mr. Freud smiling, but he is wrong, as he should have known from his own controversies. Only people who believe deeply and almost fanatically in a dream—as many of us in GSIA did—can struggle so hard without inner doubt and conflict, and without losing, in the presence of frequent disagreement on particulars, a deep sense of common purpose and mutual respect.

< 5 >

Nor do I want to make conflict seem to play a greater role in GSIA than it did; but the story of a marriage that pretends there were no spats is always a little dull. More important than internal agreement and disagreement was the position of GSIA vis-à-vis the world. Evolutionists have discussed the advantages and disadvantages, for progress, of an isolated island community. GSIA was such a community, open and hospitable to alien ideas blown in from the sea, but protected from the need to defend the tender mutants it had bred against constant confrontation with all the established mainland species. Its success speaks for the island as a locus for innovation.

The island metaphor was only one part of GSIA's external posture. We also had David and Goliath much in mind. For several of us—certainly for Bill Cooper and me—there was no greater pleasure than being the underdog, unless it was the pleasure of being the winning underdog. And we often portrayed in such terms our struggles against the Goliaths of traditional education, conventional business practice, and classical economics.

THE NEW MODEL BUSINESS SCHOOL

Having weathered its first crisis, and holding to its social science emphasis, GSIA quickly gained national visibility as the new model for a business school. European universities, moving cautiously into business education for the first time, generally found the scientism of GSIA a more comfortable model than the unfamiliar case method of the Harvard Business School. Two national studies of business education (whose directors came from liberal arts backgrounds and were extremely skeptical of business education in general) picked GSIA as the example for other business schools to imitate (R. A. Gordon and J. E. Howell 1959; F. C. Pierson et al. 1959).

Within about five years, GSIA came to be regarded as one of the two or three best business schools in the nation. To avoid constraining our ability to innovate, we did not seek national accreditation until our reputation was so well established that the accrediting body could not put pressure on us to conform to conventional ideas. . . .

The Ford Foundation, seeking to improve business education, used its golden carrots to push and pull other business schools toward the road GSIA had pioneered. GSIA faculty staffed a number of summer schools that the Foundation financed for

< 6 >

business school faculty who wanted to learn about the new methods. GSIA students regularly won the Foundation's annual awards for the best business school dissertations and its graduate fellowships. The Foundation also funded some of our research (though never on the scale we thought we deserved for our services to it). Many of our doctoral alumni soon became deans of other business schools.

POLITICS ON THE CAMPUS

Perhaps this is a good place to explain how Carnegie Institute of Technology became Carnegie Mellon University, because this happened in 1967, between the time when Dick Cyert became Dean of GSIA and when he assumed the presidency of the university. In 1967, during the presidency of Guyford Stever, a merger was arranged between CIT and the Mellon Institute, a nonprofit industrial research organization in Pittsburgh that had been endowed by Andrew Mellon. The two institutions, and the names of their major benefactors, were merged.

I do not know whose decision it was for us to become a university. The professionals at the Mellon Institute were scientists, principally chemists, who would have been quite at home in an Institute of Technology. Somehow the merger was seized on as an opportunity to proclaim a broader mission for Carnegie Mellon by dubbing it a university.

Organization theorists will be interested to know that the change in name has not been without consequence. It has supported arguments such as, "We are now a university; universities have Philosophy Departments, therefore CMU ought to have a Philosophy Department." What's in a name? A great deal, it would appear.

Campus politics and administration need to be guided by two goals: excellence and innovation. Money does not guarantee excellence. Although university salaries and faculty quality are correlated, the correlation is far from perfect. Insisting on excellence—on the university's getting what it pays for, and more if possible—at the time of critical personnel decisions (hiring, reappointment, promotion, tenure) can turn a mediocre faculty into a first-rate one.

When making tenure decisions, members of a faculty are inclined to sacrifice quality to humaneness, particularly when close associates and friends are being judged. Acting humanely is an

< 7 >

admirable human trait but it is easy to misconstrue what is at issue. A faculty tenure committee is not determining how many people will be employed in the society, but which people will be employed in a particular university. Retaining a faculty member who is less able than others who could be recruited is as inhumane to the (possibly unknown) replacement as it may be humane to the incumbent. Faculty members who are denied tenure don't go on the breadline. They move to other universities or other occupations. Universities achieve high quality when they keep these facts in view.

Innovating means not simply generating ideas but disseminating them. Ideas can be disseminated by talking and writing, and the dissemination can be greatly facilitated by building institutional homes for them. At Carnegie, we have had considerable success in generating new ideas, in creating organizations to nurture them, and in propagating them through the wider educational and scientific communities. The first innovative activity I was involved in at Carnegie was founding GSIA; that organization and its worldwide influence on business education has already been described. The second was building a psychology department that has been an international leader in developing and diffusing computer simulation and information-processing psychology. The third one was introducing computers at Carnegie Tech and building there one of the world's earliest and leading computer science departments.

A fourth effort at innovation, still developing, is reconstructing design as a scientific activity and reintroducing design into the engineering curriculum. A fifth is strengthening effective education at Carnegie, by emphasizing problem solving and the blending of liberal with professional values and approaches. The institution building associated with these innovations has largely occupied the part of my life that has been devoted to university policies and politics.

This activity is not at all separate from the main stream of my research, for the Carnegie campus provided the intellectual environment where innovative ideas could be developed and then communicated to the rest of the world. Behavioral theories of economics, bounded rationality among them, gained their visibility through the joint activities of our research group in GSIA during the 1950s. The Psychology Department provided the platform for launching the cognitive revolution in psychology. A sequence of organizations, culminating in the Computer Science Department, provided the corresponding platform for artificial intelligence.

< 8 >

The New Cognitive Psychology

The new research on cognitive psychology ... was launched from GSIA in 1956. Within a year, Lee Gregg in the Psychology Department began to take part, but no other interest was shown by that department. Lee, seeing the promise of the new approach, moved rapidly to it from the behaviorist empiricism of traditional experimental psychology in which he had been trained at the University of Wisconsin.

GSIA had had connections with psychology, in social and organizational psychology, and Harold Guetzkow had a joint appointment in GSIA and the Psychology Department. Because I was a Fellow of the Division of Social Psychology of the American Psychological Association (on the strength of my research on organizations), I also had at least minimal legitimacy in psychology. I began to propagandize for more participation of the Psychology Department in the cognitive revolution we had started.

Some GSIA funds were used to hire young experimental psychologists whom we thought might be seduced in the new directions, but that plan was not very successful. The traditions of the discipline and concerns about a successful career in psychology were too strong to allow untenured psychology faculty to join the revolt. By the time I went to RAND on my sabbatical, in 1960, I was beginning to doubt that we could accomplish the revolution from the foreign territory of GSIA, without a firm base also in the Psychology Department. I resolved to do something about it when I returned to Pittsburgh.

As I assessed the situation in the autumn of 1961, there had been little progress, and Haller Gilmer, chairman of the Psychology Department, unpersuaded by my particular vision of the future, was unwilling to promise there would be more. I decided to use some of my Brownie points with the administration to bring about a rapid change. My method was abrupt, justified in my mind by the importance I attached to the goal. The depths of my convictions on matters important to me had not gone unnoticed by my colleagues. . . .

Computer Science

Establishing a computer science program at Carnegie was much easier than introducing cognitive psychology, because we were simply filling a vacuum rather than pushing against entrenched

< 9 >

ideas. Soon after 1956, when the IBM 650 and Alan Perlis arrived on campus, faculty and students in four departments—GSIA, electrical engineering, mathematics, and psychology—began to take a strong interest in computing. About 1961, a steering committee was set up with representatives of these departments, under the rubric of Systems and Communications Sciences (S&CS).

Various members of the S&CS committee were offering, in their respective departments, courses that we would now regard as computer science courses, and because we had worked hard to maintain the permeability of departmental and college boundaries at Carnegie, students from many departments took these courses. The S&CS committee next decided to construct and administer a comprehensive exam at the doctoral level in computer sciences (in S&CS). Any department that wished could incorporate this exam as part of their examinations for the doctorate, and all four departments represented in the committee did so.

Soon, we were awarding degrees that were essentially computer science doctorates in the four departments. The University's Committee on Graduate Studies learned of this several years after the fact, but by then it was too late to do anything but give it a blessing. In that way, we became one of the first universities in the country—in the world—to train students in computer science at the doctoral level.

By 1965, the desire was widespread to take the next step—to establish a separate Computer Science Department. It was created that year, with Alan Perlis as its first, and extremely effective, chairman. From the beginning, Carnegie Mellon, MIT, and Stanford were regarded as having the three leading computer science programs in the nation, a rank we continue to hold.

The Computer Science Department kept close ties with the departments that had formed the S&CS committee, and there have always been joint appointments of faculty among them. At present, four faculty members hold joint appointments in psychology and computer science. Computer science remained in the College of Science until 1987, when it became a separate college.

ENGINEERING DESIGN

One cannot inhabit engineering schools for several decades without acquiring views about engineering education. I formed such views very early during my tenure at Illinois Tech—but probably mainly inherited them from my father. I was even moder-

< 10 >

ately active in the Society for the Promotion of Engineering Education (now the American Society for Engineering Education). My initial views were that engineering education needed less vocationalism and more science.

With my experience in GSIA and a wider view of the world, I began to view things a little differently, and began to see, too, the similarities in education for various professions, especially engineering, business, and medicine. Our goal in GSIA was to balance a professional with a scientific orientation.

As I began to understand the trends in the stronger engineering schools, I saw that the same things that were happening to them were happening to the New Model business education: science was replacing professional skills in the curriculum. I looked a little further, and saw the same thing going on in medicine. More and more, business schools were becoming schools of operations research, engineering schools were becoming schools of applied physics and math, and medical schools were becoming schools of biochemistry and molecular biology. Professional skills were disappeared from the curricula, and professionals possessing those skills were disappearing from the faculties.

The distinction between the scientific and the professional is largely a distinction between analysis and synthesis. Professionals not only analyze (understand) situations, they act on them after finding appropriate strategies (synthesis). In business, they design products and marketing channels, organize manufacturing processes, and find new financial instruments; in engineering, they design structures and devices and processes; in medicine they design and prescribe treatments and perform operations. But analysis had driven synthesis from all these curricula.

This had happened for a good reason. Analysis is at the heart of science; it is rigorous; it can be taught. Synthesis processes are much less systematic; they are generally thought to be judgmental and intuitive, taught as "studio" subjects, at the drawing board or in clinical rounds or through unstructured business cases. They did not fit the general norms of what is properly considered academic. As a result, they were gradually squeezed out of professional schools to enhance respectability in the eyes of academic colleagues.

The discovery of artificial intelligence changed this situation radically. Artificial intelligence programs generally carry out design, or synthesis. Programs were designing electrical motors, generators, and transformers as early as 1956 and, by 1961, selecting investment portfolios. Such computer programs destroyed the mystery of intuition and synthesis, for their processes were

< 11 >

completely open to examination. We could now understand, in whatever rigorous detail pleased us, just what a design process was. Understanding it, we could teach it, at the same level of rigor that we taught analysis.

As I gradually came to understand both the dilemma of the professional schools and the solution being offered by A.I., I began to urge that Carnegie Tech restore design and designers (or theorists of design) to its Engineering College. In the early 1960s the message fell on deaf ears. The scientists then in the Engineering College neither understood engineering nor believed it could be taught. They educated engineers by giving them a lot of physics and math, hoping that their students would later be able to design safe bridges or airplanes.

In 1968, I was invited to give the prestigious Karl Taylor Compton Lectures at MIT I titled my lectures "The Sciences of the Artificial," and devoted one of them to the science of design, setting forth the view I have just sketched and filling it out with a prescription (a design!) for a curriculum in design. The curriculum was motivated by my description, in the preceding lecture, of what our research had taught us about human thought processes, including design processes. There was no immediate seismic response to the lectures, but, in their published form, they began to attract more and more notice, in this country and abroad.

Gradually, Carnegie was able to recruit to the engineering departments a few faculty members who shared this view of design. Gary Powers and Steve Director were among the first. They came together in a Design Research Center, whose activities have burgeoned into a large network of research studies on synthesis processes of many kinds.

The research, in turn, is beginning to reflect back on curriculum, so that Carnegie Mellon is today a recognized leader in restoring professional skills—design skills—to engineering education. Of course, we are not bringing back the drawing board. We are teaching not just an art of design but a science of design. The main vehicle is the study of expert systems and other artificial intelligence systems that do design, thereby revealing its anatomy and physiology.

These developments have afforded me great satisfaction, particularly because, aside from providing the initial propaganda for them, I have not had to be very actively involved in bringing them about. They are now firmly rooted in the soil of the Engineering College and are proceeding under their own momentum. If one must be a reformer, that's the best kind of reform.

< 12 >

Notes

[1] Editors' Note—Bill Cooper, whom Herb Simon had known from his undergraduate years at the University of Chicago, left a significant legacy of applications research, institution founding, graduate training, and enduring friendships at Carnegie Mellon, 1946–1977. He was a founding member of the Graduate School of Industrial Administration in 1949, a founding dean of the School of Urban and Public Affairs (1968–1975), and a University Professor of Public Policy and Management Science (1975–1977). In 1982 Carnegie Mellon awarded him an honorary doctorate. He is now Professor Emeritus of Management, Accounting and Management Science and Information Systems in the Graduate School of Business of The University of Texas at Austin.

[2] William Larimer Mellon was a son of the banker Thomas Mellon, who had established the Mellon fortune at the time of the Civil War, and a brother of Andrew Mellon. He and Andrew were uncles of Richard King Mellon, who in turn was the central figure in the Mellon barony when I reached Pittsburgh and the partner, with Mayor Dave Lawrence, in bringing about the Pittsburgh Renaissance.

The editors would like to thank the Massachusetts Institute of Technology Press for permission to reprint the contents of this chapter from Herbert Simon's autobiography, *Models of My Life*, pages 135–156, 251–268. The paperback edition was published by MIT Press, Cambridge, Massachusetts, in 1996. *Models of My Life* was originally published by Basic Books in 1991.

< 13 >

THE SCIENTIST AND THE UNIVERSITY

Lincoln Wolfenstein

Lincoln Wolfenstein is Emeritus University Professor of Physics at Carnegie Mellon University. His research has dealt with elementary particle phenomenology, and more recently, with neutrino physics. Professor Wolfenstein received his Ph.D. from the University of Chicago in 1948, and taught at Carnegie Mellon for 52 years, 1948–2000.

What are the goals of the university? That is the first question one must answer. I believe the goals are (1) to transmit the knowledge and culture of mankind from one generation to another; and (2) to create new knowledge and new culture. These goals are not transient, following the latest fad, but rather reflect fundamental values of mankind. There is an unfortunate tendency in universities to set up new committees to establish new programs, to find strategic advantages, to reinvent the university. This, of course, is in part a reflection of contemporary American society, built around advertisements always pushing something wonderfully new.

In my own field of science, physics, I feel strongly the sense of continuity. The fundamental laws of motion and the law of gravity established by Newton still govern the motion of the planets and man's voyage to the moon. Science writers, and even some philosophers of science, love to herald revolutionary new developments that overthrow all our old ideas. But they do not under-

< 15 >

stand. For example, Einstein's general theory of relativity is a more accurate theory of gravity, but it does not overthrow Newton's theory, it encompasses it. The relation of a new theory to an older well-established one can be described by a "correspondence principle," a term invented by Niels Bohr to describe the relation of classical mechanics to quantum mechanics. The new theory reduces to the old in a suitable limit. I like to think of this in poetic terms (thanks to Edwin Markham):

> He drew a circle that shut me out—
> Heretic, rebel, a thing to flout.
> But Love and I had the wit to win:
> We drew a circle that took him in![1]

Continuity does not mean that we should not bring our courses up to date. In physics there has been the tradition that the first-year college course covers the foundations: classical mechanics, thermodynamics, and electrodynamics, and so hardly mentions any twentieth-century physics. I have long protested against this and even gave a special freshman course to remedy this. On the other hand, I worry about the other extreme in many humanities areas, where new courses are often invented to satisfy the latest fad.

A fundamental problem for a university is money, without which it cannot operate. I worry that in the difficult effort to raise money the university administration may confuse two possibilities: (1) we must raise money so as to achieve the goals of the university; (2) the goal of the university is to raise money. We face the same problem in science. Funds are needed to finance research and most funding is obtained from federal grants. These grants ultimately come from the US Congress, which contains only two scientists, and the majority of whose members are illiterate as far as science is concerned. This raises the question of whether scientists should try to satisfy Congress or define their goals on a strictly scientific basis.

This tension between political and scientific criteria has a long history. When Congress first voted to create a National Science Foundation (NSF) it gave scientists complete control, inspired by Vannevar Bush's "Endless Frontier." President Truman vetoed the bill because it did not give enough power to the executive branch.[2] When the NSF was finally established in 1950, the President was given the power to select the directorate. In spite of this, the funding of science in the United States has worked amaz-

< 16 >

ingly well. In particular, agencies like NSF and Department of Energy (DOE) are given funds in broad categories with specific research grants decided by review by scientific referees or panels.

More disturbing is the question of grants from the Defense Department. This research must be justified by its military goals even though much of it is research that also serves more general goals. In 1983 significant funds became available, as part of the Star Wars program, which most scientists believed was technologically unsound and strategically dangerous. Large number of scientists pledged to refuse any such funds. Shortly thereafter Carnegie Mellon established a Software Engineering Institute (SEI), which was totally funded by and integrated into Defense Department programs. Serious questions exist whether such a close association with the Defense Department best serves the goals of science or of the University.

A related issue is that of industrial support and joint industry-university programs. Often these programs may have restrictions on the release of research results, which is exactly contrary to the goals of university research. There is also the possibility that the university may be motivated by financial profits from such research. There is a growing worry that "increased industrial support for research is disrupting, distorting and damaging the underlying educational and research missions of the university, retarding advances in basic science."[3]

In planning for many years ahead both for the science departments of the university and agencies like the NSF, the question arises as to which areas to emphasize. For industrial research the answer is areas that will lead soon to profitable applications. For the university, on the other hand, the answer requires defining areas that are likely to lead to fundamental new knowledge in the next 10 or 20 years. That is often hard to predict. I believe that universities should particularly emphasize areas of science that may have no apparent applications, but which address fundamental issues such as the elementary constituents of matter, the structure of the universe, and the origin of life.

A difficult question is the relation between decisions by the university and decisions by funding agencies. In reviewing a promotion for a science faculty member an important consideration is the success in obtaining research grants. Does this mean that in a sense the university is giving up its independent decision making? I think as long as the research grants obtained (or rejected) result from a process of peer review by scientists the consideration seems perfectly reasonable. On the other hand, unfortu-

< 17 >

nately, there has been an increasing tendency by Congress to sidetrack peer review and award grants via pork-barrel politics, and sometimes even university presidents appeal to congressmen to get research money.

A problem often raised concerning peer review is that it favors conformity—"safe" research along established lines. What happens then to faculty members with some original projects totally different from what others are doing? There is no simple answer. However, in the short run, it is reasonable that young faculty members be encouraged to make their mark in established areas of research. In the long run there is the protection of the tenure system, a major purpose of which is to allow for non-conformists.

Today science seems increasingly compartmentalized. Not only do I know little about developments in chemistry or biology, there are also many areas of physics I have no time to follow. The current issue of the *Physical Review* devoted just to my area of physics is approximately 1000 pages in length. On a dirty shelf I found a 1954 issue devoted to all areas of physics with 300 pages. Similarly, for the university as a whole, there is relatively little interaction between the humanities, fine arts, and science. We need more mechanisms for bringing faculty members together for intellectual exchange, not only for occasional parties.

Some years ago I participated in a committee with the mission of designing interdisciplinary courses. There were various suggestions, but the only one that actually was given for several years was a course I organized on the Nuclear Age. The other suggestions concerned courses for noncommittee members to offer and never took off. In 1986 I taught this course with Professor Achenbaum of History and Professor Rich of the School of Urban and Public Affairs (SUPA), the predecessor of the H. John Heinz III School of Public Policy and Management. In 1987 I was joined by Professor Salamone, a political scientist in the College of Humanities and Social Sciences (H&SS). Then in 1989, the emphasis switched slightly when I was joined by Professor Pressler of the Philosophy Department. In the preparation of the course each year, I met regularly with my colleagues from across the campus in the fall before the course was to be given. While the course was being given we met regularly each week. These meetings involved a valuable exchange of views both on educational strategies and on the subject matter of the course as well as incidental discussions on more general university issues. These interactions represent one of the most important values of such courses.

< 18 >

Forty to fifty students fairly uniformly distributed between Carnegie Institute of Technology, Mellon College of Science, and the College of Humanities & Social Sciences, with occasional College of Fine Arts students, took the course. Students' responses to the course were very favorable. A typical response was "the interdisciplinary blend was particularly beneficial; I liked being exposed to all aspects of a topic." It is true that one student objected to the fact that the two professors actually disagreed with each other concerning certain policy issues.

In its last incarnation, the course was taught together with a retired diplomat, Professor Goodby, who was hired by Engineering and Public Policy for a special program on international affairs.[4] The course was called "Global Security and Science." It was focused on the "implications of modern science and technology for the developments of new weapons and their control." I have been particularly interested in the decision to build the atomic bomb, then the hydrogen bomb, and the various efforts, often led by scientists, to initiate arms control. All these decisions relate to the interaction between scientists and government. Interestingly, all those who joined with me to teach the course, soon after left Carnegie Mellon. The course disappeared when it was clear that there were no faculty members interested in continuing it.

The problem of communicating science to the general public must be a major concern. Within the university this involves science courses for students in humanities or fine arts; outside the university, faculty can play an important role helping schools and community organizations. Our goals in telling the general public about science are three: (1) to communicate the wonderful discoveries that have been made concerning the nature of the world and the universe; (2) to provide an understanding and an appreciation of the use made of public funds provided for scientific research; and (3) to help in understanding societal problems that have a significant scientific component.

None of these goals is possible unless we communicate the methodology of science: how discoveries have been made, how theories have been tested, and how the community of scientists becomes persuaded. Unfortunately science is often taught in schools as delivered truth which you better believe or else you will flunk, much as religion is preached with the warning you better believe or you will go to hell. As one science journalist notes: "Without a grasp of scientific ways of thinking, the average person cannot tell the difference between science based on real data

< 19 >

and something that resembles science— at least in their eyes— but is based on uncontrolled experiments, anecdotal evidence, and passionate assertions."[5]

One type of course I have given over the years is a science course for non-science students. The students were from all the different departments of Humanities and Social Sciences, most of whom were fulfilling a science requirement. In its last version it was called Discovery of the Physical Universe. The course started with Galileo and Newton and our present picture of planets circling the sun. It jumped to the quantum theory starting with Bohr's atomic model based on planetary motion. It ended with the Big Bang theory of the history of the universe. A common feature of these subjects was that they were counterintuitive. I try to tell the students that their first reaction should be, "That's crazy."

The whole point is how scientists came to believe these crazy ideas. The problem, of course, is that it took scientists many years, often a whole generation, to accept the new ideas, while the students have only three or four weeks on each subject. I remember when I first taught a course like this and I was trying to get students to argue back and forth about a theory, one poor student raised her hand and said, "Please, teacher, just tell us what we are supposed to believe." The reaction of the students varied from enthusiasm to great dissatisfaction. One problem was that there was no textbook that was suitable. Thus I gave students a variety of readings that I believed conveyed the sense of discovery, for example, a section from Arthur Koestler's book *The Sleepwalkers* about Johannes Kepler. Some students wanted a more textbook-like course with exercises that would help them with the next test. Many of them just wanted to pass some tests and get past this requirement.

A very different type of science course for non-science students is now offered entitled Energy and the Environment. It is primarily concerned with the third goal. It is a physics course explaining all the various types of energy, but emphasizing the application of this physics to contemporary problems. The hope is that students will be motivated to learn the physics because they realize the importance of the applications and at the same time will realize the importance of truly understanding the science in order to make intelligent political decisions which effect environmental policy.

There have been growing suggestions that we should consider our students as our customers. A survey found that stu-

< 20 >

dents today desired a relationship with their college "like those they already enjoyed with their bank, their gas company and their supermarket."[6] If this is true it is a sad commentary on today's students; in any case I believe the university must be true to its goals. When a student comes to my class or my office I will not treat him as if he were paying for a service from a store; I will serve her as if she were my own child. I can do no more or no less. I hope that student will become more fully aware of the human heritage and thereby have a more rewarding life as the result of a college education.

It is difficult to predict what the university will be like many years from now. It may be that my fifty years as a university physics professor took place in a unique period after World War II when the value of basic research was almost unquestioned. It may be that federal funds for fundamental research will be sharply cut. It may be that students will become more cynical, only wanting a degree as a way to make money. But if the university is to succeed, we must think positively. Compromises may be necessary, but we should not operate under that assumption. We should reiterate our fundamental goals and make all our plans based upon them.

Notes

[1] Edwin Markham, "Outwitted," in online companion to the Cary Nelson (ed.), *Modern Anthology of American Poetry* (New York: Oxford University Press, 2000) www.english.uiuc.edu/maps/poets/m_r/markham/poems.htm

[2] D. J. Kevles, *The Physicists* (New York: Alfred A. Knopf, 1978).

[3] Richard Florida, "The Role of the University: Leveraging Talent, Not Technology," *Issues in Science and Technology* (Summer 1999), p. 67.

[4] Professor Goodby's research interests include arms control, non-proliferation of advanced weapons, and European and Asian security issues. He served as US Ambassador to Finland, Chief of the US delegation to the Conference on Disarmament in Europe, and Chief US Negotiator for the Safe and Secure Disarmament of Nuclear Weapons. He was also the first winner of the Heinz Award for Public Policy. Teresa Heinz created the awards in 1993 to honor the memory of her late husband, Senator John Heinz. The late Senator Daniel Patrick Moynihan was also a recipient of a Heinz Award for Public Policy.

[5] Boyce Rensberger, "The Nature of Evidence," *Science* (Volume 289, Number 5476, July 7, 2000), p. 61.

[6] Arthur Levine, "How the Academic Profession Is Changing," *Daedalus* (Volume 126, Number 4, Fall 1997), p. 1.

< 21 >

Rethinking the Humanities

Peggy Knapp

Peggy Knapp is Professor of English at Carnegie Mellon. Her major research interests are in medieval and renaissance studies and literary theory. Professor Knapp received her Ph.D. from the University of Pittsburgh in 1965, and has been at Carnegie Mellon for 33 years. In 2003, Professor Knapp was awarded the William H. and Frances S. Ryan Teaching award, the University's highest form of recognition for excellence in teaching.

"Humanities" is a fraught term, etymologically connected with "humanism," "humanitarianism," "humane," and "human." It elicits great respect from some people and resentment and scorn from others. When it is linked with its cousin "humanism," it seems to marginalize the sacred by focusing on what people have done, written and created images of. The humanists of the late Middle Ages, though by no means atheists, were castigated for making human endeavors so central to their inquiries, and some powerful cultural/political groups today are repeating that gesture by objecting to the "humanistic" (read "secular") bias of American education. In a completely different kind of critique, people who link "The Humanities" with "humanitarianism" and "humane" find the current practices and studies not benevolent enough. I've heard it asked why, after all these years of (some people) studying great authors and thinkers, there is still war and

< 23 >

cruelty in the world. For still other critics of the term, "humanities" seems to claim an especially "human" quality for those who practice it, at the expense of those who study other aspects of nature or thought.

I'm not particularly interested in saving the term itself from such critiques, but I would like to suggest some ways the humanities at Carnegie Mellon ought not to be taxed with them. On the first point, it's true that we touch on "the sacred" in terms of the textual record rather than dogma, but this is the right course of action in a multicultural university setting. On the second: study in the humanities does not automatically lead to benevolence or "moral improvement." We do not *teach* particular values (except those of universities in general: freedom of inquiry, accuracy, respect for persons, integrity, and the like), we investigate the written and enacted record in order to *discuss and consider* values as our own and earlier generations have represented them. Instead of claiming that the humanities makes, or ought to aim at making, people nice, we argue that it acquaints them with a larger number of alternative models for ethical thought and enables them to use a larger array of perspectives on human affairs than they otherwise would.

The third issue is a reason I myself am a bit uncomfortable with the term: mathematical and scientific investigations are as deeply human in their impulses as the study of language, philosophy, or culture. I don't like to seem to be claiming some sort of high ground just by mentioning my area of study. Nonetheless, for thinking about such study, we do need a name. The humanities at Carnegie Mellon do participate in different discourses and are responsible for different modes of evidence than, say, physics or economics, on the one hand, or the production of art, say, painting, on the other. Our common effort might better be called language-based and interpretive, but I'll use "humanities" as a shorthand during the rest of this essay.

"Rethinking," the other term in my title, also deserves attention. In the professional arenas involved, especially historical and literary studies (in all languages), the last couple of decades have seen impressive, widely acknowledged paradigm shifts in dealing with the artifacts of culture and the written record. "Rethinking" has been a recurring motif of books from leading presses, articles in leading journals, the founding of new journals, the writing of dissertations, and the selection of new faculty in the humanities. In 1967, a conference at Johns Hopkins hosted a remarkable array of influential European intellectuals at a conference which resulted

< 24 >

in the 1970 book *The Language of Criticism and the Sciences of Man*. American professors, especially those who saw the mainstream practice of explicating literary text to display its organic unity and its congruence with an empirically established historical milieu as exhausted, eagerly began the work of rethinking the relation between language and virtually everything else.

In retrospect this long reappraisal has been called "the linguistic turn," and associated with terms like "deconstruction" and "post-structuralism."[1] Like many other intellectual newcomers, these ideas were sometimes taken to extremes, as nullifying previous knowledges in the humanistic disciplines or even subordinating all inquiry to the discursive realm, provoking, of course, a counterrevolution (the publicity surrounding the Sokal/Aronowitz debates was a symptom of the disarray).[2] Departments of history and English have for some time now been sorting out the useful and enlightening features of the linguistic turn from its misconstruals and exaggerations. Rethinking the humanities has, therefore, been going on with fervor for decades—but what should Carnegie Mellon's role be?

The "Cutting Edge" and Its Discontents

Carnegie Mellon is a university with a well-articulated identity, and the humanities must find its mission within that identity. The language in which the University has described itself over the years has been adapted somewhat—the headline for the College of Humanities and Social Sciences (H&SS) is no longer "The Professional Choice"—but has always circled around suggestions of committed work, excellence, problem solving, and the cutting edge. There is no awkwardness in our assent with the first two of these shibboleths, although we too often have to remind our colleagues elsewhere of the intellectual work it takes to analyze a philosophical argument or weigh the nuances of a long novel or densely textured poem. The problem-solving motto fits less well with our teaching and learning style than with some of the other units at Carnegie Mellon. We could, of course, insistently structure our courses around problems (either well- or ill-defined) and suggest that successful students had "solved" or "developed intelligent solutions for" those problems. In some cases this approach might work well, and students might learn a good deal, but in many others we would have to compromise the larger goals of our disciplines in order to serve that logic.

< 25 >

Sometimes students say, why don't you just tell us which is the right interpretation of *Hamlet*? (That is, which one solves the problem of meaning.) We resist that tack in order to force them to come to terms with the issues in the play themselves (which doesn't mean we don't correct errors of textual or historical fact or plain logical lapses). Sometimes they say, surely after all these years someone has solved this—what more can be said? We respond that each of them is (or can be) an informed reader with a unique perspective on the life-world Shakespeare created for his characters. Scholars who study *Hamlet* do not usually do so to isolate a problem, but to complicate their first reactions to the play and thus prepare themselves to experience it more fully and with keener intellectual tools. The experience of reading and/or seeing *Hamlet* is an episode in the lives of its audiences, not a problem with a discrete solution. People continue to stage, look at, and write about the play, and each generation finds new interpretive schemes from which to regard it. The problem-solving model, in other words, tends to undervalue the reformulations and recomplications of issues necessary for mature judgment to develop.

"Cutting Edge" is still the way the University is described in the Undergraduate Catalogue. This is a term I want to both claim for the scholarly work we do and disclaim for the way it can distort the teaching function of the University. I can justifiably claim it because my colleagues break ground all the time in the classroom (and in their contributions to national and international forums) and because the students they instruct often distinguish themselves in the graduate schools, law schools, and careers they enter after they leave us. Our department in particular has risen to the challenge of new ways of configuring the study of language and texts, including much writing that was previously marginalized, and accounting for new modes of presenting narrative (modes like film, television and Internet communication—the English Server was perhaps the most successful academic instrument of its kind). My disquiet with the term comes from the fact that not all we teach is or can be "on the edge"—much of our work is work other colleges and university faculties and students are also doing—and not every edge is the right place to be in offering undergraduate education.

Even in matters of interpretive theory, there are aspects of our teaching that must and should include older ways of looking at texts—Aristotelian as well as contemporary poetics, for example (as Lincoln Wolfenstein argues that Newtonian physics

< 26 >

must be included in a modern physics course). Even more important, the primary objects of investigation, the historical treatises, poems, and plays of earlier eras, are unique artifacts rather than merely steppingstones toward contemporary treatises, poems, and plays. If we give up recomplicating *Hamlet* and *Tom Jones* (and this has been insistently urged upon us, both from the outside and inside), we will be withholding from this generation what we ourselves wrestled with and what other college-educated people are doing now. When we use tradition wisely, courses can enable students to both experience texts in their immediacy and bring historical perspective to bear. That is, we can acknowledge that we have contexts and structures of personal feeling different from those of the original author and yet attempt to construct that author's world.

In the specific case of teaching older literatures (my bailiwick), I often ask my students to perform thought experiments in which they try to imagine themselves a person living in a particular year and place responding to a fiction—one of the pilgrims on the way to Canterbury, for example, hearing Chaucer's tales. Deliberately denying oneself one's twenty-first-century habits is an exercise in historical imagination, in that sense a return to an earlier cultural response, and presumably not cutting edge. It is also (although probably not a common teaching device nowadays) not cutting edge pedagogy; if anything, it's probably a bit retro. That particular thought experiment can only be carried out in discontinuous bursts—we can't help returning to our present mindsets—but the very interruption of customary mental habits is itself a boon to mental agility.

From time to time Carnegie Mellon's handling of teaching in the humanities has been widely publicized as "cutting edge." The History Department was given national attention not long ago for its innovation of "Applied History." English was also touted, first for shifting its emphasis from the study of literature to research into career-oriented writing tasks and then for its postmodernist/cultural studies emphasis. There were obvious advantages to being discussed in both the *Chronicle of Higher Education* and the *New York Times*. The names of our school and our departments were celebrated and that publicity probably netted more applications for undergraduate and graduate programs. In the case of English, the rush to be "cutting edge" also created divisions within the faculty, caused the department to lose some of its longtime allies in the University, and confused most students.

< 27 >

For many constituencies in the University, diversion from the older style of presenting history as "what happened" and English as the appreciation of "the best that has been thought and said" was widely seen as an unmitigated loss. Yet at the same time every serious discipline is held responsible for bringing its curriculum and course content up to date, and the adoption of the very new served the University's cutting edge definition admirably. These tensions are related to whether the humanities departments in the University ought to be considered "civilizing" features of campus life or enclaves of research and teaching for majors, a problem to which I will return shortly. In very large fields like English and history where there are serious debates about what constitutes an up-to-date approach, the problem is complicated and often frustrates good intentions. In such cases, the sharpest cutting edge is not necessarily the best building tool. When we were most famous, we were not necessarily offering the best education.

I ought to say a bit more about the "linguistic turn," experienced in the College here in the 1980s. When Carnegie Institute of Technology became Carnegie Mellon University and the College of Humanities and Social Sciences was founded, the English Department taught the whole student body a freshman course called The Literary Imagination and the History Department taught all freshmen Historical Understanding. Those courses, like the academic professions they represented, assumed the learner to be engaged in a project of understanding, of assembling facts and construing their meanings, of grasping and appreciating the meanings of an event or text. The linguistic turn challenged this "hermeneutic of understanding" by emphasizing a "hermeneutic of suspicion." At its center was the insight that language can mystify as well as disclose the realities of the past, that there is no direct, unmediated record of historical events. For example, if someone other than Tacitus (or even Tacitus himself at another age or in a different mood) had written the *Germania* describing the Germanic tribes early in the Common Era, the particular progress narrative of northern Europe we have inherited would have been constructed differently. "Critique" became the watchword for a hermeneutic of suspicion. Instead of trying to "think with" Tacitus, we needed to think about or against his account.

In this light, the verities of "Great Man History" and the succession of established "periods" of literary history (Romanticism, Victorianism) melt away docilely as ideological constructs erected to protect or establish (personal or class) privilege. There is in

< 28 >

this stance an important partial truth. Every modern historical account ought to be written with a due humility and skepticism about the written record. But the strongest version of this skepticism is that there is no narrative to write, no general historical configuration to be seen in any past era and contrasted with the present. I remember a time when the words "feudal" and "monastic" were objected to on this campus because they belonged to the Grand Narrative scheme. In the end, such sweeping skepticism makes it impossible to teach history at all because the terrain is so heavily disputed. It is widely realized now, though, that all perspectives need the support of some narrative history, even while we understand its fragility. The question is, can we preserve the gains of the linguistic turn in historical study—its encouragement of semiotic, feminist, postcolonial, and other perspectives on the inherited record—without being hamstrung by its excesses?

The effect on English studies of such pervasive tentativeness was attention to "brushing the text against the grain." Whatever *Hamlet* or *Tom Jones* had come to be thought of must now be the target of deconstructive readings; every text contains evidence, which contradicts its surface tenets. This too is an important partial truth, but its misuse, for a time, crippled any attempt to carry on rigorous literary analysis, since the text was assumed to be *merely* a tissue of ideological maneuvers and the historical formation it spoke to and about could not be characterized with any confidence. For its true believers, this position made it hard to teach or support the teaching of time-honored works. One had to move on, and that suited the cutting edge mentality very well. Nobody gets his/her name in the paper for taking a moderate position on disciplinary developments. Serious academic writing about Madonna—that's news. Our Department has since recovered from its cutting edge phase and is now looking for solidly researched, convincingly argued scholarship, from both faculty and students. Our teaching and research rests on close examination of texts, historical considerations treated with modern complexity, and methods of analysis informed by contemporary theory, but this has been a hard-earned ground.

INSTITUTIONS AND CAREERS

The humanities at Carnegie Mellon have always experienced a tension between hiring and tenuring faculty who stand high in

< 29 >

their particular disciplines or those whose talents and specialties serve needs specific to the Carnegie Mellon community—and whether that service to the campus ought to enhance its general literacy or become handmaiden to its various professional programs. Recently a colleague referred to Carnegie Mellon as not just interdisciplinary, but antidisciplinary. If true, and it often seems so to me, that antidisciplinarity is part of the deliberate strategy of defining practical problems at a high level of abstraction and assembling research teams to attack them from various points of view. This plan has worked very well for us in many areas and produced spectacular successes in some. In thinking about a faculty responsible for undergraduate humanities education, though, its wisdom seems less obvious, partly because of what I've already said about problem solving, but also because collaboration has a different face in humanities projects.

Most books and articles in the humanities have single authors. Research and writing is usually solitary. What we need are colleagues to talk with, to read books with, to share our first drafts with. And what students need from us is a variety of approaches and subject matter so they can develop an eclectic personal style of inquiry. These faculty and student needs are best met by hiring and tenuring high-achieving scholars in their fields whose undergraduate teaching styles reach all kinds of students. (This doesn't mean everybody who is famous or likely to become so. Some published discourse in the humanities is readable only by the initiate and some people who write that way can't make their thoughts more widely accessible.) We could put away the nagging division between elite research/graduate and "service" functions among the units by recognizing that non-majors also deserve instruction in the humanities by scholars who are respected in their disciplines.

Another way to look at this problem is to note that a contribution to the humanistic disciplines is made in a specific area—a time (even perhaps a period), place, genre, or interpretive strategy. Nationally, history and English are huge professions, and in them almost no one these days is known—positively—as a generalist. That is not to say that professors can't do many things well, merely that they have to concentrate their research efforts in order to become known within a professional specialty and to fulfill their responsibilities to graduate students. When they come up for promotion and tenure, they will be judged by others in the disciplines as specialists in, say, Renaissance literature or feminist theory or both. Journalistic notoriety of the kind we have

< 30 >

enjoyed from time to time rarely matters much to the referees who will be asked to assess scholarly careers.

The same tension affects tenured professors, who are called upon to make decisions in the profession (read other colleges' tenure cases, referee articles for journals, and the like). Carnegie Mellon is now numbered among the respected American Association of Universities (AAU). I'm guessing that we are unique among those universities in our attitude toward the academic disciplines. This is not to say that we should stop sponsoring interdisciplinary projects or stop asking humanists to join them; it is to say that we should respect the specific methods and knowledges of the disciplines on campus and weigh the costs, case by case, of devising an undergraduate curriculum around "problems" which require more than one discipline.

So far I have argued that the very strategies that have contributed to Carnegie Mellon's remarkable success have not aided the attempt to integrate the humanities into the university as a whole. First, I have argued specifically that the description of intellectual life here as cutting edge has distracted the contributing disciplines from their traditional bases, as they are encouraged to rush to be where no one else is yet. This is particularly damaging for the study of language, history, philosophy, and literature, although I imagine it must be disquieting for some of the natural sciences as well. Second, I have argued that a lack of respect for the disciplines (and I could mention the fact that we have so few of them, as they are named and defined in most other places) has placed the humanities in a particularly difficult bind: the young professor is chosen to contribute to exciting, but relatively non-discipline-specific intellectual activity, but his/her retention depends on achievements established by national and international standards of judgment within the discipline which his/her local career has challenged, if not publicly attacked.

Students

The best thing about Carnegie Mellon is its excellent student body. If we wish to define success in the humanities departments merely as the survival of small majors, the goal seems within reach. I am very much impressed with the learning and the adaptability of the young humanists in the College, many of whom can do so many things both locally and nationally. Their students, too, are a source of pride; majors have fewer choices of subject

< 31 >

matter than elsewhere, but they are challenged by whatever they do take, and their progress carefully watched. But if success for humanities in the University involves integrating them into campus life generally, the answer is less sanguine. It is a rare student among the non-humanities majors who has read two books (not snippets, but books) written before 1900 in a classroom setting. Every student in H&SS must take courses in calculus, statistics, economics, and social and decision sciences, two natural sciences, and, of course, computing. We insist, in other words, that all our students have at least a general sense of contemporary mathematical, scientific, and economic systems.

The rest of the University, however, does not require any student beyond the first-year writing and history courses to pay attention to the cultural systems to which they are subject in their daily lives by taking courses in history, English or philosophy. (A colleague on the Rhodes Scholarship committee recently complained to me about a leading candidate's inaccurate and over-generalized remarks about the Middle Ages, but it's hard to see how the student could have said anything more pointed when our course offerings in that area are so scanty.) It is not convincing to argue that the world of linguistic discourse is no longer relevant—only numeracy counts nowadays. The barrage of film, video, and print vying for consent and/or empathy these days requires more than ever an informed rhetorical, literary, and cultural insight. The college-educated person has traditionally been expected to share in that insight.

Nonetheless, it's not hard to see how we got where we are. Carnegie Mellon's programs are demanding, precise, and time-consuming. Distractions from such focused programs need strong justification; anything that takes a person out of the lab needs strong justification. Why, since our students are so smart, and since they can already read English, and since many are already good writers, should we distract them with study in the humanities? Moreover, humanities courses are also demanding, precise and time-consuming, and they must involve small groups of students working closely with an instructor. Interpretative skills cannot be taught effectively by simply assigning reading and lecturing on it because meaning is a negotiated transaction between the writer and reader (as would be agreed by people on all sides of the "linguistic turn" controversy). Everyone has to do it for him/herself, preferably in conversation with other perceptive readers, ideally at Carnegie Mellon in conversations with perceptive readers from all the disciplines. The gain for humanities

< 32 >

majors from more contact with the rest of the campus would be conversation with a wider range of perspectives from more members of our student community.

What would those gains be for non-humanities majors? First, there are analytic skills and logical systems, which must be invoked in non-numerical study (humanists do not avoid numbers when appropriate, but their usual practices are linguistic and rhetorical). At Carnegie Mellon, a general assumption (sometimes tacit, but often announced) is that anything that cannot be quantified cannot be studied rigorously. If this is your opinion, gentle reader, go on to the next essay; I haven't time here to dispute it. The fact that each student must experience a literary, philosophical, or historical text for him/herself, does not mean that no logical rules apply or that no rational processes are involved. Reading closely, looking into semantic change and/or ambiguity, and grasping complex relations between parts and whole are rule-governed activities, which must be taught. A very intelligent engineering student, who took a Shakespeare course with me last year, wrote at the end of the term that he had always been the first in his courses to come up with the answer, but that in reading Shakespeare he didn't see many of the implications other students saw until they were pointed out—he had to learn different intellectual strategies.

Second, college-educated people have to confront challenges as citizens and professionals which demand linguistic acuity, historical knowledge, and perhaps a measure of empathy with people different in some way from themselves. This is perhaps obvious in political and cultural contexts: anyone who wishes to understand some aspect of the world—and influence it—needs nuanced language. Professional work presents similar challenges. Hans-Georg Gadamer and many scholars influenced by him have argued that at some point scientific and technical advances must pass into the shared discourses of ordinary language.[3] At Carnegie Mellon we should be particularly aware of this issue, what with genomes and robots and nuclear waste and a depleted ozone layer to attend to. Even the best-honed expertise in relevant fields must turn to language to make its claims in the public sphere.

Most importantly, study in the humanities offers intellectual pleasure. The simplest kind is the pleasure of the chase: shaping a grammatically correct French sentence, working out a truth table, grasping the inevitability of a tragic plot. Many more follow. There are the pleasures of experiencing new scenes, meeting the flamboyant or profound characters of history or fiction, or

< 33 >

performing the mental gymnastics needed to take in the tribal culture of *Beowulf* or a sci-fi film. There are the pleasures of grasping the relations between parts and wholes, of seeing the fit (or sometimes the non-fit) between a text of any kind and its context, of finding the unexpected, the little known, or the just plain bizarre where the platitude should have been. The Carnegie Mellon classroom might then offer the pleasure of conversation with other smart people who read the same text, but respond to different features of it. This sort of pleasure can turn into a lifelong addiction, but unlike many other current addictions it rarely harms either the addict or the social order. It seems odd to me that we train many excellent actors and directors, but give very little attention to helping non-dramats to understand theater; we train poets, but few readers of poetry.

As I write, I am finishing a course on utopias, one that as many computer science majors elected to take as English majors did. In *1984* George Orwell centers his nightmarish picture of the consolidation of a totalitarian state in the destruction of history, literature, and beauty (eventually empirical science has to go as well), and the depletion of natural language. I don't mention this to insist that Orwell is right, only to describe the reactions of my students, who said (pretty much all of them agreed on this): destroy these things and you've destroyed the possibility of active citizenship, since the present regime, however onerous, will seem like the only one possible. If we want our students to value history, literature, beauty, and precise language when they run the world, we'd better give them some experience in doing so while they're here.

Notes

[1] *The Language of Criticism and the Sciences of Man: The Structuralist Controversy*, ed. Richard Macksey and Egenio Donato (Baltimore: Johns Hopkins University Press, 1970). The concentration of Anglo-American academic philosophy on issues of language became known as "the linguistic turn," especially through the influential anthology of essays on the subject edited by Richard Rorty, *The Linguistic Turn: Essays in Philosophical Method* (Chicago: University of Chicago Press, 1967), but the term soon became entwined with the work of a very different (this time a continental) tradition through the work of Jacques Derrida and others. Then it began to turn up in many humanistic disciplinary contexts. Different as "linguistic philosophy" (Rorty's term) was from deconstruction (as Derrida's practices came to be known), their shared focus on language tended to undermine an unreflective empiricism in the human sciences, as Christopher Norris argues in *The Deconstructive Turn* (London: Metheun, 1983). Positions like those of Hayden White in *Metahistory* (Baltimore: Johns Hopkins

< 34 >

University Press, 1973) and Thomas Kuhn in *The Structure of Scientific Revolutions* (Chicago: University of Chicago Press, 1963 and 1970) also contributed to a heightened awareness of linguistic and discursive aspects of knowledge.

[2] The widely-publicized hoax carried out by physicist Alan Sokal involved his publication of "Transgressing the Boundaries: Toward a Transformative Hermeneutics of Quantum Gravity" in the journal *Social Text* (spring-summer 1996). This parody of what Sokal took to be the excesses of cultural theory and its opaque argumentative style prompted sharp controversy in both academic and journalistic venues and a series of debates between Sokal and Stanley Aronowitz, a member of the *Social Text* collective, including one in Pittsburgh.

[3] In many ways Gadamer's famous pronouncement "Being that can be understood is language" in *Truth and Method* is a precursor to the concerns of the linguistic turn; Gadamer discusses what he means by it in "On the Scope and Function of Hermeneutical Reflection" in *Philosophical Hermeneutics,* trans. David E. Linge (Berkeley: University of California Press, 1977). Today some version of Gadamer's position is widely held. Donna Haraway puts it very strongly: "Science and science studies, no less than literature or philosophy, depend constitutively upon troping [indirection in language]. . . . there is no direct route to the relationship we call knowledge, scientific or otherwise" *Social Text* 50 (Spring 1997), 125.

< 35 >

Drama and the New Media

Donald Marinelli

Donald Marinelli is Professor of Drama and Arts Management at Carnegie Mellon. His current work deals with digital media, and with co-directing the Entertainment Technology Center, a joint initiative between the College of Fine Arts and the School of Computer Science. At the Center, students study a wide variety of immersive entertainment experiences — virtual reality, location-based, and internet-based. Professor Marinelli received his Ph.D. from the University of Pittsburgh, and has been at Carnegie Mellon for the past 22 years.

Describing the relationship between Drama and New Media is complicated for many reasons. In the course of such an examination, connections will surface that run the gamut from dependent and / or causal to symbiotic, and all points in-between. Consequently, one of the main challenges confronting us in an endeavor of this magnitude is in defining the terms to be used throughout this essay. It is taxing enough to consider the influence, impact, and relationship between Drama and technology in general, but focusing on the influence Drama will have on the myriad entertainment technologies existing or now germinating is especially daunting.

There are terms I will use interchangeably in this essay, and I need to identify and explain them first and foremost. The term "New Media" refers both to existing media (namely, theatre, film,

< 37 >

and television) that have been augmented by computer technology, and new forms of expression made possible by digital technology. Computer technology applied to existing media usually results in the replacement of the original analog technology with new digital technology. The introduction of digital technology most often results in greater efficiency over analog technology, as well as a significant expansion of the technology's original functionality. The rightful presumption is that digital technology (be it with "Old" or "New" Media) endows the system with new capabilities and functionalities.

Digital technology changes how the medium's content is conceived, created, captured, and compiled into stories or experiences. For example, digital video cameras and digital video editing have radically altered the entire scope of cinematic post-production possibilities. The Internet, a completely digital medium, has introduced an entirely new way of engaging in business (i.e., e-commerce), interpersonal communication (e-mail and instant chat), and myriad leisure time activities. Since the constant in everything cited above is the impact of digital technology, I will frequently interchange the terms "New Media" and "Digital Technology."

Another term that will play a major role in this essay is "Digital Entertainment." This term recognizes the fact that Drama will most influence those technological ventures that are being done for entertainment purposes. It is important to realize though that Drama in particular will continue to be influential in all aspects of human-computer interaction.

Having said all this, however, I want to pause our discussion of "New Media," and provide a little dose of "Old Media"— in the form of storytelling. This is required because I cannot discuss the relationship of Drama to "New Media" without first discussing my own personal journey to "New Media." I will do my best, though, to make it dramatic.

When I first arrived at Carnegie Mellon University in 1981, I was hired as Assistant to the Head of the Department of Drama. This was barely weeks after completing my doctorate in theatre history, literature and criticism at the University of Pittsburgh under the tutelage of former Carnegie Mellon Drama professor Leon Katz and Attilio "Buck" Favorini, head of the University of Pittsburgh's theatre department. I essentially got into Carnegie Mellon the old fashioned way: *connections*. Leon Katz, it turned out, was an old friend of the then-new head of Carnegie Mellon Drama, Mel Shapiro. A meeting was arranged for the next day,

< 38 >

and before I knew it, the Italian kid from Brooklyn who had grown up in a Jewish neighborhood was hitting it off grandly with the Jewish guy from Brooklyn who had grown up in an Italian neighborhood. Thus began my now twenty year association with Carnegie Mellon Drama.

Carnegie Mellon University has been for decades the Mecca for any aspiring actor, designer, playwright, or director. Carnegie Tech (as it was called until 1967) was *the* place to study theatre. The odds of getting accepted into the school though were miniscule. Hundreds applied each year but barely five percent were accepted. Furthermore, there was no guarantee at all that you'd finish the program. Stories abounded about freshmen being lined up on stage, told to look to their left and right, only to be informed that one of those two young actors would *not* be there next year. Some students thought they had enlisted into the US Marine Corps by accident.

Fortunately, I had circumvented that fear by realizing early in my undergraduate studies that acting was not my strongest point. It soon became obvious to me that I was never going to be cast as a leading man or any kind of romantic figure for that matter (something which was then important). I knew though that I had a great shot at being typecast as a Mafioso or a loving but dimwitted Italian uncle. These roles frankly didn't appeal to me. Bluntly, I thought I had *left* Brooklyn!

By honing my specific skills in administration, financial management, interpersonal communication and other administrative skill sets in what we now call "human resources," and by having a solid background in theatre history, literature, and criticism, I had carved out a unique niche for myself within academic theatre management. As a result, I became a member of the Carnegie Mellon Drama leadership team, and I was ecstatic.

Now, from a paternal perspective, pursuing a career in the theatre wasn't exactly what my father had hoped for his eldest son. I was supposed to be the next incarnation of the great Yankee Clipper, Joltin' Joe DiMaggio. As a rustic Sicilian 5' 7" in height, with a weight problem persistent enough to hear the phrase "pleasingly plump" all too often in my youth, and with eyesight so bad that I was legally blind without my Coke Bottle spectacles, I suspected from a very young age, however, that a career roaming centerfield for the New York Yankees was, shall we say, unlikely. Now if only my father could accept that. Upon coming to Carnegie Mellon however, I immediately called my father and told him that, within the league of college and university theatre,

< 39 >

I was indeed "playing for the Yankees." It worked. The light switched on above his head.

That he understood, and he would proudly convey the Yankee analogy to his friends for the rest of his life. In 1986, I joined the *faculty* of Drama teaching theatre history, dramatic literature, and theatre management. Life seemed complete. Oh, by the way, during the time all of the above was happening in my life, the School of Computer Science at Carnegie Mellon University did not yet exist.

Theatre is studied most often in a chronological manner, commencing with the Greeks. Greek theatre, however, included a great deal of study in theatre technology, for the Greeks had developed stage machinery that helped tell a story in the manner that Greek playwrights thought a story should be told. For example, recognizing the vagaries of fate and the unpredictable nature of the gods, Greek theatre technicians developed a machine consisting of a derrick and a crane that was capable of whisking an actor in a basket from backstage, over the *stoa* (roughly, the upstage proscenium wall), onto center stage in a matter of seconds. This device was called a *Deus ex Machina* or "God from Machine." It was so named because Greek stories and myths embraced the religious belief that gods do indeed appear and impact human lives (sometimes for good and sometimes for ill) and in Drama, at least, they did so "in person."

Another Greek stage machine, the *ekkyklema,* was used to display the horrid results of off-stage actions, such as the bodies of murder victims, battlefield casualties or other horrid sights. This device was needed because Greek dramatists believed audiences would never accept staged (i.e., fake) enactments of battle and death occurring before their own eyes. As a result, it behooved the playwright to confine all such action offstage, out of the sight of the spectators. Aristotle warned that depicting such actions on stage would lessen the impact of the play's thematic content, and make an audience reflect upon the wrong aspects of the performance. Other Greek theatre technology had more practical purposes: larger-than-life actor masks featured built-in megaphones, and boots with huge soles made the actor easier to see in the huge Greek amphitheatres, where upwards of ten thousand people would be seated. The *Deus ex Machina* and the *ekkyklema,* however, were technologies designed for their specific roles in telling the story and advancing the action.

Theatre technology has served a similar purpose in eras much closer to the present day. The most revolutionary time period

< 40 >

during which theatre technology altered the means of storytelling and play enactment occurred in the late nineteenth century. From the standpoint of performance style and genres of theatre, there is absolutely no question that the dominant performance style in North America and Europe is a style we call "realism." Interesting enough, few people realize that technology played a very large part in fueling the revolution of "realism" that occurred in the late nineteenth century. Realism was an outgrowth of naturalism, a theory that called for complete and total verisimilitude on stage, requiring actors, stage setting, and character interaction to come as close to real life as possible. The supposition presumed that audiences would more readily immere themselves in imaginary worlds if those worlds were a mirror of daily existence. The oversight of the naturalists though was in touting the primacy of stage appearance (actors and settings included) to the detriment of storytelling, which is an intentional and fundamental manipulation of time in the service of themes; i.e., meaning. Technology, as it turned out, would be the evolutionary catalyst transforming naturalism into realism.

The advent of electrical lighting in the latter decades of the nineteenth century had a great impact on facilitating a new way of enacting drama, a new way of telling stories. Prior to electrical lighting, stage lighting was done through gas lamps situated around the downstage area of the stage apron where the feeder gas lines could be accommodated more easily. They were called, appropriately enough, footlights.

The poor field of illumination provided by gas lighting resulted in theatres infusing the gas lines with lime, a compound that burned brightly and provided greater illumination to the stage area. Unfortunately though, when combusted, this lime-infused gas gave off an ugly greenish glow which, while bright, cast bright, greenish light upwards into the performers' faces. The resulting ghoulish glow made stage performers look like cadavers! This required great amounts of make-up to compensate for the pasty tones of this illumination. It was also well nigh impossible to regulate the amount of light streaming forth from the front of the stage. Performers were forced to perform in three-quarter or full frontal stage positions so as to be seen from the further reaches of the seating areas. Meanwhile, the actors would cast huge shadows and silhouettes onto the backdrop or act curtain situated upstage. Verisimilitude was impossible. Consequently, the performance style of this era is referred to as "presentational" acting. The plays of this era were largely "melodra-

< 41 >

mas" where, if anything, the lighting constraints worked in favor of the script and story.

The harnessing of electric power exerted a greater influence on stage design and production techniques than any other single invention. Stage lighting became an art form in itself. For the first time, lifelike lighting effects could be replicated and manipulated on stage. Furthermore, the entire stage space suddenly became open to the imaginary world of the play. No longer did inferior lighting technology require performances to occur downstage near the footlights. As a result of these new technological advances, the entire stage playing area was suddenly opened up to theatrical creativity. There was a subliminal irony in that artists' demands for plays with greater depth and a more realistic portrayal of the human condition, were facilitated by technology that literally opened up the entire stage area to the imagination of directors and actors alike. Thanks to the revolution of electric lighting, action could occur fully upstage, center stage, or anyplace within the playing area, and be seen fully by the audience. Stage lighting and technology fostered the development of subtlety in stage performance. The reign of melodrama was being challenged at last.

Electric lighting also allowed for the creation of exceptional lighting effects on stage, from "specials" that illuminated a single actor to area lighting that could provide visual cues to the thematic action of the unfolding story. In fact, many of the "-isms" of the early twentieth century (Cubism, Surrealism, Expressionism, Futurism, etc) were spurred on by the advent of new theatre technologies. Some of the more daring theatre practitioners, such as Gordon Craig, would ultimately dream of a theatre capable of telling a story on stage solely through the manipulation of light, as was the aspiration for Stravinsky's *Firebird Suite*. There would be no need for actors at all.

The reason I found the aspects of theatre history cited above so interesting can be traced back to the topic of my doctoral dissertation: a critical bibliography of Filippo Tommaso Marinetti, the founder of Italian Futurism. The dissertation bore the title, "The Making of a Futurist." Italian Futurism, under the leadership of F.T. Marinetti, was the first cultural movement to embrace industry and technology as the pinnacle achievements of mankind's artistic endeavors, this pronouncement being proclaimed on the front page of the Parisian daily newspaper *Le Figaro* in February 1909. In technology, the Futurists saw the ultimate aspiration for the human species, because technology was a de

< 42 >

facto concrete transformation of mankind's ontological limitations. The Italian Futurists may have begun as a movement focusing on modern poetry, but the ephemeral quickly lost out to the tangible. Through the creation of new forms of machines, mankind was now able to experience flight, to cross great tracts of land or water in a minimum of days, to construct giant steel bridges that negated geographic obstacles, to experience the sensation of speed, and, most importantly, to literally defy death at every turn. Their belief in technology was such that they sought the creation of a new generation of young people enamored of and empowered by industry. This belief system led ultimately to an ethos dominated by the machine and technology, and a resulting equivocation of life and art. In the eyes of the Italian Futurists, a belief in technology should neuter a belief in God.

The futurist merging of life and art within a new world shaped by technology, had always fascinated me. It fascinated me because I, too, shared this enthusiasm for technology, even though I wasn't exactly mechanically inclined as a young man (or as a middle-aged man, for that matter). Of equal interest to me, however, was the fact that Italian Futurism's slavish adoration of machine culture had resulted in F.T. Marinetti and many of his followers becoming ardent fascists during the dictatorship of Benito Mussolini. Though Marinetti often disagreed with Il Duce's actions, there was no getting around the fact that the futurists supported Italy's nationalistic self-aggrandizement and international belligerency. The story of Italian Futurism revealed that the interconnections between art, life, and technology could indeed be very dangerous.

As a result, more than serendipity seemed at work when, in 1995, friends of mine in the School of Computer Science received a sizeable federal grant to create a digital video database for a very "sci-fi" sounding project called Informedia. Upon hearing this news, I picked up the telephone, contacted my friend and soon-to-be-collaborator Scott Stevens, and asked if I could "play in his sandbox." Much to my utter astonishment, I was welcomed with open arms by Scott and his co-principal investigator Vice Provost Howard Wactlar. Instead of the laughter or snickers that I had feared, I listened amazed to compliments about the skills I would bring to this project, how I possessed a different way of seeing the world, and how I would make an excellent addition to the Informedia team.

Work on Informedia led to collaboration with colleagues Scott Stevens, Mike Christel, and Alex Hauptman on the Synthetic In-

< 43 >

terview technology (which I will go into greater depth about later in this essay). Concurrent with this endeavor was the establishment by then Dean of the School of Computer Science, Raj Reddy, of the Entertainment Technology Center (ETC), a joint initiative between the College of Fine Arts and the School of Computer Science. Very early in his administration, President Jared Cohon, further embraced the idea of Carnegie Mellon University being a logical location for an Entertainment Technology Center because of its strong reputation in fine arts and computer science.

The fact that I was the first Drama professor to ever cross over into the School of Computer Science was raising eyebrows across the country. Shortly after I began working in the School of Computer Science, I recall attending a Defense Advanced Research Projects Agency (DARPA) gathering in Orlando at the behest of my colleague and Entertainment Technology Center Co-director, Randy Pausch. Unbeknownst to me, I was part of the presentation. Towards the end of the meeting I was called upon to answer one simple question before the assembled gathering of computer scientists and government researchers: what exactly were the experiences and thoughts of a Drama professor residing in such a high-powered technology center as the Carnegie Mellon School of Computer Science? The context more than the question caught me off guard, because, in all honesty, I had been asking myself the same question ever since I "crossed over" from a life devoted fully to the theatre to one now very much immersed in computer science. I recall the room falling silent when I replied, "Frankly, I feel as though I have never left Drama." The puzzled expressions beckoned clarification. I continued. I pointed out that Drama is the original collaborative art form, utilizing the full dimension of human expression: speech, song, gesture, dance, movement, stage setting, background, lighting, costumes, sound (in all of its forms), as well as linear narrative and dramatic structure. What I have found is that Computer Science, especially within the realm of entertainment technology, can be as collaborative as anything we do in Drama.

I stressed that the most important point, however, had to do with the unrealized similarities between the theatrical way of thinking and the basic thought processes in computer science. I explained further. The fundamental building block of computer science, from a software perspective, is the algorithm. What is an algorithm? As defined by Merriam-Webster's Collegiate Dictionary, an algorithm is "a procedure for solving a mathematical problem in a finite number of steps that frequently involves rep-

< 44 >

etition of an operation." We understand algorithms most often as "if-then" equations, constructs, procedures, and formulas for solving a problem.

I then pointed out how we in Drama have always abided by algorithmic thinking; we just don't call it that. A director, for example, works with the actor to surmise how a particular character's actions on stage will be perceived by the audience. The logic of directing is such that in his mind's eye, the director is constructing a series of stage actions for a specific character that are designed to achieve a specific goal in the minds of the audience. For example, *IF* Hamlet enters from upstage right without saying a word, but then makes his way to center stage, glances in the direction from where Ophelia just exited, then turns to face the audience but doesn't see them—pauses—and thereafter commences his soliloquy, *THEN* the audience should perceive Hamlet as delusional, beset by indecision, cognizant of what actions should be taken but unsure of whether or not he can actually make these things come to pass. In an algorithm such as this, mathematics has been replaced by human psychology, sociology, and the social mores of a specific culture (in this instance, Danish royalty). This thought process on the part of a director occurs as a result of a formal education in philosophy, psychology, directing theory and implementation techniques, many of which are codified in directing textbooks and literature. The relationship between Drama and the "New Media," however, transcends the fundamental similarity discussed above between theatre and computer science.

The most important connection between Drama and the "New Media" is in the blurring of the line between "audience" and "actor." The theatrical metaphor is most vital and profound in the transformation of computer "user" into "actor." And, this transformation from passive viewer (in the traditional performance genres) to active participant is the result of the most fundamental change brought about by digital technology: "interactivity."

The profundity of interactivity cannot be underestimated. Interactivity is the entertainment hallmark of America's young. Interactivity is recognized as a paradigm shift of major proportions precisely because it allows one who had been merely a passive viewer to engage fully in the entertainment experience. Using the theatrical metaphor, we can say that the traditional division between actor and audience has been blurred and, in many instances, obliterated. Digital technology has gone a long way—

< 45 >

and will go further—into making William Shakespeare's famous quotation "all the world's a stage" not just correct but prescient.

Professor Janet Murray, formerly of MIT and most recently at Georgia Tech, in her groundbreaking book *Hamlet on the Holodeck: The Future of Narrative in Cyberspace*, was the first scholar to grapple with the core dynamics and attributes of interactivity. Murray posited that what truly constituted human-computer interactivity were the user attributes of *immersion, agency,* and *transformation. Immersion,* Murray states "is a metaphorical term derived from the physical experience of being submerged in water . . . the sensation of being surrounded by a completely other reality." This "submersion" in the story excites us because of a "feeling of alertness that comes from being in this new place" and the "delight that comes from learning to move within it." *Agency* refers to the ability of players to take meaningful, tangible actions within the virtual world. The main tool of agency is *navigation,* a term that refers to the ability of the player to explore the inner depths of the world through some form of interface, such as keyboard, mouse, joystick, or some other input device, perhaps one utilizing speech, sound, a head mounted display (HMD), touch screen, or some input device not yet imagined. *Transformation* refers to the player's ability and desire to relive the experience by replaying the game. Murray succinctly captures this desire when she calls it the "love of variation." Implicit in this dynamic is the desire to have an experience that may be *transformative* in its living out.

This latter reference is where the importance, influence, and pending impact of Drama truly comes to the forefront, because what Janet Murray has hit upon is the dramatic evolution of the passive theatre audience member to a computer "user," then to an engaged "player" and, finally, to a genuine "actor." The continuing revolution of computer processing power, and the development of terabytes of data storage technology, is making the impossible probable: the ability of an individual to transform him or herself into a full-fledged actor/character within a virtual, imaginary world. These immanent technologies will soon make it possible for the actor to engage virtual characters in discussion or cross-examination, to move through the virtual world in fulfillment of a purpose, and to expand the boundaries of storytelling by engaging in a reality that is nonlinear, where there is no prescripted plotline that you, the "cast member," must follow. Instead, you will be faced with as many choices in the "virtual" world as you might encounter in a similar "real" world situation.

< 46 >

From a historical standpoint, though, the language of drama was *not* the simile by which digital entertainment extolled the enormous potential of interactivity. Rather, the nomenclature of present day digital entertainment is derived from "games" and "sport," and this metaphor is appropriate because you *cannot* be a passive observer when "playing" a sport! The individual has become "engaged," and the player's actions now have a significant impact on the unfolding drama and ultimate outcome of the game or story. The reality, though, is that most of the unfolding "dramas" available in computer interaction are quite simply— "games." Most people do not realize that in ancient Greece, the earliest theatre festivals were—like the Olympics— "competitive," with cash prizes and laurels being given to the "winner."

As is paramount with the structure of games, there are rules that have to be followed. For example, in baseball, four balls means the batter gets on base; three strikes and the batter is out. Teams play for nine innings, there are twenty-seven outs; and there is no clock. Yet for all of those "rules" and "regulations," there remain an infinite variety of events that can occur during a baseball game. Decisions are made amidst myriad choices and possible actions available to the player. There are so many variables involved that seldom are two games replicated, and fans show up to see how certain decisions will lead to particular results within the sport's rule set.

Games and sports require active participation. When we combine this demand for "active participation" with the reality of generational change, we happen upon a generation of youth who not only relish the experience of active participation, but who seek to push the limits of human endurance. There is, for instance, a clear irony in the fact that *Generation X* (post-baby boomers), a generation lambasted and lampooned for its distrust and aversion to societal norms, was among the first to embrace and extol the individual empowerment offered by computer games. *Generation Y* (those born since about 1975) did them one better. Today, their legacy is alive and well in the guise of *extreme* sports and adventures that propel young people into truly death-defying acts. Among this particular demographic, the X-Games are more popular than the Olympics.

We can, at this juncture, see a convergence between the training methodology of the famous Russian acting teacher Konstantin Stanislavsky, and the interactive capabilities of digital technology. It is the goal of any actor trained in Stanislavsky's method to

< 47 >

"live in the moment" and to "live in the imaginary world of the play," both of which demand that the actor be immersed in both the physical environment of the space and the interpersonal dynamics of the characters. The requirement of both "authentic" acting on stage and the actor/player's virtual experience, is the "willing suspension of disbelief." Furthermore, digital media is striving towards the creation of human-computer interactions that are anthropomorphic in nature. Regardless of whether the villains are creatures from another galaxy, flesh-eating zombies, or crazed gunmen, game play centers on engaging the player with values straight out of Maslow's "Hierarchy of Needs."

At this point, it behooves us to investigate the specific venues of the new interactive media. The computer-generated technology that most overtly thrusts the user into a state similar to that of a genuine theatrical or cinematic environment is *Virtual Reality (VR)*. As the name professes, the reality the actor encounters here is entirely virtual. In other words, the world is a visual representation, albeit in three dimensions. The actor requires a special visual device, called a Head-Mounted Display, in order to enter this world. At present, Virtual Reality environments are as close as we get in the entertainment sphere to the Star Trek notion of "beaming" a human being into a completely different universe. With the exception of direct speech interface, the actor in a *Virtual World* environment possesses the dynamic attributes of interactivity singled out by Janet Murray: *immersion, agency,* and *transformation,* albeit in minimal form.

Another emerging technology that offers a *VR*-like experience is called a *Cave Automatic Virtual Environment (CAVE)*. Like *VR* head-mounted displays, a *CAVE* seeks to place the actor within an all-encompassing environment. *CAVEs* offer display surfaces on the three walls surrounding the actor, and can be extended to include the ceiling, floor space, and (literal) fourth wall. Whereas traditional Virtual Reality requires a special device like a head-mounted display, *CAVEs* can achieve their desired effect by having the actor wear 3D glasses, thus allowing the actor's head to move freely around the projected, immersive environment. *CAVEs* have so far exhibited many of the same limitations as virtual environments, and have not yet been able to engage the actor in an unfolding story by endowing the actor with agency, navigation, and transformation. What both *VR* and *CAVE* environments have shown is that the acting space no longer needs to be a theatre. Digital technology has created countless new venues wherein an individual can immerse him or herself in an imaginary world.

< 48 >

Synthetic Interviews, or early emergent virtual environments, is a technology developed at Carnegie Mellon University by School of Computer Science senior research scientists Scott Stevens and Michael Christel, and was one of the first attempts to create a truly *synthetic character*. Implicit in this project was the aspiration to create a *Synthetic Interview* so realistic that it would essentially pass the Turing Test for anthropomorphic synthetic characters.

The original goal of a *Synthetic Interview* was to permit experts to scale, and individuals to span time. It is a technology and technique that creates an anthropomorphic interface with multimedia data of a particular kind: video of a person responding to questions (interacting with another person). The responses of the interviewee are presented in such a way as to simulate the experience of interacting with a live person. Thus, *Synthetic Interviews* provide a means of conversing in depth with an individual or character, permitting users to ask questions in a conversational manner (just as they would if they were interviewing the figure face to face), and receive relevant, pertinent answers to the questions asked.

Throughout the development of the *Synthetic Interview* technology, Stanislavsky's notes on the creation of character were an essential educational supplement, as important to the overall process as was the software design itself. One of the most salient realizations on the part of the researchers was the degree to which gesture, breathing, gaze, eye motion and direction, blinking, pausing during delivery, and innumerable other facial attributes, were of utmost importance in conveying nuance and subtext, the intangibles that make us truly human. Without the inclusion of these essential human qualities, the synthetic character remains—*synthetic*.

The most famous synthetic character to date has been Jar-Jar Binks from the movie *Star Wars: The Phantom Menace*, and while audiences and critics alike hailed the graphic and editing skills that allowed a completely synthetic character to appear so seamlessly in a live-action movie, there was universal agreement that the synthetic character's "personality" was not conveyed successfully (unless George Lucas' sole goal was to create an enormously annoying sidekick!). Through a heightened relationship between drama and computer science, it is only a matter of time before no one will be able to detect the *real* amidst the *synthetic*. And, when that moment occurs, it will be because of the millennium-old observations of human behavior contained within the art—and heart—of Drama.

< 49 >

References

Murray, Janet. (1997) *Hamlet on the Holodeck: The Future of Narrative in Cyberspace.* New York: Free Press.

< 50 >

A Perspective on the Faculty

Joseph (Jay) B. Kadane

Jay Kadane is the Leonard J. Savage University Professor of Statistics and Social Sciences at Carnegie Mellon. He studies statistical inference, especially Bayesian statistical inference, from both a theoretical and applied viewpoint. Professor Kadane received his Ph.D. from Stanford University in 1966, and has been at Carnegie Mellon since 1971.

Introduction

The opportunity to write this essay allows me to look back on the important steps in my education and development as a professor of statistics, with an eye toward the problems and issues I am currently engaged in at Carnegie Mellon. From this reconsideration, several themes develop, and they have more to do with moral principle, community, face-to-face discussions, integrity, breadth of undergraduate learning, and interdisciplinary leadership than they do with the specific demands of my field. We as faculty are called upon to perform many functions that are not part of our training. I was trained technically, and I conjecture that many of our Carnegie Mellon faculty were trained technically to perform certain kinds of analyses and computations or to achieve certain kinds of artistic expression. Yet my university teaching and activities have led me to understand that the moral component of what I have to teach is far more important than anything techni-

< 51 >

cal. Many of us at the University are called upon to advise students, to serve on and to chair committees, and to lead departments. Again, nothing in our formal training prepares us for these roles. Faculty find models for what they do in the actions of others before them, and invent based on their own experiences. Universities are about people, and the level of apprenticeship and colleagueship that people interested in teaching and learning can have with one another. Much of the most important learning and teaching happen in one-on-one interactions outside the context of regular classes. Indeed, because of the strong influence of these relationships in my life, I am skeptical that distance teaching can provide an adequate education.

UNDERGRADUATE EDUCATION

I did my undergraduate degree in mathematics at Harvard. I chose math, not because I necessarily expected to be a mathematician, but because I thought it would be good training for whatever I finally settled on. In my undergraduate years, 1958-62, I was deeply concerned about the prospect that there might be a nuclear war, which was not an unreasonable thing to think at that time. As a result, I was attracted to the social sciences and to organizational work in international affairs. Most of my friends were majoring in various social sciences—economics, government, social relations (a hybrid department at Harvard), etc.—and most of what we discussed was politics.

Thus I was led to the efforts to reduce the danger that the Cold War would suddenly go hot, especially to efforts toward arms control and disarmament. I took Henry Kissinger's Defense Policy Seminar, but it was disappointing, since it seemed to me that he mainly used it to ingratiate himself with Washington potentates by inviting them to address us. My principal faculty contact was with Tom Schelling, a maverick economist who taught game theory and wanted to understand how the Korean War stayed limited, in that no nuclear weapons were used. I took all the courses he offered, and apprenticed myself to him. Another faculty member who influenced me was Roger Fisher, a law professor. His specialty was negotiations, finding ways to reach agreements with a view to finding mutually beneficial deals. Through him, I got the opportunity to brief Eddie McCormick, who was running in the primary against Teddy Kennedy for a Senate seat, on the Trade Expansion Act and the theory of comparative advantage.

< 52 >

Communications of all sorts with other undergraduates played a major role in my education. The mathematics department itself seemed quite uninterested in undergraduates; I never did make serious contact with anyone there. At least as influential to my development as these other faculty contacts across a range of disciplines, most particularly in the social sciences, and the apprenticeships that followed, were my contacts with other students. I remember lunches that went until three in the afternoon, because everyone had a lot to discuss.

In recounting these undergraduate experiences, I wonder how distance education, with its sense of remoteness from a residential campus, would have worked for me. The most meaningful parts of my education, contact with fellow students and apprenticeships with faculty (in my case, in subjects quite distinct from my major), would not have been possible had my access to them been purely electronic. So far, those most interested in distance education seem to emphasize the delivery of course material. My experience, however, suggests to me that the more important part of education may occur outside the classroom in a face-to-face moral and social community.

GRADUATE SCHOOL AND THE CENTER FOR NAVAL ANALYSES

As a junior, I took a two-semester course in statistics from Art Dempster and Fred Mosteller. Fred sent me to Howard Raiffa in the Business School for advice about graduate schools. At his suggestion, I wound up at Stanford in the Statistics Department, with a strong interest in econometrics. But in my first summer after graduation, I got a job at the Center for Naval Analyses (CNA), on the recommendation of Tom Schelling. My boss had been there only three weeks when I arrived. My assignment was "find something interesting to do, and do it." I apprenticed myself (again!) to Dr. John Coyle, a nuclear strategist, and thought and wrote about the counterforce doctrine, the targeting of enemy forces rather than cities, and the possibility of nuclear destabilization that might result. I worked for CNA after my first year of graduate school as well, again on matters of nuclear strategy. I kept a connection with CNA for quite some years after this, as a consultant.

In graduate school at Stanford, I hung out with, and took courses with, the economists as much as I did with the statisticians. I was especially interested in the work of Kenneth Arrow,

< 53 >

and took all the courses he offered. The Statistics Department was quite theoretically oriented. My advisor, Herman Chernoff, admitted, "We all do statistics in the Department, it's just that we don't talk about it here." I got a client in the Political Science Department and persuaded Lincoln Moses in Statistics to advise me about it. I would read the materials in Political Science, decide what I thought would be an appropriate statistical analysis, and then discuss it with Lincoln. He would straighten me out, and then I would go back to the political scientists with answers. Although totally outside the curriculum, this is how I learned the practical side of statistics.

In addition to my technical work, I was also active in the student movement at Stanford. Stanford, when I arrived in 1962, was a socially and intellectually stultifying place. Neither political nor religious meetings were permitted on campus (except for the official kind in the official chapel). The campus was nominally dry, and several students every year were killed in driving accidents returning from off-campus liquor parties. Undergraduate women could be expelled for violations of parietal rules in single-sex dormitories, but, to my best recollection, no action would be taken against the men. Some of the best graduate students every year would leave in despair over campus climate and actions taken by central administration. My group decided to stay and fight.

At the time that the Berkeley campus started to address its own cultural problems, I became Stanford coordinator of the Free Speech Movement, and helped form the Graduate Coordinating Committee. Members of these groups ran for election as graduate representatives in the Stanford Student Legislature. When we won, we took seats that had long been vacant for lack of interest. A year later, I was elected Speaker of the Student Legislature. We worked hard and managed to change many of the policies we found most objectionable, and to attract both student and faculty interest toward education in the widest sense of intellectual and personal growth.

A reasonable question, and one raised by fellow students as well as faculty and administrators, is "why care?" Why should we care about defining so broadly the range of concerns in undergraduate education? I suppose part of the answer lies in a sense of citizenship, that wherever one is, one gains from the culture of the place, and by the same token has a responsibility to enhance it. I suspect that for me, some of this sense of accepting group membership has a religious root as well, although

< 54 >

these religious identifications are not currently very salient in my life.

There is also a related issue of "leadership." From time to time, I hear rhetoric aimed at encouraging people to be leaders, but I think this is misplaced. I aspire to be flexible, able to lead when that is called for, but just as able to follow someone else's lead. A person who is uncomfortable in anything other than a leadership role can be as much of a group problem as someone who is incapable of leading.

While members of the Stanford Administration had been used to intimidating undergraduate student leaders, they were perplexed about what to do with this new group. I, for one, didn't look like a typical student radical, since I had short hair and wore a jacket and tie for appointments. Moreover, I was holding a security clearance through CNA. As long as I did my coursework and wrote my thesis, the Statistics Department would protect me from the members of the central administration. The administrators knew that they could make whatever threats they wanted to, but they would read about them the next day in the *Stanford Daily*. This helped them concentrate on the message, since they had a hard time attacking the messenger. I think they were relieved to see me leave with my Ph.D. in 1966, but a few years later when Vietnam War protests were at their height and they had to deal with the next wave of campus leaders, I must have seemed rather moderate by comparison.

YALE AND CNA (AGAIN)

My first academic job was at Yale, half in the Statistics Department and half in the Cowles Foundation for Research in Economics. The dominant figure in Statistics at the time was L. J. "Jimmy" Savage, one of the founders of the modern Bayesian movement in statistics, and a man of enormous intellectual depth. Whenever I was confused about some point in statistics, I could always ask him, and get an interesting and intelligent answer. I learned a lot, but also found myself in danger of losing some intellectual independence. The other major influence on me at Yale was Marc Nerlove, an econometrician at Cowles.

During my second academic year at Yale, Nerlove went off to visit Harvard, and Savage spent the spring in Italy. I was left teaching Nerlove's econometrics course, and standing in as Director of Graduate Studies for Savage. That spring, I was in Wash-

< 55 >

ington on a trip to consult with CNA. The friends I had worked with during my second summer at CNA had risen to be managers. They invited me back for a full-time year-round position, and I took a leave of absence from Yale. My responsibilities were to publish papers in the open literature (which would help with recruiting) and to be available to consult on projects. If there were projects whose politics made me uncomfortable (not impossible in 1968, with the Vietnam War going strong), I could decline to participate.

At CNA, I no longer had Jimmy Savage to consult with about my statistical issues. Indeed, I was the senior statistician there, and all sorts of colleagues were turning to *me* for advice. This made me more independent and self-confident in my judgments, and also increased my interest in the philosophical side of statistical inference, because I wanted to be sure that my advice was sound.

After a year at CNA, I got a rather handsome offer from Carnegie Mellon—a position as Associate Professor with tenure, and a chair in interdisciplinary studies. My sponsors were Dean Richard Cyert of GSIA, the business school, and Morrie DeGroot, head of the rather newly formed Statistics Department. I was to be half in GSIA and half in Statistics. While I liked the offer, I was not ready to leave Washington yet. Carnegie Mellon agreed that I would be on leave until I was ready to make the move, which turned out to be two years later, in the fall of 1971.

CARNEGIE MELLON UNIVERSITY

My first year at Carnegie Mellon, Cyert was also acting head of Statistics, while DeGroot was taking a sabbatical in Europe. Tragically, on the way to begin his sabbatical, his wife came down with multiple sclerosis. It became obvious that his main energies had to go toward caring for his wife, and that he would not have much attention to devote to the Department. Cyert asked me if I would step in as department head, as I was the only other tenured member. A chaired full professor, I became head of the Statistics Department. When I reflect that only six years before I had been such a pain to the Stanford Administration, I can only conclude that sometimes God has a wicked sense of humor.

The reporting structure, which sounds like a mess, actually worked out to be an advantage. I reported to the Deans of GSIA and CIT (the engineering college). I participated in the councils

< 56 >

of both GSIA and CIT, and learned a lot about management and the people involved. I especially gained from participating in the CIT Dean's Council and learning from the Dean of Engineering, Herb Toor. At the time I became head (summer of 1972), Richard Cyert (former Dean of GSIA) was beginning a 17-year term as President of Carnegie Mellon, and the Statistics Department had only six members.

We were a tiny line in the University budget. Statistics was being taught in many departments on campus, with varying levels of sophistication and success. Within our discipline, nationally and internationally, the high-prestige statistical work was mathematical, and rather divorced from applied considerations. The University context prized interdisciplinary work. Without some fast swimming on our part, we were a minnow just waiting for an academic pike to swallow for lunch.

We resolved the problem of the tension between disciplinary and University pressures by emphasizing collaborative, applied interdisciplinary efforts. To make this real to a largely junior department, we made the commitment that applied research would be judged on the basis of its contribution to the field of application, not to statistics. And if we didn't know the applied field well enough to judge, we undertook to get advice from someone who did. This assurance is necessary to give identical incentives to each member of an interdisciplinary team, and is obviously a necessary prerequisite for successful interdisciplinary work.

A department head is, of course, responsible for protecting, developing and buffering the faculty. One of the most important parts of this is to make the internal incentives put before the faculty member consistent with the external incentives and goals faced by the department. Supporting applied work in this way is an example.

We aimed for a combination of applied and theoretical work, and that is what we got. Our recruits found the wider range of intellectual activities stimulating, and what started off as a conflict of values produced instead a different paradigm: theory strengthened practice, and practice posed new theoretical questions.

As our applied work took us all over campus, more and more students started taking our courses. We worked with various departments to fashion courses suitable for their majors, and gradually they came to trust us to teach their students. And each year I would make a case for more faculty, based partly on the teaching we were doing. At one point, President Cyert, while agreeing that we deserved more resources, remarked that he was

< 57 >

having trouble extracting the resources from the departments whose students we were absorbing. But, of course, that was his job, not mine.

DEPARTMENTAL LEADERSHIP

Teamwork is a very important aspect of the culture of the Statistics Department. We work together in many ways—research, teaching, advising, supervising students and staff, making department exams, hosting guests, etc. Broad authority is delegated, with an eye to developing leadership for the future. One of the essential jobs of an administrator is to train successors, and our structure reinforces faculty taking on increasing responsibility as they became more senior.

This idea of teamwork is especially important in thinking about the relationship between faculty as advisors and students as advisees. It is not essential that each faculty member connect with each student (in fact, it isn't possible). What is important is that each student have the opportunity to connect with someone on the faculty. As long as someone on the faculty is in touch with each student, the faculty as a group is doing its job for the students as a group.

One important institution I introduced was an *ad hoc* promotion and tenure committee, combining aspects of departmental and college review. It was designed to preview our promotion and tenure cases before they moved on to official university-wide review. In addition to DeGroot and me, it contained a number of strong department heads and faculty from around campus—all the likely hungry pike, as I look back on it. This way our cases would receive serious and tough scrutiny from the start, which was a good signal both to the Department and the University. It gave the pike a stake in the Department, and was part of the process of absorbing statistics courses from around the University.

How did I learn what I needed to be department head? It certainly had nothing to do with the courses I took. In those courses, I was trained to prove theorems about the distributions of random variables. It was everything else—the political work at both Harvard and Stanford, the understanding of how organizations work that came from my social science studies, and the practical training I got on the job that made it possible.

I think this is often the experience of faculty: we are given many tasks for which we have no training at all, and for which

< 58 >

we were not selected. Cyert and DeGroot hired me because of my econometrics and search theory, but I was supposed to teach, advise, be a boss, hire good faculty and staff, deal with the personal problems of students and faculty, and avoid the pike. There is nothing in how we are trained and selected that gives us the skills we need for our many jobs.

Partly in response to this thought, I have developed over the last few years a mentoring seminar for statistics graduate students. We discuss the cultural topics not included in the more technical courses, such as how to write a paper, write a referee report, respond to a referee report, the role of editors, how to write a grant proposal, what the university tenure and promotion system is about, how to handle academic integrity issues that arise in work as teaching assistants, how to write a vita, how to find a job, etc. While such a seminar does not prepare students explicitly for the job of being department head, it does at least initiate a discussion of the wider, nontechnical context of the work.

ACADEMIC INTEGRITY AT CARNEGIE MELLON

One recent endeavor gives some flavor of how disconnected our lives are from our training. A few years ago I was chair of a Carnegie Mellon Task Force on Academic Integrity, looking into the functioning of the University's system for handling cases of suspected student cheating. As we discussed the issue among ourselves and with our colleagues, two attitudes were repeatedly voiced to us. The first took the view that student cheating is not the concern of the faculty. "It's not my job. I was hired to teach my subject. If a student cheats, he or she won't succeed in life. I'm not going to do anything about it." This amounts, in my view, to a total abdication of the faculty's role in setting an example of moral concern, and of maintaining a grading system that is fair to the students.

There is a second level of discounting that we also heard. This position acknowledges that the faculty member must deal with cheating, but regards it as the private business of the faculty member and the student. Such a view is contrary to University policy for two good reasons: to provide an avenue for students to appeal the actions of a faculty member whom they feel has unjustly accused them, and to catch repeat offenders. In some sense, the position of dealing with cheating without reporting it to the

< 59 >

Dean of Students takes the extreme of too much responsibility for the faculty member.

As usual in these matters, wisdom lies in a middle course that avoids both extremes. The faculty member must be on the alert, and confront suspicious circumstances. When cheating is found, the faculty member should take action at the course level, and report the incident to the Dean, so that the general University community can participate in reviewing the incident to see if appropriate action was taken.

The work of the task force involved developing a statement on Academic Integrity, which we brought successfully for approval to the Faculty Senate, the Student Senate, the Staff Council, and the President's Council. But getting a statement blessed by all these groups does not necessarily change behavior. Since, without an honor system, the responsibility for enforcing standards falls to the faculty, the active cooperation of the faculty is essential to confronting the issue. While the Dean of Students, Michael Murphy, cares deeply about these issues and has trained his staff accordingly, he needs the trust and help of the faculty to succeed. Accordingly, the Task Force proposed and set up a system of Academic Integrity Advisors, faculty members in each department available to advise both faculty and students about how the system works, and how their situation, whatever it is, may relate to the system. Passing a statement is only the start of changing attitudes and behavior.

I have come to see that what I have to teach about truth telling and straightforward dealing is much more important, to me and to my students, than details of statistical procedures. How odd that, having studied the technical side of empirical knowledge for so many years, I find myself believing that moral philosophy, in which I have no training, is what I must teach.

FACULTY SENATE AT CARNEGIE MELLON

Some years after stepping out of the job of being Department Head in Statistics, I was invited to become active in the Faculty Senate, most of whose members are elected by the faculty. At the time, the Faculty Organization was submitting proposals for revision of its constitution to the faculty almost yearly. This incremental approach to modernization was an annoyance, and had resulted in a set of documents that were mutually contradictory. It was impossible to run the Faculty Senate under the inherited rules.

< 60 >

The year I served as vice-chair (and hence chair-elect) of the Faculty Senate, a committee I chaired, with Toby Davis and Henry Pisciotta as members, rewrote the Constitution and Bylaws. Our basic idea was to put into the Constitution only those matters that we thought should take a vote of the faculty as a whole to change, leaving all the details to the Bylaws, which could be changed by a simple majority of the Faculty Senate. Our proposals were adopted nearly without change. We must have done okay, because the Constitution has remained unchanged since that time.

My year as chair of the Faculty Senate passed reasonably uneventfully. My work consisted primarily of trying to help a new president of Carnegie Mellon (Robert Mehrabian) become comfortable with his surroundings and understand the informal culture of the place. Just recently I was asked to serve again as chair of the Faculty Senate, under President Jared Cohon, when the elected chair and vice-chair had both become ineligible for various reasons. The spring of 2000 was taken up with the issue of granting health benefits to qualified domestic partners.

The chair of the Faculty Senate has the official and public responsibility for appointing committees and chairing meetings. There is also a private side to this office. The chair meets regularly in one-on-one meetings with the president, the provost, and various other administrative officials. These private meetings allow for many problems to be resolved before they become public issues, contributing, in that way, to the smooth running and innovative practice that Carnegie Mellon must have to reach its highest potential.

CONCLUSION

The administration of universities and colleges is becoming progressively more complex and professional. There are national and international membership groups for development, for financial aid officers, for student affairs, campus planning, and so forth. All this is for the better, as there is every reason for universities to benchmark best practices among their peers, and to avoid mistakes that have been made elsewhere. At the same time, this professionalism might lead administrative personnel to be less open and sensitive to faculty on their own campuses, since their professional relationships connect them intimately with administrative peers who may be thousands of miles away on quite different campuses, or perhaps on no campus at all. Similarly, faculty

< 61 >

need to connect to their own resident communities, develop a sensitivity to the culture of the campus, and foster a sense of place. Both faculty and administration ought to work harder at developing ties to the culture and history of their own institutions. Only in an atmosphere of genuine cooperation and self-knowledge can an organization as complex as a modern research university grow and prosper.

< 62 >

CHANGES IN ENGINEERING EDUCATION: PAST, PRESENT, AND FUTURE

Cliff I. Davidson

Cliff Davidson is Professor of Civil and Environmental Engineering and Engineering and Public Policy at Carnegie Mellon. His research and teaching interests are in the area of air quality engineering. Professor Davidson earned his Ph.D. from the California Institute of Technology in 1977, and has been at Carnegie Mellon for 26 years.

The discipline of engineering has changed rapidly in the past several decades, and, not surprisingly, engineering education has also changed. Many of the most significant changes have come in my own lifetime and have been pioneered at Carnegie Mellon. Contributions to this volume by Adnan Akay, Granger Morgan, and David Dzombak and Cliff Davidson focus on changes in the areas of mechanical engineering, environmental engineering, and technology and public policy. In this chapter I offer a general overview of engineering education in three distinct time periods: before 1950, 1950–1990, and 1990–2000. Throughout that discussion, I highlight the role of our university in providing leadership in educational innovations. I also consider what the future is likely to bring for the education of engineers at Carnegie Mellon and elsewhere in this country.

The United States expanded rapidly in both land area and population in the early 1800s, and with this development came

< 63 >

the need for construction of housing, factories, roads, bridges, and railroads. The first technical schools in the country were established in the 1820s and 1830s in an attempt to provide a highly trained workforce for these projects. However, the demand for workers could not be satisfied by the few existing technical schools; most engineers at this time were educated by self-study or on the job training (Layton 1971).

Formal technical education gained momentum by the middle of the nineteenth century. Especially important was development of the railroad as a large and powerful industry; this ultimately helped engineers to be recognized as professionals (Chandler 1965). Rensselaer Polytechnic Institute, originally founded in the 1820's, was re-organized as an engineering school in 1847. The Massachusetts Institute of Technology was founded in 1861 with a focus on engineering. Programs of study in these early institutions included courses in mathematics, geology, physics, chemistry, hydraulics, and mechanics (Bledstein 1976). By 1870, there were 21 engineering colleges; this number grew to 110 by 1896 (Layton 1971). Unlike the first technical schools, which focused on the practical side of getting the job done, the new programs emphasized engineering as a profession with considerable social status, high salaries, and service to society. They emphasized craftsman and artisan skills. The establishment of the American Society of Civil Engineers in 1852, and its rapid growth after the Civil War, reflect these changes (Bledstein 1976). The engineering discipline further expanded by the end of the century to include mining, metallurgical, electrical, and chemical engineering (Layton 1971).

It was at this time that Carnegie Technical Schools was founded by Andrew Carnegie. Originally intended to educate and train Pittsburgh's industrial workers, the four schools established in 1900 included the School of Science and Technology, the School of Fine and Applied Arts, the School for Apprentices and Journeymen, and the Margaret Morrison Carnegie School for Women. In 1912, the schools merged and became the Carnegie Institute of Technology (CIT), offering four-year college degrees including engineering. CIT essentially became a military encampment during World War I, as over 8000 soldiers trained to be auto mechanics, electricians, propeller makers, and other technically oriented professionals (Fenton, 2000).

Engineers, including those from CIT, continued to play key roles during the industrial growth of the twenties and the depression years of the thirties. Some key educational changes, how-

< 64 >

ever, occurred during these years: universities introduced laboratory courses, established honors programs, and set up distribution requirements. Furthermore, the importance of a liberal education for engineers was promoted on a national scale. Leading the effort in this area was CIT President Robert Doherty, who established the Carnegie Plan of Professional Education in 1936. The idea behind the Carnegie Plan was that even individuals trained in technical fields had responsibilities as citizens in society and needed to be educated in the humanities. Many other colleges and universities developed curricula based on Doherty's model (Schaefer 1992).

Engineering education began to change in more substantial ways during World War II. As a result of the war effort, Congress poured large amounts of funding into technical training and research. After the war, the Truman Commission called for expansion of college education for all Americans, not just the elite, and the GI Bill made that possible. By the beginning of the 1950's, government funds were available to support an ever increasing number of college students in both technical and non-technical fields.

The modern engineering curriculum was established in response to specific national needs in the 1950s. Russia launched Sputnik in 1957, marking the beginning of the Space Race. The US response to Sputnik was swift: Congress targeted engineering research and education as major thrust areas, and students flocked to engineering with new government support. According to one source, federal support for basic research grew by a factor of seven between 1958 and 1968 (Geiger 1997). The availability of research funds shifted the emphasis of many schools from undergraduate education to graduate degrees. The country during this period produced large numbers of highly specialized engineering Ph.D.s, who were joining research laboratories in industry, government, and academia.

By the mid-1970s, the number of schools competing for research funds had grown markedly, while the government began to decrease the funds available. Ph.D.s found it more difficult to get research positions in their specialty, and faculty found it more difficult to get grants to support new Ph.D. students. The windfall of the 1950s and 1960s was over.

Through the 1970s and 1980s, there was growing recognition that the world was becoming increasingly complex: people across the globe were more interdependent, requiring attention to interdisciplinary and cross-cultural issues. Furthermore,

< 65 >

underrepresented minorities attended college at lower rates than their counterparts and engineering as a discipline had among the lowest proportion of minority students. The number of women in most fields of engineering was far below the average in non-technical fields, despite recruitment efforts. And people began to question parts of the undergraduate engineering curriculum in place since the 1950s: many viewed the heavy doses of science and math before beginning engineering coursework as an over-emphasis on analytical thinking. This emphasis, some believed, shortchanged creative problem solving, which was viewed as equally important to developing analytical skills.

Some of the earliest attempts to adapt engineering education to a changing world at this time took place at Carnegie Institute of Technology, which became Carnegie Mellon University in 1967. The school had already established a reputation for education and research at the boundaries between traditional disciplines, and this provided impetus for several innovations. One of the most visible examples was the founding of the Engineering and Public Policy (EPP) Department in 1972, led by M. Granger Morgan from shortly after its establishment until the present day. This unique department has developed highly successful undergraduate double major programs with all other departments in the engineering college, as well as joint degree programs with other colleges at Carnegie Mellon. Furthermore, several faculty members in engineering have joint appointments with other colleges, and there is considerable collaborative work underway. In some cases, the collaboration focuses on how human values influence the development of technology. In other cases, the work involves how technology can be used to solve social problems. It is clear that interdisciplinary work, so important to the future of engineering education, has been part of the culture at Carnegie Mellon from a time when few others recognized its importance.

To enable students to broaden their experience in problem solving, a program entitled Analysis, Synthesis, and Evaluation—(ASE) was introduced to engineering students at Carnegie Mellon in the 1970s. A three course sequence ASE 1, 2, and 3—was set up to emphasize creativity in conjunction with increasing technical depth as students progressed through the curriculum. The concept that creative problem solving could be taught to engineers was demonstrated in this sequence.

Related to the creative aspects of engineering was the development and implementation of the science of design. In 1986, the engineering college at Carnegie Mellon established the Engineer-

< 66 >

ing Design Research Center (EDRC) funded by the National Science Foundation (NSF). The EDRC was a collaborative effort involving faculty in all engineering departments, founded by Steven Fenves, Arthur Westerberg, Gary Powers, and Sarosh Talukdar. Several new courses in engineering design were developed as part of this Center. An outgrowth of the EDRC is the current Institute for Complex Engineered Systems (ICES) founded by Pradeep Khosla and currently led by Cristina Amon. ICES is devoted to improving design using computer software and rapid fabrication techniques, and has developed innovative courses that bring together instructors in business, design, and technology.

Many other issues in engineering education were being discussed in the 1980s, but it wasn't until the final decade of the twentieth century that the field as a whole was altered in substantive ways. Improvements in transportation, communication, and information technology changed the scale and complexity of engineering projects toward the end of the twentieth century. Engineering graduates who could work at the interface with other professions were increasingly in demand. In addition, international projects became big business, and engineers who were sensitive to cultural and political issues in other countries became key players.

These factors influenced engineering education in many ways. Of primary importance, many schools recognized the need to broaden their curricula. This was accomplished in some cases by decreasing the number of required courses, which were replaced by breadth courses in different disciplines or free electives. One of the first engineering departments to develop a broad and flexible curriculum was the Department of Electrical and Computer Engineering at Carnegie Mellon under Department Head Steve Director (ECE 1995). Other departments in the engineering college followed suit within a few years. Introductory freshman courses in all six engineering departments were started in 1990 after a college-wide curriculum review led by Professor Chris Hendrickson (Director et al. 1995). Furthermore, programs were established to enable students to obtain minors in fields related to engineering. The current curriculum for engineers at Carnegie Mellon demands that students become competent in core engineering subjects while allowing them the option to develop breadth through courses in business, public policy, liberal arts, fine arts, and other disciplines. Some aspects of the current program are an outgrowth of the Carnegie Plan, while others are an outgrowth of the ASE sequence.

< 67 >

A second change in engineering education demanded by a rapidly changing world was the need to recruit engineering students from traditionally under-represented groups such as women, minorities, and international students. Universities realized the benefits of attracting these individuals into engineering, and recruitment efforts increased greatly during the 1990s. Carnegie Mellon Vice President for Enrollment William Elliott has spearheaded many of these efforts and has significantly changed the composition of incoming freshmen at Carnegie Mellon.

A third change involved the types of learning activities developed in engineering courses. More hands-on courses with laboratories, group projects, and creative exercises were set up in the early 1990s. Courses were broadened to expose students to the challenges of global competitiveness and the responsibility of engineers to society. Modules on the environmental effects of engineering projects and on ethical decision making were introduced. Furthermore, opportunities were developed for undergraduates to participate in research projects as part of the curriculum.

Consistent with the need for students to have a variety of learning experiences, Carnegie Mellon founded the Undergraduate Research Initiative (URI) in 1990 headed by one of its graduates, Jessie Ramey. The URI eventually developed a national reputation for promoting undergraduate research (Stocks and Lazarus 2000); over 400 students now take part in the annual URI research conference to showcase their projects. A majority of these students are in engineering and science, although all undergraduate colleges are represented.

Learning activities have also changed due to the increased importance of environmental constraints in virtually all engineering projects. The Environmental Institute at Carnegie Mellon, founded by Edward Rubin in the engineering college in 1991, has developed the Environment Across the Curriculum initiative to address this need. Students in the introductory engineering courses as well as in other courses are exposed to key environmental issues in their own engineering discipline. Results of research in Carnegie Mellon's Green Design Initiative have been incorporated into this educational effort.

Several organizations helped to develop these innovations, including the Accreditation Board for Engineering and Technology (ABET), the American Society for Engineering Education (ASEE), the Engineering Deans Council, and the National Re-

< 68 >

search Council. Examples of key reports include *Engineering Education for a Changing World* (ASEE 1994) and *Engineering Criteria 2000* (ABET 1998), which called for engineering curricula to include:

- development of team skills;
- improvement of written and verbal communication skills;
- discussions of multidisciplinary perspectives and development of holistic thinking;
- discussions of societal, economic, and environmental impacts of engineering decisions;
- integration of ethics into engineering decision making; and
- promotion of lifelong learning.

According to the new ABET rules, engineering programs are allowed considerable flexibility in implementing these changes. In fact, engineering schools can substitute their own goals, but must present convincing arguments for the changes and must show how their curricula satisfy the new goals. The increased flexibility helps each institution capitalize on its unique strengths, promoting excellence and leading to greater diversity among engineering programs. Such criteria from ABET are a far cry from previous accreditation rules, which specified minimum numbers of courses in each of several categories with little variance allowed.

The quality of engineering education at any institution is determined first and foremost by the quality of its faculty. Recognizing the importance of faculty development, the NSF funded a series of Engineering Education Scholars Workshops (EESW) at different institutions beginning in 1995. Carnegie Mellon organized one of the earliest workshops of this series (Straders et al. 2000). The Carnegie Mellon workshop capitalized on its world-renowned research in cognitive development, including work by Carnegie Mellon Nobel Laureate Herbert Simon, as well as the nationally known Eberly Center for Teaching Excellence, which had been working with graduate students and faculty since 1981. The Carnegie Mellon workshop included roughly 30 participants each year for five years. The participants were selected competitively from applicants nationwide. The workshops used a series of interactive sessions, panel discussions, and participant exercises to help new faculty gain an understanding of the learning process that could enable them to move toward excellence in edu-

< 69 >

cation. Other sessions at the workshops focused on mentoring and advising students, preparing proposals for educational and research grants, and managing time effectively, among other topics. Carnegie Mellon has provided its workshop materials (e.g., Davidson and Ambrose 1994) to several other schools throughout the country and internationally to assist in establishing programs elsewhere.

But only a small fraction of engineering faculty attend EESWs or similar programs, and few engineering Ph.D. programs include a pedagogical component. How then can engineering faculty develop the understanding they need to become effective educators? Many schools have Teaching Centers with experts who can work with faculty toward a better understanding of the learning process. We have found engineering faculty at Carnegie Mellon and elsewhere to be particularly receptive to this approach, for several reasons. Engineers understand the nature of the consulting relationship and feel comfortable collaborating with people like faculty developers, instructional designers, and educational technologists. Furthermore, engineers believe in the team approach, which is part of the engineering culture. Perhaps most important, they appreciate process-oriented models—such as those that describe the learning process—and such an understanding is vital to effective teaching. This approach has been used successfully by the Eberly Center to help faculty at Carnegie Mellon improve their teaching and has been examined by other universities, in this country and abroad, intent on making improvements to curriculum and instruction.

Having considered historical changes in engineering education and the role of Carnegie Mellon in bringing about some of these changes, we now conclude with a brief look at engineering education in the future. In a rapidly changing world, it is inconceivable that our colleges and universities would remain static. The Internet has changed the way we obtain information; some professional journals have already ceased traditional publication and are now available only on-line. Distance learning, videoconferencing, and telecommuting are common. Laptop computers are used for everyday lectures. New software and hardware are enabling university faculty to be more efficient in virtually all of their tasks. Most of these new tools are created through engineering, and it is reasonable to expect that engineering educators will make maximum use of these and future technologies to assist them.

Besides adopting new tools, however, the nature of engineering education is also changing in a more fundamental way. Boyer

< 70 >

et al. (1990) pointed out that too many universities are attempting to focus on research rather than defining scholarship more broadly. They argued that the national interest would be better served if higher education would consider integration, application, and teaching as scholarly activities—activities other than research that bring national attention to the university. For this to happen, new reward structures must be developed. Bringing about such changes in administrative policy will be a major challenge at most research institutions, but it is already starting to happen. Indeed, the current Dean of Engineering at Carnegie Mellon, John Anderson, has developed a committee structure to consider these changes.

Furthermore, if engineering is to provide greater help in solving societal problems, there must be stronger links between the engineering discipline and other fields, such as science, humanities, business, and policy. This implies a critical role of the faculty in providing a broader education for the next generation of engineers. We also need stronger links between higher education and elementary/secondary schools to expose younger students to what engineers do, and we need partnerships with government decision makers and with practitioners in industry. Only through these types of outreach and interdisciplinary efforts can engineers be educated to solve the complex problems facing the nation and the world. And through broader definitions of scholarship, we can expect engineering educators to influence teaching and learning far beyond their own classroom—and beyond their own discipline.

Acknowledgments

The author wishes to acknowledge Dr. Susan Ambrose, Director of the Carnegie Mellon Eberly Center for Teaching Excellence, who provided considerable information and insight as well as reference materials for this chapter.

References

Accreditation Board for Engineering and Technology (1998) *Engineering Criteria 2000*, ABET Publication.

American Society of Engineering Education (1994) *Engineering Education for a Changing World*, Washington, DC: ASEE, October 1994.

Bledstein, B.J. (1976) *The Culture of Professionalism*. New York, NY: W.W. Norton and Company, Inc., pp. 194–195 and 287–331.

< 71 >

Boyer, E. (1990) *Scholarship Reconsidered: Priorities of the Professoriate*. Princeton, NJ: The Carnegie Foundation for the Advancement of Teaching.

Chandler, Jr., A.D. (1965) "The Railroads: Pioneers in Modern Corporate Management," *Business History Review,* Volume 39, page 17.

Davidson, C.I. and S.A. Ambrose (1994) *The New Professor's Handbook: A Guide to Teaching and Research in Engineering and Science*. Bolton, MA: Anker Publishing.

Director, S.W., C.T. Hendrickson, R. Kail, and P. Laughlin (1995) "Undergraduate Curriculum Revision Assessment." Carnegie Institute of Technology report, Carnegie Mellon University.

Electrical and Computer Engineering (1995) "Electrical and Computer Engineering at Carnegie Mellon—A New Curriculum." Carnegie Mellon University report.

Fenton, E. (2000) *Carnegie Mellon 1900-2000: A Centennial History*. Carnegie Mellon University Press.

Geiger, R.L. (1997) "Research, Graduate Education, and the Ecology of American Universities: An Interpretive History." In Lester F. Goodchild and Harold S. Wechsler (eds.), *The History of Higher Education*. Needham Heights, MA: Simon & Schuster Custom Publishing.

Layton, Jr., E.T. (1971) *The Revolt of the Engineers: Social Responsibility and the American Engineering Profession*. Cleveland, OH: The Press of Case Western Reserve University.

Schaefer, L.F. (1992) *Evolution of a National Research University: 1965–1990*. Pittsburgh, PA: Carnegie Mellon University Press.

Stocks, J. and Lazarus, B. (2000) "Ten Years of Discovery: Undergraduate Research at Carnegie Mellon." Carnegie Mellon University report.

Strader, R., S.A. Ambrose, and C.I. Davidson (2000) "An Introduction to the Community of Professors: The Engineering Education Scholars Workshop." *Journal of Engineering Education*, Volume 89, pages 7–11.

< 72 >

SCIENCE, TECHNOLOGY, AND THE INNOVATIVE BUSINESS SCHOOL

Yuji Ijiri

Yuji Ijiri is the Robert M. Trueblood University Professor of Accounting and Economics at Carnegie Mellon's Graduate School of Industrial Administration. He has a broad set of interests in the social sciences, with major publications in the fields of accounting, economics, management, mathematics, statistics, and computers. He received his Ph.D. from Carnegie Mellon in 1963, and has been on the faculty at Carnegie Mellon for 36 years.

THE MILLENNIUM PERSPECTIVE

The start of the new millennium offers an opportunity to take a super-long-term perspective by using a thousand years as a unit of measurement instead of the normal one year, ten years, or a hundred years. This reminded me of a delightful 1978 film and its follow-up 1982 book called, *Powers of Ten*, by Charles Eames et al. in which an image of Earth and its surroundings was enlarged by a power of ten in 41 steps by decrementing the power of the scale from 10^{25} to 10^{-16}. This made me feel less fearful about extremely large or extremely small objects. The new millennium seems to give me the same feeling about time.

The "millennium perspective" may not necessarily assure any better insight into the distant future but it certainly offers a chance

< 73 >

to look back thousands of years and view contemporary issues from this super-long-term historical perspective. The same contemporary issues may look quite different depending upon which power of ten is chosen as the unit of the time scale.

For this reason, I was delighted to receive an invitation to write this essay on "The Innovative Business School." I wish to thank the editors as well as Doug Dunn, then Dean of the Graduate School of Industrial Administration, for this opportunity, and their help during the writing.

I decided to choose as the basic theme of the essay the recent explosive development in science and technology and its impact on business and business education. During my three and a half decades on the Carnegie Mellon faculty, I have been very much interested in and frequently astonished by discoveries and breakthroughs in science, technology, and mathematics.

About ten years ago, I started taking notes and clippings regularly from newspapers, magazines, and journals on news in these fields as well as news in business, partly as a hobby and partly with their classroom uses in mind. The collection of these materials formed a valuable basis for writing this essay.

Of course, I could have stated the basic theme in a few words—science and technology as the central forces of the current revolutionary changes affecting business and business education—and have gone on to talk about what the Innovative Business School should be or should do in the future. However, I preferred to have the focus of the essay not on prescriptions but on "reasoning" based on what seem to be the inevitable forces acting on business and business education.

Therefore, a brief review of recent discoveries and breakthroughs is included in this essay, though some of them may be well known. By focusing on reasons, I hope that a common understanding of these basic forces may be obtained, even though disagreements on specific prescriptions for business schools may still remain as implementation issues. Let me start with a brief review of Alvin Toffler's three waves of revolutions starting around eight thousand years ago.

AGRICULTURAL AND INDUSTRIAL REVOLUTIONS

In his 1980 best-seller, *The Third Wave,* Toffler highlighted three waves of revolutions in human history: the First Wave is the Agricultural Revolution that occurred roughly eight thousand years

< 74 >

ago; the Second Wave is the Industrial Revolution that started about three hundred years ago; and the Third Wave is the revolution that began during the last two or three decades.

Interestingly, Toffler tried to name the Third Wave revolution and considered a number of alternatives, including, for example, "Scientific-Technological Revolution (STR)," the term he credited to Russian futurists for its first use. But in the end he rejected the idea of naming the Third Wave altogether, fearing that any name he chose might be too restrictive.

The driving force of the First Wave was the simple idea of planting seeds instead of hunting and migrating. The driving force of the Second Wave was steam engines and a host of other technological innovations. The driving force of the Third Wave we are faced with now seems to include not only technological innovations but also discoveries in basic sciences. In this sense, the Russian futurists' term seems to look more fitting now than it might have been twenty years ago when *The Third Wave* was published, and I wish to use it for convenience in this essay even if it may still be too restrictive.

It is interesting to note a common ingredient in all of Toffler's three revolutions: They are all economically "beneficial" for human beings as a whole, offering something enormously valuable at a relatively small cost. Not all revolutions are beneficial in this sense. In fact, history is full of "destructive revolutions" driven by war or famine or other political and natural disasters.

Beneficial revolutions are often brought about by creative ideas, technological innovations, and scientific discoveries. They produce "free gifts" for human beings. The Agricultural Revolution produced "free food," a permanent source of food that human beings could count on year after year at a relatively small cost. Agriculture proved to be a much more efficient way of getting food than hunting and migrating. The Industrial Revolution brought about a variety of gifts that may be collectively called "free productivity." Increased productivity was achieved in many phases of production and many kinds of products by using concepts of "mass production" of "standardized products" by "specialized labor."

While the net benefits brought by these two revolutions were overwhelmingly positive for society as a whole, there were losers in each. Planting required territorial rights over a longer time period than hunting had. As a result, fights over food became much more intense, claiming many more lives than before, even though food became more abundantly available for society as a

< 75 >

whole. The Industrial Revolution created losers, like the so-called "Luddites," who could not or would not adapt to the new production efficiency. Their businesses became noncompetitive and lost their place in the market.

Looking from the perspective of these two earlier revolutions, the third revolution, the Scientific-Technological Revolution, is also producing "free gifts." However, their variety is considerably larger than the variety in earlier revolutions. For this reason, I would like to examine the third revolution in more detail, with attention to its three component elements. These three parts are: (1) Internet, Computers and Robotics; (2) Microbiology and Medicine; and (3) Astrophysics and Space Stations.

INTERNET, COMPUTERS, AND ROBOTICS

I will discuss this part in two stages, "Internet and Related E-Commerce" and "Computers and Robotics", each with its own distinct "free gift," even though the two stages are closely related.

The Internet Revolution has brought "free communication"— free worldwide, instantaneous communication. This free communication is a tremendous gift to human beings. The Internet offered a common means of communication, a common base of knowledge, and a common market for buying and selling—all worldwide. E-commerce was built on this benefit of technology. Not only sales to consumers, the so-called "Business-to-Consumer, or B2C," but worldwide, instantaneous auctions and other forms of buying and selling changed the way sales and procurements are carried out by many businesses, the so-called "Business-to-Business, or B2B." This mass marketing is as revolutionary as mass production was in manufacturing.

There have been losers, however, such as those in traditional distribution channels who suffered from the transition to e-commerce as the Internet short-circuited the distance between the producer and the consumer. Also, many of those who worked in or invested in dot-com companies suffered from stock market fluctuations caused by unreasonably high expectations and excessively high levels of investment.

However, the benefits of "free communication" have been overwhelming. The ups and downs of e-commerce seem to be transitional problems that are destined to occur in any revolutionary change. In the long run, such huge, irresistible benefits to the society will not likely be denied just because of short-run costs or los-

< 76 >

ers. This explosive use of the Internet might be viewed as an early signal, if not the earliest, of the start of the third revolution.

The next stage in which major breakthroughs are occurring is in computers and robotics. They go beyond the Internet Revolution and concern the bigger issue of the Information Revolution, which seems to be on its way at full speed.

Just to take a few developments in the past year or two, molecular computers are definitely in the implementation stage according to a July 1999 announcement by Hewlett Packard and the University of California-Los Angeles. In May 2000, a Japanese team reported success in solving an "NP-complete problem" using DNA computing, which has the theoretical potential of attaining speeds 100 million times faster than supercomputers. But the most earthshaking development in this area seems to be "quantum computers." In August 2000, IBM announced a major breakthrough that may bring quantum computing from the theory stage to the implementation stage rather quickly. They succeeded in building an experimental quantum computer using five computing elements called "qubits." This is a fine start considering that 30 qubits are thought to be the magic number beyond which classical computers will not be able to compete. Furthermore, in January 2001, two teams of scientists, one at Harvard University and another at the Harvard-Smithsonian Center for Astrophysics in Cambridge, independently discovered a way of halting a light pulse and storing the information it carried, for up to 1 millisecond, before regenerating it on command. This is viewed as a major step toward the development of quantum computers. Thus, quantum computers will undoubtedly bring in a new era of computing with their unprecedented speed and memory.

Artificial intelligence, a new discipline created by Herbert Simon and Allan Newell at Carnegie Mellon over four decades ago, continued to make significant contributions. A chess-playing computer, "Deep Thought," was first developed at Carnegie Mellon and further enhanced at IBM with the name changed to "Deep Blue." This computer defeated World Chess Champion Gary Kasparov in May 1997 with two wins, one loss, and three draws. This is a tremendous achievement in the field of artificial intelligence.

Coupled with artificial intelligence, the field of robotics has seen a number of major achievements, including Carnegie Mellon Robotics Institute's numerous contributions in fields such as integrated manufacturing, field robotics, medical robotics, and space robotics. In August 2000, a fascinating development was reported

< 77 >

by Brandeis University researchers: the creation of a robot that designs and builds other robots—a sort of self-evolving, self-generating machine that may be called the first generation of "digital Darwinism."

Another interesting development has to do with robots designed to make office work more efficient—a sort of "white collar robot." Most major corporations now have telephone answering systems with elaborate layers of menus and sometimes voice recognition capabilities. Furthermore, industrial robots designed to deliver parts to the factory production floor are now finding applications in the offices of high tech companies, moving around office corridors and delivering mail and packages.

These computers and robots are all designed to save human labor or do what humans cannot do because of limitations on their physical or computational capacity. They offer "free labor" since after the original investment their operating cost is negligible in many cases. Thus, in addition to the "free communication" brought about by the Internet Revolution, we can now enjoy the benefit of "free labor." There are losers, to be sure—workers who have been replaced by robots. However, these are tremendous gifts to human beings as a whole, which, at least in concept, allow people to work less and spend more time on things they prefer to do: travel, exercise, or education or whatever.

MICROBIOLOGY AND MEDICINE

Many people would agree that microbiology and medicine are at the top of the list of fields with the most potential to change society and business in the near future. The developments in these fields underscore the point that the term "Information Revolution" might indeed be too narrow, as the force has spread far beyond information, affecting the substance of society.

The floodgate was opened in February 1997 when Scottish scientists succeeded in cloning sheep. In microbiology, there is said to be a night and day difference before and after "cloning" both in terms of researchers' efforts and of funding the field attracts. Scientists in the field say "BD" and "AD," meaning "before Dolly" and "after Dolly," using the name of the sheep used in the successful cloning. Dolly has been rapidly followed by reports of cloning of other animals. An attempt to resurrect an extinct species using cloning was reported in December 2000 in a joint project between US and Spanish researchers.

< 78 >

One of the most fundamental achievements in microbiology is the decoding of the entire DNA sequence of a human chromosome reported jointly in December 1999 by the scientists at Celera Genomics of Rockville, Maryland and the international group of scientists in the Human Genome Project. In June 2000, Scottish scientists reported the ability to alter sheep genes with unprecedented precision—a discovery that a scientist in the field called the Holy Grail of biology.

In December 2000, Swiss drug manufacturer Novartis reported a revolutionary leukemia treatment that produced an extremely high remission rate of 95 percent. Armed with the knowledge of the exact DNA sequence of the defective copies of a chromosome, researchers developed the drug to attack only cells carrying such defective copies, thus virtually eliminating side effects. This approach is viewed as revolutionary as it has an impact far beyond the cancer it is designed to treat. This drug, which was approved by the US Food and Drug Administration in May 2001 after an unusually swift, two-and-a-half month review, was also found to work exceedingly well for a previously incurable intestinal cancer known as GIST.

In February 2001, scientists at Celera Genomics and the Human Genome Project mentioned above announced that they could find only about 30,000 human genes, far less than expected, since even a fruit fly has 13,000 genes in comparison.

Another significant achievement is the November 1998 discovery and isolation of embryonic human "stem cells" that can grow into every kind of human tissue, such as muscle, bone, or brain. Repairing nerves with stem cells was reported in July 1999, and many other applications quickly followed. In February 2001, a scientist at the University of South Florida reported that simple infusion into the bloodstream of cells from umbilical cords appears to greatly speed recovery after stroke in animal experiments, with human experiments planned in a year or two.

Here again, these medical developments offer the most valuable gift for human beings, a gift of "free life," since the patient literally receives a new lease on life. How will the benefits of this revolution be diffused? As with the earlier gifts of food and a labor substitute, the gift of healing and long life poses a challenge for society by calling for ways to accommodate the rapidly increasing and aging population. Adaptation to this gift is an especially great challenge to both social science and human ethics.

< 79 >

Astrophysics and Space Stations

One more field of science may be singled out because of an explosion of new facts and findings, although their impact on society and business is much more indirect and uncertain than the two others mentioned above. That is the field of astrophysics.

Ever since the Hubble Space Telescope (HST) was launched in May 1990 and its problems remedied in December 1993, the HST has brought mankind detailed views of the sky, including pictures of a star being born and a star's death throes. Scientists found in January 1996, after focusing HST on a narrow sector of the sky, that there are as many galaxies in the sky as there are stars in the Milky Way, making it necessary to revise the estimated size of the universe by a massive factor. In August 1999, the first image arrived from Chandra X-ray Observatory, opening a new field of X-ray astronomy. In September 2000, the design of another super-telescope, a million times more powerful than Chandra X-Ray, was reported.

In April 1997, physicists at the University of Rochester and the University of Kansas reported observations of radio waves from over 100 distant galaxies that may upset the major tenet of cosmology about the uniformity of the universe. Furthermore, in July 2000, the results of experiments reported by researchers at NEC Research Institute in Princeton, New Jersey showed the speed of light was indeed surpassed.

One of the most exciting issues in the field seems to be the existence of water on other planets because of the possibility of sustaining lives on the planets and of humans migrating to them. In March 1998, a NASA robot spaceship, Lunar Prospector, circling around the moon found significant quantities of water-ice at both lunar poles—enough to support a large, permanent human colony. In December 2000, evidence sent from the Mars Global Surveyor spacecraft showed signs of sedimentary deposits suggesting that water was once at work on that planet.

Commercialization of the $60 billion International Space Station (ISS) is now being promoted. In April 2001, the first paying space tourist, who reportedly paid $20 million to Russian Aviation and Space Agency, was flown on a Russian Soyuz space capsule to rendezvous and dock with the ISS for a ten-day trip in space. Many other paying space tourists are expected to follow. Space travel is no longer science fiction but rather a commercial reality.

This field of science will be offering "free space," at least allowing people to enjoy space at a small fraction of cost that would

< 80 >

have been necessary only a decade ago. Its significance in terms of economic benefits and costs, however, has yet to be identified and analyzed.

Currently, we may not put much value on "free space," since there is still enough inhabitable space available on our planet. But well before the end of this millennium, people will realize the importance of this gift of "free space" generated by the third revolution. Why? Because even at a modest one percent-a-year compound growth rate, the population will be 1.01^{1000} or 20,000 times the current world population before the current millennium ends, putting the US population alone somewhere in the trillions. This exponential population growth will place unacceptable pressure on the space for habitation currently provided by our planet.

All of these developments indicate that dramatic changes are taking place in science. Microbiology before and after cloning, communication before and after the Internet, space knowledge before and after Hubble, and probably computing before and after quantum computers can all be viewed as being as different as night and day. It should be remembered that all of these exciting events in science and technology are happening in a very short span of just a few years.

A Scientific-Technological-Business Process

We should not, however, think that after scientific discoveries and technological breakthroughs, the rest is carried out automatically. Society must have fluid capital and an army of managers with entrepreneurial spirit, in private and public sectors, to steer the economy and business enterprises. They are indispensable to make the distribution of benefits from the scientific discoveries and technological breakthroughs efficient and equitable for society. Without this distribution, even the most beneficial discoveries for human beings would be bottled up somewhere, as we often observe in countries where fluid capital and managerial talents are in short supply.

Furthermore, during the transition phase, management problems created by adaptation to the revolution can be enormous. To take an extreme example, assume that there had been a breakthrough in dealing with energy and all of a sudden "free energy" became available to society. This may not be totally science fiction as in March 1989 two researchers at the University of Utah thought they had succeeded in cold fusion. Let us suppose, then, energy

< 81 >

became freely available in massive quantities and in portable and controllable form at a very small cost. Free energy would be a tremendous gift to human beings and to the economy. It would attract an unbelievable amount of capital. Over-expectation and over-investment could easily occur and they could just as easily go bust. In the long run, however, free energy would be so irresistible economically that no society could afford to discard or suppress it.

In the short run, however, there would be a painful transition period involving those who have invested in or work in electricity, oil, gas, coal, nuclear, and other energy industries. In terms of economic impact on energy suppliers, free energy is far worse than dumping by foreign competition because here the "dumping" would continue permanently. Some countries might try to provide soft landing to affected industries by means of subsidies during the transition period, but others might do nothing.

Thus, management problems related to dealing with a large transition involving a significant portion of the economy might be enough to convince people that discoveries and breakthroughs, however important they may be, are only part of the story in getting the benefits delivered to society.

The opposite of free energy, a severe electricity shortage in California in the spring of 2001 produced skyrocketing prices for electricity and natural gas, rekindling interest in conservation, exploration, and the search for alternative energy sources. Fuel cells, for example, produce energy cleanly and can convert 60 percent of the energy in natural gas into electricity as opposed to the 35 percent efficiency of conventional power plants; but, at the moment, they are caught in the high-cost, low-demand deadlock, which could be broken by scientific and managerial breakthroughs.

Considering the critical nature of these management issues, it seems to make sense to view the process of bringing the "beneficial revolution" to its efficient fruition as a "scientific-technological-business" process. If the premise of revolution is accepted, it may be possible to draw a few conclusions from it and to use them to guide the future of business and business education, particularly at Carnegie Mellon. Let me explore three major themes below: (1) Constructive Mutations; (2) Merging Disciplines; and (3) A Paradigm Shift.

< 82 >

CONSTRUCTIVE MUTATIONS

One conclusion we can draw from the above observations is that e-commerce and the related Internet Revolution are only parts of a bigger revolution and many more parts are on the horizon. This implies that from now on, for a considerable period, society will be in a constant state of transition. Therefore, the revolution impacts everyone involved in business, industrial, and government administration. Transition management is needed to adapt industries and companies to the changes in order to maximize gains or minimize losses from the revolutionary forces.

There seems to be one common rule that can be applied to management in non-routine environments with a higher than normal level of uncertainty. Generally speaking, in a period of revolutionary changes, diversification and experimentation will become much more important than what we experienced in the last century. "Constructive mutations" become important in the context of increased uncertainty that shockwaves will bring about. I will demonstrate the concept of "constructive mutations' with a story about pine cones.

A small fraction of pine cones on a tree drop to the ground unopened. Under normal circumstances, they are wasted since they fail to achieve the purpose of getting their seeds spread widely by the wind. But they are heatproof and in forest fires they survive and carry the seeds to produce the next generation of pine trees. In normal times, these pine cones would be called mutants, which do not contribute to the survival of the species, and yet they save the species in an emergency. This is a good example of constructive mutation.

Another example of the importance of diversity was reported in August 2000. In China's Yunnan Province, an international team of scientists directed farmers to plant a mixture of two different types of rice instead of a single type. This simple change alone radically reduced the incidence of disease called rice blast, and resulted in crop increases worth billions of dollars. It is a modern-day version of the "free food" phenomenon observed during the Agricultural Revolution.

Preservation of diversity should be a priority for organizational planning. There are in fact many artificial life programs, but they all seem to have three essential elements: the reproductive capability to create a new generation, the memory capability to pass knowledge on to the new generation, and the mutation capability to give the species the necessary variety. Without the

< 83 >

mutation capability, a species can easily be destroyed in a single catastrophic event. The more homogeneous it is, the greater the risk of extinction.

The survival of the species is at issue. If the frequency of forest fire increases, more mutant pinecones will be needed to preserve the species. Similarly, as more shockwaves are thrust upon society and businesses, more mutations and the resulting diversities will be needed to preserve enough varieties for the survival of the unit, whether the unit is the society or one of its subgroups. In an environment in which changes take place frequently, we should develop the habit of observing and varying our routines. This will help us determine the differential impact of different kinds of adaptations to our environment.

In this regard, we can now see why so many scientists are serious about the possibility of a permanent human colony on another planet. It is not just scientific curiosity, but a tremendously large-scale pine cone project to deal with the contingency of the Earth becoming unlivable for whatever reason: a comet crash, nuclear war, global warming, a damaged ozone layer, or overpopulation on a massive scale. Ironically, this space revolution could put human beings in a migration mode similar to that which existed before the Agricultural Revolution.

In the face of challenges that call for experimentation and diversity, I think current business school curricula are getting dangerously similar. This reflects the relatively peaceful business environment of the second half of the 20th century: A peacetime mentality with emphasis placed on managing on-going businesses. What might be necessary in managing transitions, however, may be a business version of wartime mentality, in which the rules themselves can change rapidly.

MERGING DISCIPLINES

Second, I think we will have more frequent and intense interactions between people in science and technology and those in business and management. Managers with basic knowledge of science and technology will have considerable advantages over those who do not because at every phase of management, their judgments and decisions will be guided by such knowledge and perspectives.

In fact, I think at least some business schools may start putting science and technology at the core of the business curriculum along with economics, behavioral science, and quantitative

< 84 >

methods. These traditional core disciplines are designed to deal with forces that have an impact on business. As science and technology become increasingly important forces affecting business, they too should be incorporated into business education so that students are aware of the role they play in shaping business.

Obviously, such science and technology courses cannot cover details of any particular field, but they should aim students' antennae toward science and technology so that they gain scientific as well as business perspectives in evaluating and adapting to discoveries and breakthroughs. A course titled "A Historical Perspective on Science and Technology Impacting Business" might be a useful starting point.

The earlier analogy of dumping by foreign competition makes it clear why business should be knowledgeable about developments in science and technology. Not only can they wipe out an industry overnight, but since their gifts are valuable to human beings as a whole, developments in science and technology will have full public support. These developments offer fatal threats, as well as enormous opportunities. Managers and investors without sensitivity to science and technology can easily miss out on opportunities or make wasteful investments. It seems clear that business education should respond to the demand for new knowledge, skills, and perspectives created by the Scientific-Technological Revolution.

At the same time, I think some science and engineering curricula might start covering business and management topics, as many students in these fields are attracted to the entrepreneurial opportunities that are opened up by scientific discoveries and technological breakthroughs. Another way of achieving this goal might be to admit scientists and engineers and give them business educations, as Carnegie Mellon's Graduate School of Industrial Administration started doing in the 1950s. Furthermore, students with liberal arts backgrounds can also play important roles in transition management, especially if they gain knowledge and perspectives in science and technology. For these reasons, the educational trend for business-oriented students is clearly toward the merging of academic disciplines.

A Paradigm Shift

Third, I would like to consider a paradigm shift in business education. Thomas Kuhn argued in his 1962 best-seller, *The Structure*

< 85 >

of Scientific Revolution, that a "scientific revolution" required a shift in a scientific "paradigm" rather than just a gradual accumulation of discoveries and breakthroughs. Recent discoveries may very well constitute such a paradigm shift. While Kuhn's use of the term referred to the revolution internal to the field of science, the term could also be used to describe the external changes brought about by scientific discoveries and technological breakthroughs.

A business school version of a "revolution" defined by Kuhn might mean that there has to be a paradigm shift rather than a gradual accumulation of educational achievements. One of the likely candidates for this paradigm shift might be the shift from the function-based curriculum (marketing, finance, accounting, etc.) with its vertical orientation to an industry-based business curriculum (oil and gas, healthcare, consulting, etc.) with a horizontal orientation. In fact, some public accounting firms have switched from the traditional auditing, tax, and consulting sections to industry-based sections, each utilizing specialists in auditing, taxes, and consulting. This shift reflects a change from producer-friendly organizations in a product-scarce society to customer-friendly organizations in a customer-scarce society. When goods are scarce, a company may be organized to maximize its production efficiency. When customers are scarce, a company is more likely to move to an organizational structure that maximizes customer convenience.

While business schools or "tracks" in business schools oriented toward specific industries already exist (e.g., hotel management schools or e-commerce tracks), more business schools may develop programs with ties to specific industries. A paradigm shift may go even further, in some cases, toward the merging of traditional industries for the convenience of consumers. Internet bookstores may carry electric appliances, serve as banks or on-line grocers, or even function as ticket offices.

In particular, a revolutionary wave that is most likely to hit business in the near future seems to be coming from microbiology and medicine. Significant scientific and medical breakthroughs overflowing with potential business opportunities are already reported almost monthly. Genetic engineering start-up companies have been rapidly increasing in the past year. A medical/business joint degree is a quite likely possibility.

While computers process information only, biomedical equipment must process physical objects. As a result, the biomedical field requires considerable capital investments on heterogeneous

< 86 >

equipment. Hence, the infrastructure of this field is quite different from that of Silicon Valley. But it will need a supply of capital and management talents just as much.

The industry-based partition of educational knowledge is built on the premise that knowledge across industries is becoming more and more heterogeneous, partly due to differences in regulations, political relations, customer preferences, and other infrastructures surrounding the industry. These differences make it essential to have separate and tailored approaches to management. In contrast, the disciplinary separation within an industry is getting more and more blurred because problems to be solved rarely occur as solely marketing problems, solely finance problems, or solely problems of operational management.

Perhaps the business school of the future will be more tailored to specific industries, although undoubtedly the generic MBA program will continue to exist. Indeed, the need for a medical/business school might be one of many opportunities that are created by scientific discoveries and technological breakthroughs.

THE INNOVATIVE BUSINESS SCHOOL

Innovative business schools, if not all business schools, will undoubtedly pursue the necessary adaptation to the changing environment proactively. Innovation calls for not just doing things differently, but also doing things efficiently and effectively relative to values and conditions that may prevail in the future.

This means that the success of the innovative business school critically depends upon (1) the vision to accurately forecast what values and conditions may prevail in the future; (2) the strategy to determine the best way, however unconventional it may be, to adapt the business school to the values and conditions that have been forecast; (3) the courage to commit resources to implement the strategy under carefully calculated risks; and (4) the wisdom to prepare for contingencies by preserving the necessary diversity even against common sense.

Business schools must make choices on a number of dimensions, but lengthening lifespans and rapid technological change are likely to significantly influence those choices. Let us take a few examples.

First, business schools must create a balance between regular MBA education and continuing education, including the Executive MBA. As life expectancy increases, people will work

< 87 >

longer; and as a result, there will be more demand for continuing education. The balance will most likely shift much more toward continuing education than what we have seen in the past.

Second, the same trend also implies that the balance between foundational subjects and practical subjects included in business curricula will likely shift toward the latter. Some may criticize the shift as another factor contributing to myopic management, while others may welcome it as something long overdue in business schools

Third, the rapidity of change in science and technology implies that the balance between tenure-track instructors and non-tenure-track/freelance instructors will also shift. We might see a greater shift towards the latter since the tenure system will be strained enormously if a specialist on a subject that is likely to be short-lived has to be hired as a tenure-track faculty member.

Fourth, technological improvement changes the balance between on-campus education and distance education, moving it in the direction of the latter. At the same time, the balance between synchronous and. asynchronous instruction will move toward the latter. In addition, technology will promote internationalization of education as instruction education for students in remote places becomes much easier and less expensive.

Fifth, we may expect that there will be more and more alliances among business schools and between business schools and other disciplines. These will be formed to create joint programs, joint degrees, and joint ventures of educational activities across disciplines, universities, and nations.

Many of these trends and possibilities have already been observed in many schools but they are expected to proliferate at a much more rapid pace in the future, offering many options to innovative business schools.

The Future of Carnegie Mellon

Before closing, I would like to highlight two new announcements made in December 2000 that will further enhance Carnegie Mellon's fitness to deal with the revolution. One is the joint announcement by Carnegie Mellon and the National Aeronautics and Space Administration (NASA) regarding the formation of the High Dependability Computing Consortium in Silicon Valley at Carnegie Mellon's West Coast Campus. The other is the announcement of a plan to establish a joint biotechnology research

< 88 >

center with the University of Pittsburgh, especially with its School of Medicine, and the University of Pittsburgh Medical Center (UPMC) Health System.

I also wish to highlight the fact that Carnegie Mellon's Graduate School of Industrial Administration (GSIA) and School of Computer Science (SCS) were the first in the country to introduce a program leading to the Master of Science in Electronic Commerce. GSIA, ranked No. 2 after Dartmouth among business schools in the world by a *Wall Street Journal* survey, seems to be very well situated to explore how other forms of joint ventures might be possible inside and outside the University.

In summary, Carnegie Mellon's School of Computer Science is unquestionably a world leader in the discipline that is at the heart of the current revolution. In spite of its small size, Carnegie Mellon is blessed with considerable diversity in disciplines that range from natural sciences to engineering, from humanities to social sciences, and from fine arts to public and business policy and management. Carnegie Mellon's small size is a great blessing as interdisciplinary interactions are key to success in the future.

After examining all these recent events and issues in science, technology, and business, I must say I was very pleased to realize how well Carnegie Mellon University is situated to succeed in the period of the Scientific-Technological Revolution as "The Innovative University."

< 89 >

Learning Other Languages: The Case for Promoting Bilinguality Within an International University

G. Richard Tucker

G. Richard Tucker is Professor of Applied Linguistics and Head of the Department of Modern Languages at Carnegie Mellon. His research as an applied linguist deals with various aspects of second language learning and teaching. He is a recipient of the Eliott Dunlap Smith Award for Excellence in Teaching. Dr. Tucker received his Ph.D. from McGill University in 1968, and has been at Carnegie Mellon since 1992.

Every European country has a national policy for introducing at least one foreign language into the elementary school curriculum of every child (Dickson & Cumming 1996). And, a provocative study commissioned by the British Council (Graddol 1997), after examining an array of economic, demographic and political indicators, concluded that by the middle of the 21st century the linguistic monopoly of English will give rise to an oligopoly in which Chinese, Hindi, English, Spanish and Arabic will compete for attention, with bilingual proficiency becoming an absolute necessity for participants in the global economy. More recently, Voght (2000, 269) has argued that, "The colleges and universities that prosper in the future are those that will, among other things,

< 91 >

focus foreign language curricula on the needs of students specializing in business and other professions while modifying their business and professional courses and programs to include foreign languages, international perspectives and cross-cultural content."

What is the likelihood that students in American universities and colleges will graduate with bilingual proficiency and cross-cultural competence as a matter of course? And what role can Carnegie Mellon play in this bridging and adaptive process?

The number of languages spoken throughout the world is estimated to be approximately 6,000 (Grimes 1992). Although people frequently observe that a small number of languages such as Arabic, Bengali, English, French, Hindi, Malay, Mandarin, Portuguese, Russian and Spanish serve as important link languages or languages of wider communication around the world, these are very often spoken as second, third, fourth or later-acquired languages by their speakers (see, for example, Cheshire 1991, Comrie 1987, Edwards 1994). The available evidence seems to indicate that governments in many countries deliberately present a somewhat skewed picture of monolingualism as normative by the explicit or implicit language policies that they adopt and promulgate (Crystal 1987). Thus, fewer than 25 percent of the world's approximately 200 countries recognize two or more official languages—with a mere handful recognizing *more than two* (e.g., India, Luxembourg, and Nigeria).

However, despite these conservative government policies, available data indicate that there are many more bilingual or multilingual individuals in the world than there are monolingual. In addition, many more children throughout the world have been, and continue to be, educated via a second or a later-acquired language—at least for some portion of their formal education—than the number of children educated exclusively via a first language. And we know that innovative educational programs involving some form of bilingual education have been with us for at least five millennia—for example, since 3,000 B.C., in ancient Mesopotamia, when Sumerian and Akkadian were used as the two languages for training scribes. In many parts of the world, bilingualism or multilingualism and innovative approaches to education, which involve the use of two or more languages, constitute the normal everyday experience (see, for example, Dutcher 1994, World Bank 1995).

< 92 >

Within this broad global context, which supports and encourages innovative language education for a majority of students, I find it to be an enduring paradox of American life and education that bilingualism, becoming bilingual, and the encouragement of innovative language education programs within the core or basic curriculum of public education are so often viewed as *problematic, difficult,* and *undesirable.* Why should this be, and what is the likelihood for change?

Consider the following observations:

- When Columbus is reputed to have landed, approximately 700 indigenous languages were spoken in North America; linguists now estimate that only 187 are now spoken. Of the 187, children are *no longer learning* 149.
- Our country was historically a very rich one linguistically. Two hundred years ago, the German-speaking population was about as large (roughly nine percent) as the Spanish-speaking portion of our population today.
- Two individuals played key roles in bringing the study of so-called "modern" foreign languages (e.g., languages other than Latin, Classical Greek, and Sanskrit) into the mainstream of the curriculum—Benjamin Franklin and Thomas Jefferson. Franklin helped to erase the popular myth that a modern language could only be learned *after* mastering Latin, while Jefferson was instrumental in the establishment of the first professorship in modern languages at the college of William & Mary, and in ensuring a central role for modern languages at the University of Virginia.
- In the period from the middle 1800s until about 1915, almost 75 percent of our secondary school students studied a foreign language. In addition, many public schools, in cities such as Baltimore, Boston and Cincinnati, offered bilingual education as a regular part of their educational curriculum.
- As a consequence of World War I, in which the German Empire was our enemy, there was a precipitous decline in the proportion of students studying German in our schools. The state of Nebraska, in fact, banned the teaching of German in the public school system. It was not until 1923 that the Su-

< 93 >

preme Court (*Meyer* v. *Nebraska*) overturned that ban.

- During the period from 1925 until the early 1980s, no more than 20–25 percent of secondary school students studied foreign languages. Although enrollments have rebounded slightly since then, they are still markedly below earlier levels.
- Simultaneously, during the decade of the 1980s and continuing to the present day, there has developed a seeming groundswell of support for federal and state legislation designed to promote the use of "English-only" (see Tucker 1997). This move seems to have been fueled by a tide of escalating anti-immigrant sentiments throughout the country. The vitriolic rhetoric surrounding these discussions significantly undermines attempts to discuss, define, and implement a coherent, broadly based national language policy. The discussion led by those advocating English-only legislation focuses on the supposedly debilitating effects of bilingualism, on the negative social and economic consequences that seem to accompany bilingual policies, and on the harm to national unity and well being that inevitably accompanies the encouragement of individual and societal bilingual proficiency.

The situation is such that at present a large majority of American university students and graduates—a major source of new entrants to the service industry workforce—do not have sufficient bilingual proficiency or cross-cultural competence to be able to offer their services to international clients. Foreign university graduates and workers, however, almost all of whom speak English in addition to the language(s) of their country, are able to penetrate the American market effectively.

EDUCATION AND OUR CHANGING DEMOGRAPHY

The move toward monolinguality by the native-born English-speaking population is occurring at a time of rapidly changing national demography, and concomitantly a rapidly changing demography for our school systems and for the workplace. As a nation, we are becoming markedly more culturally and linguistically diverse (Roberts 1993). The number of foreign-born as a percentage of the total population, and the percentage of indi-

< 94 >

viduals who typically speak a language other than English at home, have increased significantly since 1980. More and more of the entrants to our schools and to our workforce are so-called language minority individuals, and this trend will continue for the foreseeable future.

Consider the following observations (excerpted from Crandall 1995):

- During the 1980s, more than nine million individuals immigrated to the US—more than at any time in the 20th century, except for the period from 1905–1914.
- Between 1980 and 1990, the Asian-American population more than doubled; the Hispanic-American population grew by more than 50 percent.
- In the five years from 1986 to 1991, the nation's school-age population grew by approximately 4 percent; but the percentage of limited-English-proficient youngsters in our schools rose by more than 50 percent.
- It was estimated that approximately 30 percent of all students in 1990 were minority group members along with 12 percent of all teachers, but that by the year 2000 approximately 38 percent of pupils would be minority and only 5 percent of all teachers.

Clearly, as the composition of the American population continues to change, individuals who possess at least some degree of even latent bilingual proficiency will increasingly comprise the pool of prospective students and members of the workforce. However, if present educational practices continue, these individuals will *not* be encouraged, nor in many instances will they even be assisted to nurture or to maintain their native language skills as they add English to their repertoire. (See, for example, the discussion surrounding the implementation of Proposition 227 in California.). These individuals will likely make up a rapidly expanding pool that Wallace Lambert (1980) has characterized as "subtractive bilinguals." I turn now to offer a few comments about language education programs for students in American schools. In discussing these programs, I will draw on my experience developing a language model for a school district in the Pittsburgh region. The model that we proposed and helped implement will be detailed later.

< 95 >

LANGUAGE EDUCATION FOR MINORITY STUDENTS

For the most part, we have failed to develop or implement educational policies designed to conserve the heritage language resources of our language-minority students (see, for example, Brecht & Ingold 1998). In addition, the available data suggest that language-minority students (and, in particular, those who are so-called limited-English-proficient youngsters) do not perform as well academically as their language-majority counterparts (del Pinal 1995); they often—as a class—do not develop the academic English language skills that they need to participate effectively in educational instruction; they drop out of school in disproportionately higher numbers than their English-proficient counterparts; if they do remain in school, they are less likely to proceed to colleges or universities; if they proceed to college or university, they are less likely to study professional subjects such as engineering or medicine; if they find employment, they are less likely to be retained and more likely to earn lower wages than their counterparts. The prognosis is not a particularly positive one given the prevailing educational practices, although there are many (e.g., August & Hakuta 1997, Brisk 1998) who argue persuasively for a change in current policies.

LANGUAGE EDUCATION FOR SO-CALLED MAJORITY STUDENTS

What is the prognosis for developing bilingual language competence in our language-majority students? By all accounts we are *not* achieving the level of success in foreign or second language teaching programs necessary for these students to compete effectively in the commercial world of the 21st century. Although the absolute number of students enrolled in modern foreign language programs at the post-secondary level has increased substantially from 1960 to 2000, enrollments in relative terms have actually *fallen* from 16.1 per 100 college students in 1960 to 7.9 per 100 in 1998 (Brod & Welles 2000). Nor do American students, for the most part, study abroad. During their academic career, fewer than ten percent of American post-secondary students study abroad. By contrast, in 1998–1999, there were approximately 490,000 international students studying in the United States. At that time, there were only 114,000 American students studying abroad—and a large proportion of those were studying in English-speaking countries or studying in English-medium programs in other countries (Desruisseaux 1999)! At Carnegie

< 96 >

Mellon University, fewer than five percent of our students study abroad during any given academic year.

The picture is equally bleak at the elementary and secondary levels, which are the feeder institutions for our colleges and universities. There it is estimated that fewer than 30 percent of our elementary schools (reaching approximately 15 percent of the population of elementary school students) offer any foreign language study. Although a majority (approximately 85 percent) of our secondary schools offer some form of foreign language instruction, the programs reach only about 50 percent of the students, and then the most common sequence of study is for two years. Thus, a majority of the relatively modest number of individuals who do have an opportunity for foreign language study achieve disappointingly low levels of proficiency in their chosen languages (Branaman & Rhodes 1999). As Richard Lambert (1993, 84) has observed "the foreign language effort in the United States is a mile wide but an inch thin." Yet another indicator of the marginalization of foreign language study within the American core curriculum is the observation that to date, the evaluation of language proficiency has not been included as a part of the National Assessment of Educational Progress, although the NAEP governing board has recently adopted a recommendation to assess the Spanish proficiency of 12th grade students for the first time on a trial basis in 2003 (Kenyon et al. 2000).

There has been a great deal of discussion in professional educational circles in recent years about the effectiveness of so-called *foreign language-immersion programs* and of *developmental bilingual education* programs—and indeed they do appear to be pedagogically effective (see, for example, Sack 2000); but it is estimated that fewer than 50,000 American youngsters participate in one or the other of these types of programs, that is less than .01 percent of the cohort.

Thus the available evidence suggests that unfortunately US schools and colleges have been strikingly unsuccessful in either expanding or in conserving our country's language resources. But the available social and economic indicators suggest that we have a crying national need for dramatically expanded language resources. What makes addressing this need so urgent?

A National Need

I turn now to a brief discussion of our students, what they will likely be doing in the future, how they will support themselves,

< 97 >

and how they will (or will not) help our nation to prosper economically and socially. With increasing globalization, the nature of our world is changing dramatically, and the men and women with whom our daughters and sons will be trading, negotiating, and engaging in joint ventures will be changing drastically in the decade ahead. If the world's population were shrunk to 100, keeping all ratios intact, the distribution would look like this (*ACTFL Newsletter* 1993):

- There would be 57 Asians, 21 Europeans, 14 Western Hemisphere people, and 8 Africans
- 70 would be non-white; 30 white
- 70 would *not* be able to read
- 50 would suffer from malnutrition
- 80 would live in substandard housing
- 70 would be non-Christian; 30 would be Christian
- only 1 would have a university education

Cetron and Gale (1993), among others, have examined the challenges faced by our schools and workplaces as they attempt to prepare students and later employ them. They offer the following observations about the approximately 45 million American children who will be enrolled in public schools at the beginning of the 21st century, and the workforce they will enter:

- In our schools, one million youngsters will continue to drop out annually at an estimated cost of $240 billion in lost earnings and foregone taxes over their lifetimes.
- The number of at-risk students will increase as academic standards rise and social problems intensify.
- In the workplace the major management issues will be quality, productivity, and the decline of the work ethic.
- The decline of employment in agricultural and manufacturing industries will continue.
- The emerging service economy will provide jobs for 85 percent of the workforce.
- A new category of "knowledge workers" will result from the unprecedented growth of information and knowledge industries. Knowledge workers will fill 43 percent of available jobs
- On the international scene, alliances such as those created through NAFTA, GATT, increasing ties with the Pacific Rim, and other multinational linkages, will increase rapidly.

< 98 >

- These alliances, welcomed in so many parts of the world, provide potential opportunities for American workers—but to date these trade agreements have been riddled with *pitfalls* for us.

That is, our schools will be called upon to develop in all students a sophisticated repertoire of literacy, numeracy, problem-solving and decision-making skills, while simultaneously assisting them to develop, or to conserve, bilingual language proficiency and cross-cultural competence. The majority of our negative experiences with NAFTA and other global alliances to date can be attributed to the glaring lack of expertise in languages other than English and lack of cross-cultural competence on the part of US professionals. Fully two thirds of our gross domestic product is now accounted for by "services." By removing artificial trade barriers, treaties allow US professionals to provide services freely in the signatory nations in exchange for access to US markets by foreign professionals. Providers of services must be able to speak the target language with a high degree of fluency and have basic comprehension of the cultural assumptions and norms of the society in which they are operating. This has not proven problematic for foreign professionals wishing to enter the American marketplace. *But this requirement has virtually paralyzed our workers wishing to gain access to foreign markets* (Brecht & Walton 1995).

Addressing This Need

This problem must be attacked on at least four fronts: (1) by developing intensive, yet flexible, options for second language study by students in elementary and secondary schools and in colleges and universities—options that draw upon the often ignored linguistic and cultural resources that students can bring to classes; (2) by implementing basic interdisciplinary cross-national and cross-linguistic research to investigate and describe more thoroughly the process of second language learning and teaching, both in the classroom and in natural language learning environments; (3) by developing innovative and coherent graduate training programs to prepare students to do the types of research called for or to teach in the proposed programs; and (4) by the broad diffusion of practical, timely, and relevant information to educational practitioners and policy makers. In the sections to follow, I

< 99 >

shall describe two exemplary programs intended to improve the ultimate level of language proficiency and cross-cultural competence of our graduating students. The first example is chosen from the primary/secondary level of education; the second, from the university level.

AN ILLUSTRATIVE EXAMPLE FROM THE PRIMARY/SECONDARY LEVEL

Recent federal legislation enacted in the United States, the Goals 2000: Educate America Act, calls for American students to leave grades 4, 8, and 12 having "demonstrated competence over challenging subject matter including English, mathematics, science, [and] foreign languages . . ." If American students are to leave grades 4, 8 and 12 with demonstrable proficiency in a foreign language, the number of foreign language programs at all levels will need to be significantly expanded and improved. This is particularly true at the elementary level. The importance of including foreign language study in the elementary school is also supported by the research on the amount of instructional time required for developing functional proficiency in a foreign language and by the widely held professional view that language competence can only be achieved in well-articulated, sustained sequences of foreign language instruction. In the following section, I describe briefly an innovative foreign language education program that is currently being implemented by the Chartiers Valley School District in southwestern Pennsylvania.

GENESIS OF AN INNOVATIVE PROGRAM

In May 1995, Richard Donato, of the University of Pittsburgh, and I were invited to attend an informal meeting with the Superintendent of Schools of Chartiers Valley School District and several of his administrative staff. The superintendent opened the meeting by articulating a vision for his students and for his district—a vision that included doing something different, something daring. He proposed that a new program be developed so that *all* the district's pupils would study a common foreign language throughout their entire scholastic career—from kindergarten through grade 12. He described clearly how American secondary school graduates in the 21st century will be competing for positions in which students with bilingual language

< 100 >

proficiency will possess a comparative advantage over their monolingual English-speaking counterparts. He predicted that tomorrow's graduates will compete for positions in Beijing, Paris, Tokyo and Zurich, and not just for openings in Baltimore, Chicago, Detroit and New York.

A number of questions were raised at the initial meeting. Was the superintendent's vision plausible? If so, in which language(s) should instruction be offered? Were there teachers available? Would the community support such a program? Would the members of the school board support such a program—and provide the necessary budgetary authorization? How could the school district and the universities (Carnegie Mellon and the University of Pittsburgh) work collaboratively to their mutual benefit? The group decided to form an Elementary Foreign Language Committee to oversee the planning and implementation of a new and innovative foreign language program. Committee members consist of the director of curriculum who chairs the group, the superintendent, principals from the elementary and intermediate schools, selected elementary school teachers, the chair of the secondary school foreign languages department, and the university collaborators. As appropriate, subgroups or individuals carry out specific activities, which they report back to the Committee.

CHOICE OF LANGUAGE AND TIMETABLE FOR IMPLEMENTATION

One of the first issues confronting the group was choice of language(s). A number of options were considered, including French, German, Japanese, and Spanish. At the time, the district offered French, German, and Spanish to students in grades 9–12 on an elective basis. A number of factors were considered, such as likely availability of prospective teachers and materials, potential community support, and utility of proficiency in the target language for graduates. For pragmatic reasons, the decision was made to select one language only, and to make its study *compulsory for all children*. At this point, the Committee decided that it would be useful to conduct a community survey to ascertain level of support for the program and to obtain feedback concerning the choice of language. A survey instrument was developed, piloted, revised, and administered to a broad sample of parents as well as to all members of the school board. The results revealed broad general support for an innovative foreign language education program, and support specifically for the teaching of Spanish.

< 101 >

The second major issue was whether to begin the program from the bottom up, that is at the kindergarten level; from the top down, that is working backwards, a year at a time from grade 9, where instruction then began; or from both ends, to meet in the middle. After much discussion centering around issues such as scheduling, teacher availability, and the necessity of ensuring long-term articulation, a decision was made. We decided to propose to the school board the implementation of a Spanish Foreign Language in the Elementary School (FLES) program in September 1996 for all kindergarten children in the district. It was also decided to extend the program to grade 1 in September 1997; to grade 2 in September 1998, with the systematic introduction of one new grade cohort each year. With this plan, the district will have a fully articulated foreign language program from kindergarten through grade 8, as well as for grades 9–12, in the year 2004. The Board of School Directors formally approved this plan in April 1996.

DEVELOPMENT OF AN ACTION PLAN

After deciding on the target language (Spanish) and the model for implementation (bottom up), the Committee next turned its attention to: (1) recruiting an appropriate teacher for the start-up class, (2) planning for curriculum development activities, (3) informing members of the community about the new program, and (4) orienting other teachers and administrators working in the system. These activities continued during the winter and spring of 1995–96.

The Spanish program was begun in September 1996, with 11 classes comprising a total enrollment of 223 kindergarten students. Each class meets 20 minutes per day, five days a week. The Spanish specialist goes to the students in their regular classroom and, in effect, team-teaches with the regular classroom teacher. Growing spontaneously from the enthusiasm for the program, a strong collaboration between the kindergarten teachers and the language-teaching specialist developed and continues to mark this program as unique. The kindergarten teachers established close contact with the FLES teacher and freely shared materials during the curriculum development phase of the program at the same time that they themselves learned Spanish through the lessons in their classrooms. This program, from its inception and with its teacher, was clearly positioned as an integrated part of the kin-

< 102 >

dergarten program and as an equal participant in the total school curriculum. The program has proceeded as planned. Additional teachers were hired, and new kindergarten cohorts were offered Spanish instruction in each subsequent year. The lead cohort of children and those that followed continued their study of Spanish as they progressed through the educational cycle. In Fall 2003, the lead cohort will begin grade seven. Additional information about this program can be found in Tucker, Donato and Murday (in press).

FORMATIVE EVALUATION OF THE PROGRAM

Members of the Committee decided that it would be important for all of the stakeholders (e.g., the pupils, their parents, and members of the school board) to systematically and continually evaluate the progress of the pupils. Accordingly, curriculum-based interview protocols have been regularly developed, pretested, revised, and administered with the assistance of the university partners. The results of the formative assessment of the children in these early years have met the expectations we had for their progress. The children's listening comprehension exceeded their oral production; their production was limited to learned material; production began as single word utterances and formulaic expressions; signs of emerging syntax began to appear, but the children focused more on the content of their utterances than on their form; language mixing was not uncommon; and the children developed good pronunciation ability in Spanish.

The children and their parents have been unanimously positive about the Spanish program and about wanting it to continue. Likewise, the views of the regular classroom teachers and the administrators have been equally positive and supportive. None expressed the view that the Spanish program was somehow detracting from other elements of the school district's program.

A number of factors contributed to the success of this project to date, and continue to do so. The first is the key role of the superintendent. By his active participation in all of the Committee meetings, he has provided immediate and visible credibility and value to the activity. He continually reminds the Committee that they are embarking on an innovation by "navigating uncharted waters" that will have far-reaching consequences for the school district in terms of its visibility and reputation. We have also been struck by the extent to which the Committee members—mostly

< 103 >

monolingual and monocultural—have embraced the goal of multiple language proficiency and cross-cultural competence for their students. They act "as if" they themselves were multilingual and multicultural. This program shows great promise for producing students who, upon their graduation from secondary school, will possess demonstrable bilingual proficiency and cross-cultural competence. Clearly, they will constitute a pool of applicants for university programs whose major challenge will be to nurture and to further enhance the abilities that these students will bring to their college campuses.

AN ILLUSTRATIVE EXAMPLE FROM THE UNIVERSITY LEVEL

Despite an imperative to succeed, a majority of US colleges and universities seem to be strikingly unsuccessful in expanding our country's language resources. It is within this context that a program oftentimes referred to as "Languages Across the Curriculum" may make a major contribution. Such a program can provide the basis for implementing a flexible option for supplementary foreign language instruction by drawing on the linguistic and disciplinary resources, which international faculty members and students bring to their campus. The idea of integrating language instruction and academic content is not a new one. The topic has received a great deal of attention in the past decade from both foreign language educators and those concerned with English as a second language (see, for example, Klee 2000, Straight 1994, Stryker & Leave 1997). Interest in this approach is not restricted to work in the United States, and Crandall (1993) describes comparable initiatives underway in countries such as Australia, Canada, and South Africa.

Support for content-centered language instruction comes from both second language acquisition theory and pedagogical practice (see, for example, Crandall & Tucker 1990). A further rationale for enhancing the incidence of foreign languages across the curriculum is provided by Rivers (1992) in her timely discussion of the internationalization of post-secondary education. She calls attention to the importance of internationalizing the content of the curricula, as well as the life of the campus. For a variety of reasons, then—pedagogical, social, and theoretical—language educators on many campuses have increasingly begun to establish dialogues with their colleagues in other departments and disciplines. These, in turn, have led to a variety of innova-

< 104 >

tive programs designed to improve the "international competence" of American students.

TEMPLATE FOR AN INNOVATIVE ACROSS THE CURRICULUM PROGRAM

Information is provided below with respect to this program at Carnegie Mellon. At our University, the work is typically supervised by both language faculty and content-area faculty (or graduate assistants) in different departments. Students are encouraged to carry out language studies in the context of their ongoing studies in other areas. (See, for example, the appendices in Rosenthal 2000).

Requirement
Language credit at Carnegie Mellon may be attached to any course, independent study, or project unit for which a student receives content-area academic credit. The program is available at the discretion of the responsible content-area faculty member, who should be sufficiently skilled in the chosen language to be able to evaluate the *technical* content of a student's work. The student, content-area faculty, and language faculty negotiate a plan for the semester's work, designed to consume approximately three hours per week, adding three units of credit to a nine-unit course. Depending on the student's language proficiency and the nature of the content-area course, a variety of activities are appropriate, including:

- extra reading assignments in the foreign language
- preparation of oral or written reports in the foreign language
- discussions about the material in the foreign language
- translation of documents to or from the foreign language

Eligibility
A student's eligibility for the program is determined jointly by the content-area and the language faculty. Beginning language students are usually *not* eligible for the program; intermediate language students must have sufficient language skill to usefully pursue content-area work. An advanced language student must show that participation in the program would have substantial

< 105 >

benefits (e.g., learning specialized vocabulary or discourse patterns in an academic area of interest). Students who continue to meet these requirements may register for the program multiple times during their careers at Carnegie Mellon.

A Typical Example

During a recent spring semester, one faculty member offered students in Organic Chemistry II the opportunity to take "Language Across the University" in either French or Japanese. Five students elected to participate in French. All had at least intermediate-level competence in French, and two had lived briefly in France. The faculty member served as the content-area specialist. He identified a half dozen journal articles on organic chemistry written in French. The journal articles paralleled the topics that students were covering in the regular chemistry course. The students wrote synopses of each article which he examined for content and which a Modern Languages instructor critiqued for grammar and composition. The students were required to revise and resubmit synopses and to discuss the contents with their chemistry professor on a regular basis. The participating faculty member noted that the students were extremely enthusiastic about this course. Each wanted to study a foreign language—some to sustain a level of proficiency previously developed, others to enhance their current level of intermediate skills—but none had time to pursue foreign language study unless it were integrated with their chemistry program. These students accomplished the milestone of learning that they could read scientific articles in a foreign language and use the language for productive purposes.

Scenarios such as these are played out at a number of campuses across the United States although a majority of programs are in what might be referred to as "pilot" or "experimental" stages. Snow (1998) provides a summary of recent work in this area with a comprehensive annotated bibliography, while Kruger and Ryan (1993) and Snow and Brinton (1997) provide useful reviews of current literature in foreign language education and ESL, respectively.

Although the extant programs appear to be pedagogically viable, it should be noted that there appear to exist on many campuses a number of administrative obstacles to overcome prior to their widespread implementation. For example, programs such as this can easily fall victim to their own success, since they often depend entirely upon the good will of participating content and language faculty members. That is, there often appears to exist

< 106 >

no regular mechanism to provide additional funding for this purpose. This funding would permit a department to offer, for example, release time to a faculty member who has assumed responsibility for supervising a specified number of students over a particular period of time. There should also be a mechanism for recognizing that this faculty member has made an educational contribution that should be valued at the time of reappointment or promotion. The use of a foreign language as a vehicle for studying relevant content material of demonstrable interest appears to hold great promise for the future.

CONCLUSION

What then is the likelihood that students in American universities and colleges will graduate with bilingual proficiency and cross-cultural competence as a matter of course? The cumulative evidence from research conducted over the last three decades at sites around the world demonstrates conclusively that cognitive, social, personal, and economic benefits accrue to the individual who has an opportunity to develop a high degree of bilingual proficiency when compared with her monolingual counterpart (see Tucker, in press). The message for educators is clear: begin foreign language training early, implement a carefully planned and well-articulated sequence of study, involve trained committed teachers, and incorporate the language program into the broader course of studies. This advice will be as applicable to the elementary and secondary level as it is for the university, if we are to prepare graduates for productive participation in our global society. We are far from achieving this goal, but if educational policymakers in the next decade come to view language as both a national and a natural resource, we should be able to bring about dramatic improvements in the abilities of our graduates.

References

August, D. & Hakuta, K. (eds.) (1997) *Improving Schooling for Language-minority Children: A Research Agenda.* Washington, DC: National Academy Press.

Branaman, L. E. & Rhodes, N. C. (1999) *Foreign Language Instruction in the United States: A National Survey of Elementary and Secondary Schools.* Washington, DC and McHenry, IL: Center for Applied Linguistics and Delta Systems.

< 107 >

Brecht, R. D. & Walton, A. R. (1995) Meeting the challenge of GATT: The impact of cross-cultural communications on the US balance of trade. Washington, DC: *NFLC Policy Issues*. National Foreign Language Center.

Brecht, R. D. & Ingold, C. (1998) Tapping a national resource: Heritage languages in the United States. ERIC Digest. EDO-FL-98-12.

Brisk, M. E. (1998) *Bilingual Education: From Compensatory to Quality Schooling.* Mahwah, NJ: Lawrence Erlbaum.

Brod, R. & Welles, E. B. (2000) Foreign language enrollments in United States institutions of higher education, Fall 1998. *ADFL Bulletin, 31*: 2 (Winter), pp. 23–29.

Cetron, M. & Gayle, M. (1993) *Education Renaissance: Our Schools at the Turn of the 21st Century.*

Cheshire, J. (ed.) (1991) *English around the World: Sociolinguistic Perspectives.* Cambridge: Cambridge University Press.

Comrie, B. (ed.) (1987) *The World's Major Languages*. New York: Oxford University Press.

Crystal, D. (1987) *The Cambridge Encyclopedia of Language*. Cambridge: Cambridge University Press.

Crandall, J. (1993) Content-centered learning in the US. In W. Grabe (Ed.) *Annual Review of Applied Linguistics 1993. 13.* pp. 111–126.

Crandall, J. (1995) Reinventing (America's) schools: The role of the applied linguist. In J. E. Alatis (Ed.) *Georgetown University Roundtable on Languages and Linguistics 1995.* Washington, DC: Georgetown University Press.

Crandall, J. A. & Tucker, G. R. (1990) Content-based instruction in second and foreign languages. In S. Anivan (Ed.) *Language Teaching Methodology in the Nineties.* Singapore: Seameo Regional Language Centre.

del Pinal, J. (1995) *Hispanics-Latinos: Diverse People in a Multicultural Society.* Washington, DC: Bureau of the Census.

Desruisseaux, P. (1999) 15% Rise in American Students Abroad Shows Popularity of Non-European Destinations. *Chronicle of Higher Education. 46*, 16, pp. A57–A62.

Dickson, P. & Cumming, A. (eds.) (1996) *Profiles of Language Education in 25 Countries.* Slough, Great Britain: National Foundation for Educational Research.

Donato, R., Antonek, J. L. & Tucker, G. R. (1994) A multiple perspective analysis of a Japanese FLES program. *Foreign Language Annals, 27*, 3, 365–378.

Donato, R., Tucker, G. R. & Antonek, J. (1996) Monitoring and assessing a Japanese FLES program: Ambiance and achievement. *Language Learning. 46*, 3, 497–528.

Dutcher, N. in collaboration with G. R. Tucker (1994) The use of first and second

< 108 >

languages in education: A review of educational experience. World Bank, East Asia and the Pacific Region, Country Department III. Washington, DC.

Edwards, J. (1994) *Multilingualism*. London: Routledge.

Graddol, D. (1997) *The Future of English?* London: The British Council.

Grimes, B. F. (1992) *Ethnologue: Languages of the world*. Dallas: Summer Institute of Linguistics.

Kenyon, D. M., Farr, B., Mitchell, J., & Armengol, R. (2000) Framework for the 2003 foreign language national assessment of educational progress. Pre-publication edition adopted by the National Assessment Governing Board May 13, 2000. Washington, DC: Center for Applied Linguistics.

Klee, C. (2000) Foreign language instruction. In Rosenthal, J.W. (ed.) *Handbook of Undergraduate Second Language Education*. Mahwah, NJ: Lawrence Erlbaum Associates. pp. 49–72.

Krueger, M. & Ryan, F. (eds.) (1993) *Language and Content: Discipline- and Content-based Approaches to Language Study*. Lexington, MA: D.C. Heath.

Lambert, R. D. (1993) Language learning and language utilization. In Moore, S. J. & Morfit, C. A. (eds.) *Language and International Studies: A Richard Lambert Perspective*. Washington, DC: National Foreign Language Center. pp. 179–185.

Lambert, W. E. (1980) "The two faces of bilingual education." *NCBE Forum*. 3.

National Standards in Foreign Language Education Project. (1996). *Standards for foreign language learning: Preparing for the 21st century*. Yonkers, NY: ACTFL.

Pesola, C. A. (1992) Notes from the president. *FLES News*, 6 (1). 3.

Rivers, W. (1992) Internationalization of the university: Where are the foreign languages? In Alatis, J.E. (ed.) *Georgetown university round table on languages and linguistics 1992*. Washington, DC: Georgetown University Press.

Roberts, S. (1993) *Who we are: A portrait of America based on the latest US census*. New York: Random House.

Rosenthal, J. W. (2000) Shared concerns and new directions. In J. W. Rosenthal (ed.) *Handbook of Undergraduate Second Language Education*. Mahwah, NJ: Lawrence Erlbaum Associates. pp. 347–354.

Sack, J. (2000) Riley endorses dual-immersion programs. *Education Week*. 19. March 22.

Snow, M. A. (1998) Trends and issues in content-based instruction. In Grabe, W. (ed.) *Annual Review of Applied Linguistics 1998*. 18. 243–267.

Snow, M. A. & Brinton, D. (eds.) (1997) *The Content-based Classroom: Perspectives on Integrating Language and Content*. New York: Longmans.

Straight, H. S. (ed.) (1994) *Languages across the Curriculum. Translation Perspectives VII*. Binghamton: State University of New York Press.

< 109 >

Stryker, S. & Leaver, B. L. (eds.) (1997) *Content-based Instruction in the Foreign Language Classroom.* Washington, DC: Georgetown University Press.

Tucker, G. R. (1997) Developing a language-competent American society: Implications of the English-only movement. In Bongaerts, T. & de Bot, K. (eds.) *Perspectives on foreign-language policy: Studies in honour of Theo van Els.* Amsterdam: John Benjamins. 1997. pp. 89–98.

Tucker, G. R. (1999) A global perspective on bilingualism and bilingual education. In J. E. Alatis (Ed.) *Georgetown University Roundtable on Languages and Linguistics 1999.* Washington, DC: Georgetown University Press.

Tucker, G. R., Donato, R. & Antonek, J. L. (1996) Documenting growth in a Japanese FLES program. *Foreign Language Annals. 29*, 4, 539–550.

Tucker, G. R., Donato, R. & Murday, K. (2001) The genesis of a district-wide Spanish FLES program: A collaborative achievement. In Walters, J. & Shohamy, E. (eds.) *Perspectives and Issues in Educational Language Policy: A Volume in Honour of Bernard Dov Spolsky.* Philadelphia: John Benjamins.

Voght, G. M. (2000) New paradigms for US education in the twenty-first century. *Foreign Language Annals. 33*, 3, 269-277.

World Bank. (1995) Priorities and strategies for education. Washington, DC: The International Bank for Reconstruction and Development.

< 110 >

WOMEN IN COMPUTER SCIENCE: THE CARNEGIE MELLON EXPERIENCE

Lenore Blum

Lenore Blum is Distinguished Career Professor of Computer Science at Carnegie Mellon. Her research interests are many and varied, ranging from model theory and differential fields to a theory of computation and complexity for real numbers. She received her Ph.D. from MIT in 1968, and has been at Carnegie Mellon for four years.

OVERVIEW

In 1995, the Computer Science Department at Carnegie Mellon began an effort to bring more women into its undergraduate computer science program. At that time, just 7 percent of the close to 100 entering freshman computer science majors were women. Five years later, the percentage of women in the entering class had increased fivefold. In 1999, women were 38 percent of the incoming first-year computer science class; in the fall of 2000, approximately 40 percent of the entering class was composed of women.

How did this remarkable change come about and what does the explanation tell us abut Carnegie Mellon as an innovative university? Rather than an endpoint, the increasing number of women in the program signifies the beginning of a crucial period of transition for women in computer science at the University.

< 111 >

We are now faced with the challenge of ensuring that women—as well as men—in the program thrive. We are committed to this process. We anticipate that the impact of our efforts will be truly transformative—not only by bringing more women into the computer science program, but by enhancing our position as a leader in the field, strengthened by the interests and concerns of a diverse student body.

Before outlining the factors that have been crucial to the success of our efforts thus far, it is worth noting that such dramatic increases in the number of women in computer science do not appear to be widespread. In fact, the widely cited statistics from articles like "The Incredible Shrinking Pipeline"[1] and "The Incredible Shrinking Pipeline Unlikely to Reverse,"[2] indicate that the percentage of women entering computer science programs and careers in the US has declined precipitously during the past decade and suggest that this is unlikely to change. Whether or not this conclusion is valid, it is the view of many observers in the field, and indeed was noted by Rita Colwell, Director of the National Science Foundation, in her keynote address at the Y2K Grace Hopper Celebration of Women in Computing. Carnegie Mellon's experience challenges a perceived trend, and may offer inspiration, ideas, and concrete suggestions to others who wish to follow in our path.

What accounts for our success? The following have helped our efforts:

- A vision for the program articulated by key faculty and administrators. They have argued that a more diverse program is good not only for potential students, but crucial to the intellectual health and future of Carnegie Mellon's computer science program, and critical for the entire field.
- A solid base of research from which to make change and educate faculty and students.
- Respected and experienced researchers, faculty and administrators at the helm of the effort, working to bring others on board.
- An articulate and committed group of women undergraduate and graduate students who have gained the recognition and respect of the faculty and administration.
- A growing reputation for Carnegie Mellon as a place that wants women and values their presence.
- Support from the president of the University that has enabled us to bring speakers to campus, orga-

< 112 >

nize events, workshops and outreach activities, provide funds for students to attend professional meetings, and assess the impact of our efforts.

In this chapter we document changes that have occurred during the past several years and examine the reasons for the increase of women in our program. We also present and summarize the impact of activities designed to help create a community of women in computer science with the goal of enhancing the educational and social experiences of undergraduate and graduate students. We indicate some of the challenges and stumbling blocks we have faced, and our plans for the future.

THE ADMISSIONS STORY

It may be helpful to say a few words about the history and structure of computer science at Carnegie Mellon. The Computer Science (CS) Department and its Ph.D. program were inaugurated in 1965; the undergraduate major was not instituted until 1988 (first as a Math/CS major and then in 1992 as a CS major). Typically, students enter the computer science major as freshmen. In 1988, the Department evolved into the School of Computer Science, which now comprises seven departments, including the core Computer Science Department, centers, and institutes of education and research.[3] Each of the divisions offers graduate programs; the Computer Science undergraduate program remains housed in the Computer Science Department. For more information see: http://www.cs.cmu.edu

During its first several years, the undergraduate computer science program was plagued by very low numbers of women—a problem it then shared with most doctoral programs.[4] In 1995, when efforts were made to understand and change this problem, the number of women in our undergraduate computer science program was negligible.

The admissions process occurs in three stages—application, admission, and enrollment—over which the university winnows its applications and creates its entering class of enrollees. The trends at each of these three stages indicate remarkable progress in recruiting applications from qualified women for Computer Science and motivating exceptional applicants to become part of the entering class. Here are the major trends:

< 113 >

- A steady rise in the numbers of both male and female applicants to the undergraduate program has been noted over the past five years. This increase, however, has been steeper for women than men. The number of women applying to the program has more than doubled (from 160 in 1995 to just over 400 in 2000), exceeding even the substantial increase in applications by males.
- A concomitant rise in the number of women admitted to the program, even as the threshold requirements for admission have remained extremely high, has also occurred. In 1995, 54 women—a little more than three out of every ten female applicants—were admitted into the program, while in 2000, 158 women—almost four out of every ten in the female applicant pool—were admitted.
- Of those women admitted to the program, increasingly higher percentages chose to attend. The yield more than doubled, from 15 percent in 1995 to 32 percentin 2000. The yield among male applicants has remained fairly constant. In 1995, the yield for male students admitted to the university was close to double that of females, but by the year 2000, yields for both genders were comparable.

Below I will examine the factors that contributed to this notable increase in opportunities provided for women, and opportunities seized by women, in the field of computer science at Carnegie Mellon.

RESEARCH AND INTERVENTION

Allan Fisher, then Associate Dean for Undergraduate Computer Science Education, spearheaded an intensive effort to understand and change the representation of women in the undergraduate program. He collaborated with Jane Margolis, a social scientist and expert in gender equity in education, on a research study aimed at deeply understanding the nature of the problem and establishing a sound base of knowledge from which to develop interventions. Funded by a grant from the Sloan Foundation, the project was based upon hundreds of interviews with both male and female CS students about their histories with computing, interests, motivations and aspirations, reasons for majoring in computer science at Carnegie Mellon, and their experiences in

< 114 >

the undergraduate program. Conducted over a four-year period, the project was able to track many students throughout their time at Carnegie Mellon. By interviewing students once a semester over a period of years, the researchers witnessed the ups and downs of their experiences, and changes in attitudes over time. Most importantly, they were able to identify crucial periods in students' attachments to the field, and factors that contributed to or inhibited their ability to succeed.

The study yielded significant insights into the many layers of the problem, in terms not only of bringing women into computer science, but also of retaining them. Problem areas identified had to do with the experience gap, confidence doubts, curriculum and pedagogy, and peer culture.

The authors of the study concluded that:

> Females' interest in computing is more likely to be one interest among several others. They are more likely to place a high value on the context of computing, the links between computers and other fields, and the contribution to society that computers can make. We refer to this orientation as 'computing for a purpose.'... Among the women, there is definitely less tinkering, less unguided exploration, less obsession with computing, and a less proprietary stance towards the computer.

The research was useful in developing a blueprint for action, confirming hunches, and serving as an informational resource for faculty and other potentially supportive parties.

As a result of these findings, several initiatives were developed. One of these involved summer institutes for teachers of advanced placement courses in American high schools. Our institute taught high school teachers a new computer language, mandated by a revised Advanced Placement (AP) end-of-course examination, but also focused on the gender gap. It made Carnegie Mellon's own program more visible to teachers who would be in a position to encourage more women to apply. But the institute also focused attention on ways to recruit more women into AP computer science courses in high school. In 1997, for example, just 17 percent of AP computer science test-takers were female, the lowest of any AP exam that year.[5]

In 1995, prompted by impending revisions in the AP CS exam, the National Science Foundation (NSF) issued a call for proposals to prepare high school teachers for the change. Allan Fisher saw this as a fortuitous opportunity to work with teachers to ad-

< 115 >

dress gender gap issues while they were motivated to gain new expertise. Thus the Summer Institute for CS Advanced Placement Teachers was conceived. With a grant from the NSF, Fisher—together with Jane Margolis, computer equity expert Jo Sanders, and Assistant Dean for CS Undergraduate Education Mark Stehlik—ran two weeklong sessions each summer during the years 1996, 1997, and 1998. The goal of the program was twofold: (1) to prepare high school computer science teachers to teach C++, a major component of the revised AP CS exam; and (2) to talk to teachers about the gender gap in computing and what they could do about it.

During the course of the three summers, approximately one in six of all Advanced Placement CS high school teachers in the US (240) participated in the program on the Carnegie Mellon campus. It is likely that, both directly and indirectly, these teachers played a significant role in the increased numbers of high school women considering majors in computer science—and at Carnegie Mellon, in particular. Indeed, anecdotal evidence from interviews with students supports this claim. For example, one first-year student interviewed directly linked her decision to apply and enroll at our university with her AP CS teacher's experience at our summer institutes. The teacher would make jokes in class, and wink at the student and say, "That's your school. They really want women." This teacher also showed off the website containing pictures from the institutes and raved about the faculty he met there. Other women students have told similar stories.

Over the five-year period from 1996 through 2000, the portion of women applicants to our program from high schools whose computer science teachers had attended our summer institutes, increased more than threefold, from 5 percent to 18 percent. In the same period, the portion of male applicants from those schools doubled, increasing from 12 percent to 23 percent.

Both the summer institutes and our success with students of high school teachers in the institutes received considerable positive local and national press. These teachers spread the word about Carnegie Mellon to their peers. AP teachers are more likely than typical high school teachers to belong to professional networks and thus have opportunities to disseminate their experience informally, as well as formally, to their peers. Thus, the reputation of Carnegie Mellon as a place that values and cares about female students was almost certainly a factor accounting for the increased numbers of women applying to our program.

< 116 >

At about the same time, Allan Fisher also conveyed to the Admissions Office his goal of a gender-balanced program, and tied it to the vision of broader leadership qualities in the field. Computer Science was far more than programming and was not simply a follow-on to years of play with computers. One thing he felt important was to get the message out that "no prior programming experience" was necessary to enter our program. The image of a computer science student as someone (usually male) who had played with computers since early childhood was widespread. As a result, many prospective students assumed that those with a more extensive computing background had a better chance of being admitted. Several women have said that Fisher's message encouraged them to apply to Carnegie Mellon.

A Supportive Community: The Women@SCS Advisory Council

The backbone of current efforts to ensure a positive learning environment for women in the School of Computer Science is the Women@SCS Advisory Council. The Advisory Council was created in the fall of 1999 and has since met weekly during the academic year. Membership includes undergraduate students representing all four years and graduate representatives from the various departments within the School of Computer Science.[6] Advisory Council meetings, and ensuing conversations, whether in person or virtual (the Council logs voluminous email correspondence), produce the Council's priorities and evolving agenda for action. A current priority is community building.

The Advisory Council was created by a confluence of events in the School of Computer Science. We had just witnessed a striking increase in the number of women in the first-year class. We were organizing social events that would bring women in the graduate computer science programs together. At the same time, an articulate and thoughtful group of undergraduate women were expressing their opinions about changes needed in the undergraduate program. I had just arrived at Carnegie Mellon, and thought that by pulling together the many elements already in place, we could rather quickly create a comprehensive program to increase the participation of women in computer science. From long experience in this area, I also believed that the issues raised and changes proposed would make sense for, and benefit, the entire program. Key faculty and administrators were supportive

< 117 >

of this direction. Thus, forming a Council that would bring together these positive forces seemed the natural way to start.

WOMEN@SCS ADVISORY COUNCIL

From the start, the Women@SCS Advisory Council had been a proactive, action-oriented group. While many of its efforts were in fact recommended in the research findings reported by Fisher and Margolis, other activities grew directly from discussions among its members about the needs of women in the program. The fact that the Council arose from within the School of Computer Science, involving "insiders" from all levels of the program, has been key to its success. Its efforts have been spurred on by people intimately familiar with the field, giving the group legitimacy.

In its first year, the Council had three primary goals:

- To foster a supportive peer environment and an academic and social community of women in all levels of the CS program;
- to communicate to faculty and administration the needs of women in the School of Computer Science, and to act as consultants, providing suggestions and information on how to improve the program; and
- to organize outreach activities for girls and women at various levels in the hopes of increasing the numbers of women.

Here we outline some specific Council activities and initiatives. During the first year, major attention was paid to undergraduate concerns. The most extensive single activity of the Women@SCS Advisory Council has been the Big Sister / Little Sister program, which pairs upper-class students with first-year and sophomore CS majors. It was formed to strengthen the bonds of women in SCS and encourage a forum for discussion and support. 34 students participated in the Big Sister / Little Sister program during its first year, 48 during the second year.

Other community-building activities have included student-faculty dinners, undergrad-graduate student dinners, dessert socials during exam periods, and group outings, such as a guided tour of the 2000 Carnegie International. In addition to the social aspects of community building, Women@SCS events also focus

< 118 >

on the professional. For example, the Council periodically sponsors panels with visiting women computer scientists on topics such as "Women's Career Choices: Costs and Benefits Along the Way" and "Grad School or Industry—What should I do?" A tradition begun at the end of the first year is the "Passing the Torch Dinner" where seniors share their wisdom.

One of the most valuable roles of the Council has been to act as a resource and sounding board for the faculty and administration about issues affecting undergraduates. These issues can be quite specific. For example, the Council provided feedback to the Associate Dean for Computer Sciences Undergraduate Education on his recruitment presentation to prospective CS majors, met with course instructors to suggest improvements, and reviewed training videos for teacher assistants.

But what is likely to have the most profound impact on the Department is the Council clearly pointing out that the CS undergraduate curriculum as currently construed serves male students far better than females. The first two years of our undergraduate CS program are extremely technical, with a heavy programming component. Many of the courses either assume students already know the requisite programming language or that they can pick it up on their own. One might describe these years as "boot camp" for computer science. It is not until the third year that our program becomes more flexible and students have the opportunity to be involved in multidisciplinary projects. The upside is that by the time our students are juniors, they pretty much have the technical ability to do anything they choose. The downside is that many women feel discouraged well before this time.

In a "white paper" she circulated at a meeting with faculty, Ting-Chih Shih, an undergraduate Council member (and our webmaster) provides some perspective:

> Most men come into the computer science curriculum having had many years of experience in programming, exploring the hardware and the software of computers, and learning on their own. Most females start with little or no experience in computer science. Some females have in-class experience in programming during high school and like it for its problem solving aspects and the joy of having programs work. Some men seem to be fascinated by the machine itself and being able to take control of the machine. But females seem to see the computer as a tool to achieve what they

< 119 >

wanted to do and therefore do not get as much enjoyment going through the process of dealing with the machine.

Upon entering college, females are faced with many more men who seem to have more experience and get better scores effortlessly. As a result, they start to doubt their ability to learn computer science. They begin thinking that learning computer science takes innate talent and no amount of hard work will pay off. . . . They start to lose confidence and forget their initial interest in computer science. Statistics show that females with grades equal to or better than those of their male peers have less confidence.

At Carnegie Mellon, females begin to lose confidence because introductory courses . . . seem to work towards men's advantage and make female students feel inferior. . . . The ways lectures are presented seem to appeal to men more. In general, females feel that the birds-eye view of a problem and the end result are more relevant than the coding details in between. Some professors fail to emphasize the purpose and the end result of assignments. Students spend most of their time programming for assignments. Because male students have had more experience coding they finish assignments earlier without struggling as much as female students. Since, for most females, the hardest part about the courses is writing programs, they may think that computer science is just mastering how to program. . . .

A more integrated approach to computer science, one that introduces multidisciplinary possibilities earlier in the curriculum, would seem reasonable.

The Council has been, and continues to be, a source of information about women in computer science for the campus community and the community-at-large. One of our first endeavors was to develop the Women@SCS web site (http://www.cs.cmu.edu/~women) with the goal of becoming a "destination" for people desiring information regarding women in computer science—both at Carnegie Mellon and elsewhere in universities and industry. It is a "must see" to get a feel for the scope of our activities.

The Carnegie Mellon experience received national attention at the Year 2000 Grace Hopper Celebration of Women in Computing in Hyannis, Massachusetts, with standing room only for

< 120 >

our panel. Eleven of our students attended the conference. Five of them[7] participated on the panel with Allan Fisher, Jane Margolis, and myself, sharing their perspectives and experiences. The students were runaway hits with their keen insights and great good humor. Their upbeat message to others: "Take one step at a time, and go for it!"

The Council continues to reach out to prospective SCS students. Activities have included panel discussions and social gatherings for prospective undergraduates during Sleeping Bag weekends, Open Houses for prospective graduate students, and informational letters sent to admitted students. We have participated in outreach activities geared towards engaging middle and high school girls in science and technology. Here are two examples of what we have done in this area:

- Expanding Your Horizons Conference for middle school girls. We developed a hands-on workshop where teams of girls built and programmed small robots. Forty girls participated.
- Take Our Daughters To Work Day. Robotics graduate students gave demos of their projects to girls ages seven to twelve.

IMPACT

We are continuing to canvas students, faculty and the administration to assess the impact of Women@SCS Advisory Council activities and to determine how we can be more effective. During our first year, Faye Miller, who had worked with Allan Fisher and Jane Margolis on their assessment, conducted interviews with 15 undergraduate women, one-on-one, in interviews and focus groups.

Of the students interviewed, those on the Advisory Council appeared to benefit most, not only from the activities they participated in, but also from being on the Advisory Council itself. The experience of being sought out by faculty, truly listened to, and respected as experts on their own experiences, was one of the most profound effects.

> [The Council] affected the way I viewed how the administration cares about the students, and ways to get things changed around the school. I didn't have any idea it could have so much of an impact. I also didn't

< 121 >

realize how much of an impact I could have on my peers and freshmen.

Just getting involved in the committee has had a big impact—you start knowing there are people you didn't know existed before.

I planned the [student/faculty] dinner, and hearing that others got things out of it means a lot to me. It makes me want to do more, boosts my confidence in that area.

During the first year, graduate women benefited less directly from their participation on the Council since efforts were focused primarily on pressing issues affecting undergraduates. While graduate women were particularly integral to the Council's outreach activities, graduate issues received much less airtime during meetings.

The women not on the Council appeared to fall into two camps. In the first were those who were moderately interested in the council's activities, had attended some events, and generally thought the group valuable. Although these students had some knowledge of our activities through e-mail and word of mouth, many were unclear about the range of our goals. They were students who might have been more active participants if they had been more aware of the Council's aims.

The other set of students had no interest in the activities organized by the Council. They said they didn't have any particular needs that the Council could meet. They said they were comfortable with the gender ratio in SCS, and were reluctant to say that there was *anything* unique about being a woman in computer science.

This quote from a graduate student, posted on a mailing list discussion about the creation of the Women@SCS Advisory Council, echoes succinctly what we heard some undergraduates say:

When I first arrived at Carnegie Mellon, I didn't see much point in women-specific groups and activities— I didn't care if other women wanted to have them, but I didn't think they had much to offer me, and I definitely didn't want to be seen as part of any gender-defined opinion bloc. After six years here, though, my feelings have changed somewhat. . . .

However, when asked what their biggest issues are *as CS students*, the women we interviewed talked about the same things

< 122 >

that women on the Council pointed to as gender-related—self esteem gap, experience gap, and being accused of "getting in because you're a girl." Regardless of whether they identify themselves as interested in "women's issues," many undergraduate women may have interests in some of the goals of the Women@ SCS Advisory Council. We ought not to ignore them as potential participants.

In assessing impact, issues of retention must also be addressed. In the early years, attrition among women in computer science was high; more recently, the situation has been improving. However, comparing male and female attrition rates is difficult, because the actual number of women, even just a few years ago, was so small. One woman transferring out might mean a loss of 10 percent of the women in that class. We are pleased that of the 50 women in the 1999 freshman CS class, 47 were enrolled as sophomores in the fall of 2000. However, until the program stabilizes, we do anticipate that additional transfers out of CS are likely. While retention is certainly one of the goals of the Women@SCS Council, we concur with Peter Lee, Associate Dean for Computer Science Undergraduate Education:

> [Retention] seems unnecessarily negative to me, and at any rate seems to aim too low. The goal, it seems to me, is to take advantage of the great recruiting success and produce a crop of graduating women who will be the future leaders, world-class scientists, visionaries, and captains of industry. . . .

There is a growing perception among the faculty and administration that the student body is more interesting than ever before. But also, awareness of pressing issues such as the curriculum, advising, and climate appears to be increasing, particularly among core faculty involved in undergraduate teaching and key administrators.

Associate Dean Peter Lee consults frequently with Council members and has been a strong supporter and advocate of the Council's role. He has given presentations—for example, at a faculty meeting and to the President's Advisory Board for the School of Computer Science—articulating opportunities and challenges afforded by the increased numbers of undergraduate women and outlining what faculty can do.

There has been a comprehensive reexamination of the entire undergraduate computer science curriculum. Revisions have been instituted in the entry level programming sequence to accommo-

< 123 >

date students with varying degrees of prior experience. Four faculty committees have also been convened with the mandate to examine and make recommendations to the Department on: (1) the early curriculum; (2) metrics/benchmarking; (3) student life/research/advising; and (4) deep thinking (math/foundations). Chairs of these committees have met with the Council and are incorporating Council suggestions in their deliberations.

Finally, it is worth commenting on the relationship between the Fisher-Margolis gender studies and the changes we are witnessing, particularly among the faculty and administration. Clearly, the Fisher and Margolis research directly informed the design of the summer institutes for the teachers' program and the material used to recruit the teachers. This, in turn, over time, dramatically impacted the CS enrollment statistics. This research also directly informed the initial modifications of the first-year curriculum and the recruitment of Carnegie Mellon faculty directly involved in the entry-level program. However, until quite recently, most other faculty members in the Computer Science Department have been either unaware of, or only marginally interested in, that research. Indeed, it has been the presence of the women themselves, their numbers and the publicity they have brought, that has caused many faculty to take note and become motivated to look to the research for insights, explanation and guidance. The research now plays an invaluable role in identifying effects of differential experiences and culture, articulating and pointing out resulting patterns of behavior (for example switching out) and in guiding the creation of productive strategies for change. Many women inappropriately switch out of computer science, not because they find their interest elsewhere, but rather because their initial high interest and enthusiasm for computing has waned due to "eroded self-confidence."[8]

Ongoing Activities and Next Steps

The scope of Women@SCS Advisory Council activities continues to grow as we meet new challenges and new opportunities present themselves. With the increase of women in computer science at Carnegie Mellon, we are starting to see changes in female students' confidence levels and feelings of belonging. The three undergraduate presenters at the Grace Hopper conference, respectively a senior, sophomore, and freshman during the Council's first year, presented what amounted to a "Before, During and

< 124 >

After" testimonial of the positive effects of the changes that had taken place. The transition from the self-doubting "Why am I here?" reaction of a woman freshman in 1996, who had had four years of high school programming, to the "What's the fuss? It's just normal" reaction of a woman freshman in 1999 was striking, even for those of us intimately familiar with our program.

Thus, as we strive to move towards "critical mass" in computer science at Carnegie Mellon, it will be important—and fascinating—to document changes in the climate and culture of computing, particularly changes in attitudes and behavior of both women and men. Building on the earlier Fisher and Margolis research, we can now ask: Which issues disappear, which persist, and which new ones arise? And how do we deal with these changes?

As an example, the question of admissions criteria has been a volatile topic of discussion among students. Women students we interviewed frequently mentioned hearing from their peers that they "got in" to computer science only because they were female. As one student put it:

> I think there is some sense that girls got in because they are girls. . . . It really undermines your self-esteem, it makes you question why you got in, like if you didn't really deserve to get in, if you are not fully qualified, it makes you question your chances for success.

As it becomes more "normal" for women to be part of the computer science community, this particular issue will disappear. Even so, a challenge for the faculty and administration will be to address admissions questions raised by students in a more direct way.

The experience gap between men and women entering the program has implications for the curriculum and for women's sense of belonging and confidence. For example, women in our interviews suggested that the Women@SCS Advisory Council could organize workshops to teach UNIX (which is needed for certain classes but never taught) and answer questions that the women feel are "stupid" and so are embarrassed to ask of male peers or male TAs. We might consider additional TA training, or find alternative sources of help.

There has been some e-mail debate among faculty about what students should be taught, and what they need to learn on their own. The Dean writes:

< 125 >

It is painful to watch new students tripping over the arcanae of UNIX. On the other hand they (recent CS alumni) thought a virtue of their CMU education was that they had 'learned how to learn' such—without much help.

Another faculty member replied:

These are issues that lots of Carnegie Mellon students understand when they enter, and we currently expect the rest of them to pick it up on the street corner. The issue, of course, is less gender than it is prior experience and orientation toward tinkering with the system—it's just that those are substantially gender-correlated.

Some of the curricular and pedagogical difficulties are perpetuated partly because many CS faculty do not have ongoing contacts with undergraduate students outside their own courses. Faculty often are not aware of the undergraduate students' whole program and the competing demands on their time and mental and psychological energy.[9] Academic advisors get to know students in deeper ways than other faculty. In the undergraduate program, only two faculty members, Mark Stehlik and Jim Roberts, have substantial formal contact with students outside of classes. Informal mechanisms, such as periodic lunches and/or seminars as suggested by Peter Lee, could be instituted to provide faculty with more student contact and a deeper and more global understanding of both the curriculum and students' programs. The Women@SCS Advisory Council is ready to provide input and assistance with such endeavors.

One area we have only touched on, and would like to pursue in the following years, is student professional development. For example, there are opportunities on campus for undergraduates to obtain funding for research projects, and there are forums for students to present their research to the larger community. Until now, male students have been the sole representatives of computer science at these forums. As more women go through our program, we expect this to change. But also, the Council could take initiative to encourage and support women to pursue and present their research.

During the first year, major attention was paid to undergraduate concerns. As a consequence, although the graduate students played essential roles as mentors and advisors, their own needs

< 126 >

and interests were not sufficiently met. Thus, during the second year, the Council split into two groups, an undergraduate advisory board and a graduate advisory board, each with its own agenda and activities. Although each group now meets separately, both come together periodically, particularly to plan joint projects and events.

Professional issues are a major focus of the graduate student advisory board. Graduate students are eager to meet with and hear from accomplished women in the field. Thus, an important graduate student activity has been organizing meetings with visiting women computer scientists. A next step will be a formal Distinguished Lecture Series.

New outreach opportunities present themselves all the time. For example, we have been asked by a local private girls' school to present a two week mini-course for sophomores and juniors that would delve more into the intellectual aspects and ideas of computer science, rather than just programming. We have not had the resources or time to respond to this request, but we hope to pursue this opportunity in the future. We already have a tentative blurb to advertise such a course to interested girls:

> What is Computer Science anyway? No, it is not word processing, it is not e-mail and it is not surfing the Web. Yes, it is the deep ideas, ingenuity and wild imagination that created all this and more! Experience the fun with some of the Carnegie Mellon women computer scientists who are creating the robots, wireless technology and search engines that for sure will be part of your future.

Along these lines, and inspired by the success of our workshop for middle school girls ("Is there a robot in your future?"), a subgroup of the Council has begun discussing the feasibility of a Women@SCS Educational Games and Software Project. Clearly, there is a need for high quality material that would be appealing to and valuable for girls. While some excellent material is starting to emerge, we feel in a unique position to contribute, given the enormous pool of talent, expertise, resources, skills and insights available at Carnegie Mellon. As part of this effort, we are planning a mini-conference on "Girls, Technology and Education."

Finally, an exciting recent development is the formation of a nascent SCS alumnae network. Already we have alumnae representatives on the Council and an e-mail list containing over 100

< 127 >

names. We expect that this group will become an increasingly important resource, particularly as more women graduate from our program. Indeed, by being a natural source of "role models" and mentors for our current students, our alumnae can serve to inspire and guide our students as they consider and move into careers in computer science, both within academia and beyond.

CONCLUSION

Increasing and maintaining the presence of women in computer science at levels equal to men necessitates taking a hard look at, and changing, business as usual. In the past, the culture, environment, and expectations of the undergraduate CS program have served to meet the needs of male students more than female students, although it certainly has not been optimal for many male students as well. Many of the changes we have been advocating, particularly regarding curriculum, advising and pedagogy, are not gender-specific, and can benefit all students in the program. Indeed, with our visibility and prestige, what we accomplish has potential to have widespread impact. The next several years at Carnegie Mellon are full of potential. We have made considerable strides. Presidential support has played a major role in enabling us to implement quickly new projects to foster community and to anticipate and to respond constructively to problems and issues as they emerged. Sustaining momentum and moving ahead in directions we have outlined will require ongoing attention and commitment from the faculty and administration.

Notes

[1] Camp, Tracy. "The Incredible Shrinking Pipeline," Colorado School of Mines. http://www.mines.edu/fs_home/tcamp/cacm/paper.html
An edited version of this paper appears in *Communications of the ACM*, vol. 40, no. 10, pp. 103-110, Oct. 1997.

[2] Camp, Tracy, Miller, Keith, and Davies, Vanessa. "The Incredible Shrinking Pipeline Unlikely to Reverse," Colorado School of Mines and University of Illinois at Springfield. http://www.mines.edu/fs_home/tcamp/new-study/new-study.html

[3] These are: the Center for Automated Learning and Discovery (CALD), the Computer Science Department (CSD), the Entertainment Technology Center (ETC), the Human-Computer Interaction Institute (HCII), the Institute for

< 128 >

Software Research, International (ISRI), the Language Technologies Institute (LTI), and the Robotics Institute (RI).

[4] The Computer Research Association "Taulbee Survey." http://cra.org/statistics

[5] http://www.collegeboard.org/press/senior97/table14.html

[6] See: http://www.cs.cmu.edu/~women/

[7] Jorjeta Jetcheva, Brigitte Pientka, Lisa Nelson, Leah Miller and Tiffany Chang.

[8] In their working paper, "Women in Computer Sciences: Closing the Gender Gap in Higher Education" (http://www.cs.cmu.edu/~gendergap/confidence.html), Jane Margolis, Allan Fisher and Faye Miller discuss "the difficulty for women students to experience and hold on to 'intrinsic interest' in computer science in an environment that can undercut their confidence, motivation and sense of belonging in the field . . ."

[9] In contrast, graduate students in the Computer Science Department are paired with advisors within a month of entering the program; they meet regularly with advisors thereafter. At the end of each semester, the entire computer science faculty gathers for 1 to 2 days (during the infamous Black Fridays) to evaluate each graduate student's progress to date and to compose individual letters applauding successes, stating concerns, and outlining expectations for the coming semester. Advisors are responsible for presenting their students' cases and are often given suggestions by the rest of the faculty on how to advise their students better.

< 129 >

—

A RENAISSANCE IN THE EDUCATION OF MECHANICAL ENGINEERS

Adnan Akay

Adnan Akay is Lord Professor and Head of the Mechanical Engineering Department at Carnegie Mellon University. His research and technical interests lie in the fields of acoustics and vibrations. Professor Akay was awarded a Ph.D. from North Carolina State University in 1976, and has been at Carnegie Mellon for 11 years.

INTRODUCTION

This chapter describes some of the innovative changes that have taken place over the last several years in mechanical engineering education at Carnegie Mellon University. To assess these changes, I take a retrospective look at these innovations and relate them to those that have been taking place in the external environment and to the renewed, deeper interest faculty have in engineering education—an interest that centers around how students can best learn to become engineers. These innovations, some of which are still underway, respond effectively to the changing needs of society and the individual student. We begin with a review of changes in the external environment and then discuss how these changes have impacted learning and education in our Mechanical Engineering Department. The chapter concludes with an exploration

< 131 >

of the environment within Carnegie Mellon that makes innovations possible and valued.

Engineering education has captured the attention of many over the last decade. This renewed emphasis stems in part from the social and political fallout from events related to higher education in general, including rising tuition and related costs. Engineering education in particular, however, has attracted unsolicited recommendations and demands from industry for changes in the way we educate engineers.

The changes recommended by many in industry, academe, and government revolve around the perceived present and future needs of industry and society. These recommendations for the practice of engineering over the next few decades are quite specific: an engineer will be expected to have effective interpersonal skills, a high comfort level with new technologies and their place in society, and the ability to anticipate and prepare for the future needs of the workplace. Some suggest that these much-needed attributes are those of "Renaissance" engineers. In using this term, we posit the need for a new man in a new era.

The attributes and interests of the students entering universities have changed significantly over the last two decades. These changes reflect the economic, social, and technological changes in society. In the area of technology skills, for example, the students' empirical knowledge base metamorphosed from one based on tinkering with hardware to one of tinkering with software. Such subtle transformations also reflect changes in society and require accommodation in the education universities offer students.

Universities like Carnegie Mellon offer educational opportunities to students to prepare them for the future. These opportunities are presented through the formal curriculum and in less formal activities such as student societies, seminars, and special projects that make up the "hidden curriculum." In planning to develop educational opportunities for students, universities often feel the need to consider the perspectives of employers as well as future directions of engineering practice. Universities must also consider the increasing demand for engineers in non-engineering sectors of the economy; engineering education is becoming a preferred preparation for many other jobs and professions. Educational expectations also reflect the differences in the talents, expectations, and interests of students who enter a university. We feel that this is the time for customizing education and tailoring it to the individual student (an academic version of mass

< 132 >

customization), and that Carnegie Mellon is well situated to play a leadership role in that effort.

REASONS FOR CHANGE

Several significant changes coincide with the renewed emphasis in engineering education:

- The shift from defense to civilian engineering at the end of the cold war sharpened competition in the industrial sector.
- Globalization of trade, coupled with more widespread knowledge networks and a broader worldwide technological base has further fueled competition.
- Rapid advances in technologies, including those in the domain of information, have altered commercial and engineering transactions.
- Consumer desires have become much more sophisticated, requiring "mass customization" of products such as automobiles, bicycles, and clothing.
- Increased public recognition of the limits of natural resources and the burden on the environment have also influenced engineered products.

While coping with changes like these, over which it has very little control, industry is primarily concerned with satisfying shareholders by improving its productivity. Productivity depends on new technologies, educated workers who can use these technologies, and better management (that understands technologies). Successful organizations of the next century will need to distinguish themselves through development of their people, technologies, and products. Products must have a faster concept-to-market time at low cost and increased quality. Customer demands eventually will lead to mass customization of today's mass-produced products.

Already, new technologies challenge the core competencies of companies to replace their entire product lines. New enabling technologies, such as computer-aided engineering tools, have revolutionized design and production. Information technology enables collective brainstorming from a diverse set of sources. The impact of computational technology paves the way for complete simulation of complex processes and systems and will col-

< 133 >

lapse the design-manufacture cycle to a fraction of its duration today. Thus, the need exists to keep abreast of the developments in technologies that may have direct or indirect influence on an industry's core competencies or enabling technologies. To be successful, companies need to have:

- processes and strategies for development and acquisition of technologies;
- strategic product development and delivery processes; and
- career-long professional development processes that complement engineering education.

While universities contribute to technologies through research, the primary expectation of industry from a university is its contribution to the "people" part of the triad of people, technologies, and products. Industries often view new engineers as bearers of new technologies and turn to them to help transform the workplace. Such expectations place an increased pressure on universities to educate students skilled in the new technologies and possessing a culture of innovation.

RENAISSANCE ENGINEER

What are the attributes of an engineer who can function successfully in such a rapidly changing environment? Today's requirements suggest that a successful engineer will have an exquisite command of the current state of the profession and astute interpersonal skills. With those qualities he or she will know how to be a team player and team leader of a diverse work group, with international experience and effective communication skills. A successful engineer constantly renews his or her knowledge and skill base and is able to predict the needs of the workforce and to prepare accordingly. These are the attributes that describe a renaissance engineer.

Implications for engineering education follow the projected needs of industry to the extent that attributes of an entry-level engineer and those of a successful senior engineer can be correlated. Presuming that the attributes described form the basis of a successful career in a successful company, universities can provide the first four of the 44 years of continuing education in an engineering career.

< 134 >

Leading indicators at career entry level of a potentially successful engineer may be further described as follows: breadth in technical areas with a good understanding of mathematics, classical laws of science and design applications; competent use of engineering tools for design, simulation, and analysis of complex systems; effective communication skills; and a comfortable working use of information technologies and knowledge bases. An entry-level engineer will have international acumen and cultural awareness, work comfortably as part of a diverse team, and will not only have an exposure to entrepreneurship, but will also be a self-starter.

Companies now prefer not to invest two years in training new graduates to introduce them to engineering practice, as they did in the past. They expect a new graduate to be able to make sound assumptions, use diverse sources of information, balance theory and empirical results, and not be intimidated by engineering problems. Engineers at any stage in their careers are expected to honor commitments, to give credit, to seek out responsibility, and to be open and honest.

Among these expectations, several appear to be new to traditional engineering education: emphasis on interpersonal skills, familiarity with engineering practice, and versatility with information and simulation technologies.

ENGINEERING EDUCATION AT CARNEGIE MELLON

At many institutions the structure of a traditional engineering curriculum does not bring an engineering student into close contact with engineering faculty for the first year, and sometimes for the first two years. Under such circumstances, the enthusiasm for engineering with which a student arrives on campus wanes, resulting in high attrition rates. About a decade ago, Carnegie Institute of Technology (CIT), the College of Engineering at Carnegie Mellon, instituted a new course in each of its six engineering departments to introduce that particular engineering field and its faculty to students in their first year. A seventh course, Biomedical and Health Engineering, has since been added. Students have to take two such courses before deciding at the end of their first year which engineering field to pursue.

In order to address the changes in the fields of engineering that have blurred the boundaries between the traditional disciplines and also to afford students the opportunity to delve into areas other than engineering, CIT departments also moved to-

< 135 >

ward more flexible curricula, allowing a set of unrestricted electives that students can utilize to customize their education. Such changes to the traditional engineering education followed thoughtful discussions and careful planning and have since become models of exemplary engineering curricula around the country and the world.

In addition to Mechanical Engineering, Carnegie Mellon has five other engineering departments. They are: Chemical Engineering, Civil and Environmental Engineering, Electrical and Computer Engineering, Material Science and Engineering, Engineering and Public Policy (which offers dual degrees with other engineering departments) and a program (soon to be a department) in Biomedical and Health Engineering, which also offers dual degrees with other engineering departments. The flexible curricula of the departments make it easier for students to pursue dual degrees with other departments of the University as well as to obtain minors in an array of areas. In developing their curricula, the departments examined the needs of the professions they serve and responded appropriately.

The mechanical engineering field continues to undergo changes in its practice and in the research that mechanical engineering faculty conduct. While the basic laws of physics and the fundamental aspects of engineering will stay with us, their applications have changed significantly. Fuel injectors have replaced carburetors, solid-state controllers have replaced the now classic governors, and electronic watches have overtaken watches with gears. Analogously, the development of fast Fourier transforms (FFT) by Cooley and Tuckey in the '60s not only led to replacement of heterodyne filters by digital filters, but also opened up the possibilities for numerous new products and processes that directly impact mechanical engineering. Micro-electro-mechanical systems (MEMS) have already made inroads in several industries. The current investments in nano-technologies surely will find applications in a broad range of products in years to come. All such advances expand the design domain of mechanical engineers.

As a result of advances in technologies, the mechanical engineering profession continues to change from being a branch of engineering dealing with the design and production of machinery to one that addresses societal concerns through analysis, design, and manufacture of systems, at all size-scales, to convert a source of energy to useful mechanical work. While the change seems subtle, it has broadened the domain of mechanized engineering.[1] These changes address micro- and nano-scale devices

< 136 >

and systems, advances in bio-systems, information technologies, and environmental issues. In addition to the explosive increase in knowledge within their fields, mechanical engineers must increasingly cope with knowledge in other relevant fields to effectively command a much larger design space.

Several years ago, the faculty in the Mechanical Engineering Department at Carnegie Mellon carefully studied many issues related to mechanical engineering and the expectations of future engineers. The faculty suggested several structural changes to the curriculum and a number of innovative approaches to teaching, as well as an increased level of interaction with students. The discussions yielded considerable agreement on the following propositions:

- Engineering requires critical thinking.
- Integrated subjects within and across engineering, and a cross-disciplinary focus provide a better engineering education.
- Effective engineering design and analysis increasingly fall between the traditional disciplines.
- Accommodation to the diversity of student talents and interests promotes enthusiasm and student success.

The ultimate goal of these discussions was to help our graduates find multiple career opportunities upon graduation and to rise rapidly to leadership positions in their chosen endeavors. Following many discussions and consultations, the faculty, over a period of a few years, introduced a number of changes to the curriculum, to the courses, and to the extracurricular activities that present additional opportunities for education.

INNOVATIONS IN MECHANICAL ENGINEERING EDUCATION

Educating a student to become an engineer involves curriculum, extracurricular activities, and linking with the practice of engineering. Being a department that supports a technology-focused research culture enables us to leverage our research strength to establish an innovative undergraduate educational environment enriched through collaboration with industry. The improvements we have made and continue to make in the education we offer our students relate to the curriculum, to the educational environment in the department, and to our links with industry.

< 137 >

Curriculum

Traditionally, engineering education tries to balance the fundamentals that engineers will need during their career and the skills that they need to start functioning as engineers upon graduation. The dynamic nature of the engineering enterprise makes it impossible and unwise to attempt to teach our students everything they need to know to function during their careers. To restate the obvious, their education should include a strong set of fundamentals and the recognition of the need for and the ability to continually learn.

In discussions regarding curricular matters, faculty always keep in mind that an effective engineering curriculum focuses on what mechanical engineering is all about: *analysis, design, and manufacture of systems of all scales*. To that extent, all mathematics, science, and engineering courses that are part of an engineering curriculum relate to analysis, design and manufacturing.

We have introduced a *flexible curriculum* that emphasizes the fundamentals and gives students significant choice in designing their academic agenda to meet their career goals. Several unrestricted electives allow diverse career options in academic planning. A flexible curriculum allows students to develop their natural talents in addition to acquiring a solid engineering education. When students elect a course that used to be required, they are more enthusiastic about it.

Integration of courses better prepares students to deal with engineering problems. Toward this goal we have developed new courses that combine subjects previously taught separately. We would like to go further in integration and utilize material from seemingly unrelated courses to introduce students early on to the interdisciplinary nature of engineering. A more focused and more integrated curriculum also leads to more communication among faculty. Faculty members have coordinated the assignments and experiments for different courses allowing students to view the same physical embodiment from different technical perspectives. As an added benefit, increased offering of multidisciplinary and applications-oriented courses brings students closer to engineering practice. Integration of topics should start in the first year as it does in the Introduction to Mechanical Engineering course.

In addition to enabling acquisition of knowledge through empiricism,[2] *open-ended laboratories and advanced technology tools* bring in the creative aspects of engineering and also provide skills required for the information technology age. Having laborato-

< 138 >

ries that are accessible to students continuously can promote active learning and discovery. Further, ability to set up new experiments to try new ideas enhances students' creativity and enthusiasm. Hands-on activities should be integrated with analysis and simulation tools, and students should be exposed to such integration during their first year. Such tools need not require separate courses but should be integrated into the required fundamental courses. Faculty in the fundamental mechanical engineering courses now incorporate computer-aided modeling and experimentation that introduces students to the simulation and design-manufacturing practices of industry. This kind of approach allows nearly all faculty to become involved in the computational and associated laboratories of the courses.

Social sensibilities, teamwork, and leadership qualities can be introduced as part of the required curriculum. For example, design courses focus on social themes, such as design for the elderly or handicapped children. Making courses of this kind open to students from disciplines like art, psychology, and business provides a natural forum for addressing engineering issues such as timeliness, cost, quality, environment, health, and safety. This has the added benefit of introducing engineers to non-engineers. Engineering students are required to acquire a significant part of their education from parts of the University other than engineering. Unrestricted electives offer them opportunities to delve into areas other than traditional engineering, and it is this exploration and choice that we contend make them better engineers.

The Department recognizes that developing each attribute discussed here does not require a separate course, but rather a common educational emphasis in a variety of courses. This emphasis would ensure that the essential elements of an engineering education are integrated throughout the entire curriculum in a way that develops a common culture and method. With this goal in mind, the faculty and staff of the Department also provide students opportunities to learn about *technology tools* via non-credit shop courses, Web tutorials, and short courses in C++ programming outside the curriculum.

Educational Environment

The educational environment can play as important a role in engineering education as does the curriculum. Extracurricular activities help prepare students to function as leaders and decision makers in the engineering world of the future. In addition to their technical skills and broad education, interpersonal skills

< 139 >

developed through such activities are sought after by business and industry.

Involvement of students in defining aspects of their education strengthens their education and provides additional opportunities for leadership, decision-making, and teamwork. In the Mechanical Engineering Department such interactions take the form of meetings and events. Examples include:

- regular meetings between faculty and student advisory groups;
- town meetings with the faculty that the students host;
- student-faculty breakfasts, picnics, and dinners that the students organize;
- annual awards that students give to faculty for their role in the students' education;
- student societies; and
- participation in faculty committees to develop new laboratories for undergraduate education and to oversee computational facilities that the students use.

Students find it helpful to have an overview of what they will learn during their education. An overview can be in the form of a "skills matrix" that lists all the major skills an engineering student must acquire during a four-year education and where they can acquire them. Plans are underway to distribute such a matrix to students as they enter the Department to provide the basis of a "contract" with students and also to help them put in perspective the skills component of their education.

Links With Industry and Engineering Practice

In preparation for the career-long professional development process of an engineer, the education acquired at a university sets the initial conditions in the first four years for the following 40 years. Employees, together with their employers, need to assume the responsibility to insure continuance of that education. An effective educational process requires a partnership between industry and universities.

Professional societies, industry roundtables, advisory boards, and industry panels provide useful and necessary feedback. In addition to feedback, active involvement by industry can provide companies with partnership in co-educating engineers of tomorrow. One such involvement focuses on *structured internships*

< 140 >

that are integrated into the curriculum. Analogous to the traditional co-op programs, internships take place only during summer months, thus making a three-month period during each of three summers part of the curriculum located at a company. The student's department can structure internships so that they are woven into the curriculum. A student can have a mentor in industry and an advisor at the University. Such arrangements can also facilitate industry-based projects at universities and have the added benefit of further involving faculty with industry. Industries will not only serve as partners in educating future engineers but will find that they have access to the best minds. As a first step, the Mechanical Engineering Department has hired a staff member to assist in the development of industry contacts for internships. Future plans include institutionalizing internships and integrating them into the curriculum as outlined.

The changes described above enable us to educate mechanical engineers who, in Peter Drucker's words, are "knowledge workers."[3] These changes also move us from the traditional engineering education, with its focus on logical-mathematical, spatial, and practical intelligence to the interpersonal and intrapersonal domain.[4] The latter two, in addition to the others, are essential attributes for a renaissance engineer and a leader. The new flexible curriculum encourages students to cultivate the full range of natural abilities and interests.

Measure of Success

How do we know whether the changes and recommendations made above will help prepare the renaissance engineer? We cannot know with certainty because the true assessment of their success requires many years into their careers. We can only judge from data we collect now. Here are some of the indicators we are looking at:

- the enthusiasm and numbers of students enrolling in the Department;
- the feedback received in exit surveys from graduating seniors;
- the range of professional opportunities offered to graduates;
- feedback from industry; both the recruiters and employers; and

< 141 >

- feedback from a Departmental advisory board that includes alumni, industry, and academic leaders.

These indicators suggest that the improvements made have been successful, encouraging us to continue on this innovative path.

In part as a result of implementation of some of the changes discussed here, the number of students in the college of engineering at Carnegie Mellon who elect mechanical engineering has increased substantially over the past five years and, more significantly, the proportion of women students has nearly doubled in the same period. We have not only moved beyond the traditional curriculum of engineering, but have also moved beyond the nearly exclusive male base of recruitment for the field. The renaissance engineer knows no gender. (See Lenore Blum, pp. 111–129.)

THE PROCESS OF PROGRESS

Who and what are the drivers of change in academe? The constituencies are diverse. They certainly include students, alumni, and employers of graduates. The diversity notwithstanding, it is the faculty who are the major agents of change. It is the faculty who bring about and implement changes in education. Additional factors that may cause changes include political-social climate, funding agencies, and advances in technologies or knowledge base.

Carnegie Mellon, as an institution, has a culture and leadership that is committed to innovation. The Mechanical Engineering faculty shares in the University's commitment. It has conceived and implemented the innovations described here and continues to revise and review its educational process. The same faculty members who are the agents of these changes also conduct a very respectable research program and supervise graduate students. Each faculty member is a renowned expert in her or his field. Our faculty, like that in almost all University departments, teach a mix of undergraduate and graduate courses and nearly all of our faculty are involved in the computational and experimental aspects of the fundamental mechanical engineering courses.

So what makes Carnegie Mellon exceptional? Suggesting that the culture of the Department and the University makes it pos-

< 142 >

sible both to lead in the chosen fields of research and offer exceptional education would be accurate but would not describe the picture adequately. The individual faculty members within a department create the environment and a level of work ethic that values innovations in education and research equally. Viewing a university as an institution of learning, where knowledge is generated and disseminated (through publications *and* education of students), helps to diminish the demarcation brought about by reward systems that assign artificial value to isolated responsibilities of faculty.

The administrative structure of Carnegie Mellon strongly supports initiatives, such as the ones the Mechanical Engineering Department has been undertaking, through decentralization. Colleges, and to some extent, departments have the responsibility—and the mandate—to conduct their own affairs. Such an approach gives the faculty in the departments the freedom, and the challenge that accompanies it, to do their very best in the way they value it.

Concluding Remarks

An evolving recognition by the faculty of the changing nature of engineering, developed through their interactions with industry and colleagues elsewhere, led them to reconsider the educational opportunities that the Mechanical Engineering Department offered its students. With the goal of trying to bring their education closer to the practice of mechanical engineering, but with the added skills expected of the new engineering workforce, the faculty developed a flexible curriculum that now permits students to tailor their education to their needs, talents, and goals for the future. The courses within the curriculum take advantage of industry-standard software tools as well as state of the art experimental facilities to enhance learning. Making parts of the courses and laboratories open-ended allows students to become more active in their learning, thus maintaining their level of enthusiasm.

Acknowledgments

The faculty members of the Mechanical Engineering Department at Carnegie Mellon deserve considerable credit for the steps they have taken to develop and implement this innovative program.

< 143 >

Notes

[1] *Mechanical Engineering in the 21st Century. Trends Impacting the Profession.* A Report to the Committee on Issues Identification, American Society of Mechanical Engineers. Prepared by Hudson Institute, Inc., 1999.

[2] M. Polyani, *Personal Knowledge.* Chicago, IL: University of Chicago Press, 1958.

[3] P. F. Drucker, *The Age of Discontinuity.* New York: Harper & Row, 1969.

[4] For the first articulation of the idea of multiple intelligences, see H. Gardner, *Frames of Mind.* New York, NY: Basic Books, 1983. See also H. Gardner, *Multiple Intelligences: The Theory in Practice.* New York, NY: Basic Books, 1993 for a fuller version.

< 144 >

COMPUTERS IN BIOLOGY: THEN TO NOW

William E. Brown

William Brown is Professor of Biological Sciences and former Head of the Department of Biological Sciences at Carnegie Mellon University. His research interests span a wide range of disciplines, but a primary focus is on understanding the relationship between structure and function, with a particular emphasis on the role of proteins. He is a recent recipient of an award for excellence in teaching from the Mellon College of Science. Professor Brown received his Ph.D. from the University of Minnesota in 1971, and has been at Carnegie Mellon for 30 years.

Where is computing taking the biological sciences at Carnegie Mellon? It is three decades since the new biological sciences department was formed within the Mellon College of Science at Carnegie Mellon, and I have been here almost all of those years. Biology had been taught in Margaret Morrison Carnegie College prior to the existence of the Mellon College of Science, but it was a different biology. Bob Rice, on the Carnegie Mellon faculty 1954–79, led the effort to create a new biology department, focused on molecular biology, cell biology, genetics, biochemistry and biophysics. The new biology has flourished, and made a major contribution to the university's strategic thrust in the basic sciences and biotechnology. Central to this success was the creation and use of new tools, dependent on computers. This chapter will provide a personal perspective on the transforming effect of com-

< 145 >

puters on research and education in the new biology at Carnegie Mellon over the past three decades.

When I arrived at Carnegie Mellon in 1973, after a post-doctoral fellowship at Yale, sophisticated equipment comprised things like a rotating anode for x-ray generation that collected data on film to determine the three dimensional structure of a protein; an ultracentrifuge that was used to measure the mass and shape of molecules and biological complexes; or a Cary spectrophotometer for measuring the changes in spectral properties of proteins and DNA. These were manual devices that provided excellent data that then required manipulation, analysis and interpretation, which was done by hand or using a mainframe computer.

At that time, mainframe computers were used to analyze large sets of data. Jobs were submitted to a central facility on punch cards, and you crossed your fingers that the cards were in the right order and that the instructions had been punched correctly. For many of us in research, one of the great revolutions in computing came with the availability of the Digital PDP series of computers, which allowed us to do our processing in our own laboratories.

Just before coming to Carnegie Mellon, I had spent a great deal of my time as a post-doc translating programming from a large IBM 370 mainframe to our lab's new PDP 11–45. With the PDP 11–45, data analysis was possible in our lab, even though graphics for visualizing the structure of molecules remained a job for mainframes, or were generated by hand. (To show how far we have come, current handheld computers have more computing power than the PDP-11.) But at that time, it was a landmark—we finally had control of our own data processing, even though the process confirmed a warning that had been given to my wife, Linda, when I first starting working in the crystallography lab at Yale. At the time, a fellow post-doc warned Linda never to let me start working with computers because they were the greatest time-sink ever invented. Without a doubt that warning has proved true over the years.

When I first arrived at Carnegie Mellon, I chose to revert back to classical biochemical research tools—performing calculations with paper and pencil, a hand-held calculator or even a slide rule (you know, one of those things that engineers used to wear strapped to their belts). I used the equipment available across the street at the University of Pittsburgh's Department of Crystallography to work on protein structure determination, while con-

< 146 >

tinuing my pursuit of structure and function using bio-organic methods in my own laboratory.

The decade of the seventies, however, was an exciting time for biology at Carnegie Mellon. The newly formed department was growing and we were very fortunate that President Cyert supported us and had a vision for the future of the biological sciences. In biology, the 1970s was the decade of DNA manipulation. The discovery of restriction enzymes and the power of molecular genetics made it possible to cut, move and paste selected pieces of DNA and to express the products of genes—proteins— in large quantities. In this way, the structure and function of proteins could be studied. While enormous strides had already been made in understanding the structure of such naturally abundant proteins as Sickle Cell hemoglobin S and human myeloma proteins, we were now entering the period when analysis of the functioning of low abundance proteins such as *E. coli* DNA polymerase I was possible. Computers were not a major part of this revolution, but they were integral to the structural work of two of the department's biophysicists—John Nagle, exploring membrane structures, and Roy Worthington, working on two-dimensional structural analysis of membranes.

Throughout the seventies and eighties our capabilities for analyzing proteins expanded enormously and this expansion was mirrored by advances in our technological capabilities in the life sciences at Carnegie Mellon. There were early advances in structure analysis using Nuclear Magnetic Resonance (NMR) by Aksel Bothner-By and Josef Dadok. The first floor of Mellon Institute housed their 250 MHz NMR instrument and the computer used to analyze their data. I once heard Aksel talk about the development of the 250 MHz instrument and its successor 600 MHz instrument. He used the image of a student hanging from a bar in the 250 MHz machine versus an operator at a computer console electronically controlling the magnet in the 600MHz version. The rapid development and impact of computers on technological advancement in the life sciences can be seen not only in the physics and engineering marvels that went into designing NMR instrumentation, but in the automation of functions. The alignment of today's NMR instruments and the massive data acquisition and processing are done virtually automatically by the computer.

The eighties saw new advances in our ability to perform analysis in biology. In the early eighties, IBM provided computers to faculty to develop innovative applications of software for research and education. We were to develop these applications

< 147 >

in our "spare time." For some of us the challenge was less daunting because we had at least seen a DOS prompt before and used Fortran. These computers were the "desktop" machines of the day: IBM XTs and ATs with 8 MB of memory and black-and-white video displays. Having long before ignored the warning about computers as a time-sink, I found myself writing code in Fortran for a program to teach genetics. I had fun writing the program, and actually made it work, but I found myself sucked into the time-sink, using my "spare time" to develop a tool that was never used. For one thing, I don't teach genetics. It was, however, a great learning experience for me. This program and projects by other faculty in the department that actually were used were the beginning of educational computing in biology.

In the early eighties, the department established a protein analysis facility with support from NIH (National Institutes of Health) to purchase a state-of-the-art amino acid analyzer complete with its own PDP-8 computer for data acquisition and instrument operation. This analyzer was capable of measuring the composition of very small quantities (nanomoles) of protein or peptide and thus allowed us to identify, quantitate and sequence amounts of material that were orders of magnitude smaller than previously measured. Basic programming for instrument operation was read into the computer using paper tape with coded sequences of punched holes translated from a Teletype input. In addition, paper tape was the backup data output for the hardcopy Teletype printout for the analyzer. The PDP-8 computer was dedicated solely to instrument operation and providing data in a useful format. Further manipulation of the data, including calibration and subsequent composition determination, was performed manually. This instrument, state of the art when it was purchased in 1985, set the tone for the next wave of computers in biology and most other sciences—computers used as dedicated machines to automate procedures and instruments.

During the eighties, three technological milestones changed biology profoundly at Carnegie Mellon. The first was the development of NMR technology as a tool with many applications. Aksel Bothner-By and Joe Dadok had already established Carnegie Mellon as a leader in NMR spectroscopy. The arrival of Chien Ho as head of the Biological Sciences department and his subsequent founding of the Pittsburgh NMR Center in Mellon Institute led to using NMR as a structural tool in both biology and chemistry. Mellon Institute was becoming one enormous magnetic field. This expansion of its NMR facilities made it pos-

< 148 >

sible to attract some of the best NMR spectroscopists to Pittsburgh. The addition of MRI capabilities in the nineties allowed for natural connections between structural scientists and the neuroscientists and transplantation scientists in Pittsburgh.

The second milestone was the establishment of the Center for Light Microscope Imaging and Biotechnology (STC), an NSF-sponsored Science and Technology Center, under the leadership of D. Lansing Taylor. Combining fluorescence technology with cell biology and the development of new light microscope imaging technologies, the Center quickly made us appreciate cell processes in living cells and tissues not only in two dimensions but in three. Fortunately, the parallel development of computing and networking capabilities made it possible to process large data sets and finely control instruments with real-time feedback devices.

The third milestone, which occurred in 1986, was the establishment of the Pittsburgh Supercomputing Center (PSC), a joint venture between Carnegie Mellon and the University of Pittsburgh, with Westinghouse Electric Corporation. Its home is in the Mellon Institute. The PSC made it possible for the STC and the NMR Center to imagine experiments with no limit on data processing capabilities.

The parallel and almost simultaneous establishment of these three centers in the mid-eighties thrust biological sciences at Carnegie Mellon to new levels of technological capabilities and prominence. It also established that computers together with computer science were a natural fit in biological research at Carnegie Mellon.

Most of us mortals, however, were still thinking about computing in small ways. Although the STC and the NMR Center, which generated massive amounts of data, were looking to the Supercomputer Center for data processing, the rest of us were not. Most of the researchers in biological sciences were finding that desktop computing was growing at a pace that could accommodate almost all of the work we performed. Primarily we were users of software for data analysis and graphics. For most of us the next great revolution in biology computing was the appearance of the Apple Macintosh computer. After all, biology is a visual science and is about process—that is, how things move and interact in a cell, tissue or organism. The Mac brought graphics to the desktop both for modeling research and for visualizing biological processes in education.

The Mac quickly brought usable computing to every lab; the DOS prompt that had paralyzed neophytes disappeared. The

< 149 >

computer was no longer just to drive instruments and collect data, but was now a creative tool. It was now first the common word processor that allowed free exchange of documents and data between labs. Everyone could and did use the computer. Our greatest problem was knowing when a particular version of software was stable enough for us to change over to it and determining if it would be compatible with everyone else in the department. Even more important, the computer now enabled us to convey with drawings as well as animations complex systems that before were difficult to imagine or describe. Macs became the common denominator except where special applications required PCs. Today many labs find themselves with both platforms. Equipment interfaces are dominated by PC software and students coming to Carnegie Mellon have greater PC experience that they did a decade ago. Many faculty and those performing graphic applications, however, have remained loyal to Macs.

In addition to the revolution taking place in our ability to conduct research and conduct our daily business, the advent of the personal computer dramatically changed how we thought we should teach. Peter Berget pioneered our efforts to provide a means to distribute information over the network. At first, simple word processing documents were delivered using an Appleshare file server and programs such as Fetch (I loved watching the little Scotty dog run across the page!) were used to retrieve documents from the server. Then, in 1990–91, Peter established and ran our first real network server using the Gopher protocol. This seemed like a natural application for the department to choose, because Peter and I were both Minnesota Gophers. Alas, Gopher did not prevail on the national scene.

By 1992 documents were being transformed to HTML files and this signaled the advent of an individual teacher or researcher's ability to create materials for delivery to classes and colleagues. Peter advocated that we have a presence in this new medium and made that possible by his enthusiastic teaching of others and his establishment of one of the earliest servers on campus, for this specific purpose. The server also made it possible to describe our educational programs and make materials accessible to the larger community. This truly launched the development of educational computing, since it provided a means to deliver distance education to destinations both within our own university and outside it.

Computers in education at all levels became the tools of the future. Early biology software was written for the Mac because

< 150 >

of its graphics capabilities. Computerized tools made illustration of processes easy, even though the sucking sound of the "time sink" was still audible. This time both the tools and the computers were simpler. Furthermore, we made quick advances at Carnegie Mellon because one of our great strengths is our collaborative approach to both science and education. Teams of developers appeared that included teachers, designers and programmers. While tools for presentation were available, most were not altogether user-friendly. Like Fortran had been earlier, HTML was the new foreign language on campus. Especially before the tools became more user-friendly, those of us in biology who wished to pursue these activities were fortunate to work with infrastructure centers supported by the university. We profited from the services provided by Diana Bajzek and her colleagues in the TELab (Technology-enhanced Learning Lab) and those that came through the Center for Innovation in Learning. We described biological content we wanted to convey and they helped us visualize how it might be presented for delivery in the classroom.

One such collaboration illustrates the cooperative nature of this enterprise. It was 1993 and the buzz was about distance learning and just-in-time learning. We were asked to put together a presentation for the National Institutes of Health (NIH) Council to demonstrate how the Internet could be used to deliver content to the classroom. Phil Miller from Computer Science, Peter Berget in Biological Sciences, Diana Bajzek and her colleagues in the TELab, a fourth grade teacher, a tenth grade teacher, and I were given ten days to put together a demonstration of what we had conceived as a National Biomedical Information Kiosk for centrally distributed educational information and programming. The concept was to provide a repository of educational modules on NIH-sponsored research topics for use by teachers and students in grade-appropriate presentation format. It was also an opportunity to demonstrate the use of a multimedia presentation over the Internet. (We took along a videotape of the presentation just in case the Internet failed us!) The team designed a module on the digestive system with grade appropriate activities, using input from the teachers. The team completed the project on time; each member contributed his or her expertise to make it successful. While the kiosk did not materialize, the ideas have found their way into today's interactive websites at NIH and the Howard Hughes Medical Institute. What is most important to us at Carnegie Mellon is that it demonstrated the successful use of interdisciplinary teams to develop biology courseware.

< 151 >

This same idea was the basis for a set of workshops I ran from 1990 to 1998 for science teachers from the Pittsburgh Public Schools. Our children, when they were small, had a DOS-based Commodore computer. As they grew older, they progressed to the Mac SE. By the time they reached high school in the late eighties, I assumed that they would be using computers in their science classes. After all, I had been receiving catalogues advertising Mac and DOS software in biology, chemistry and physics. To my surprise, I found that while there were computers in their schools, they were locked in clusters because most teachers were not trained in their use. Thus began my quest to open the clusters to the students by making the teachers feel comfortable with the technology.

As we had learned at Carnegie Mellon, we needed to make computers an enabling technology, not to make everyone an expert in the technology. So I ran summer workshops for groups of teachers from many different science disciplines. The teams could then return to their schools and help one another solve problems they had all faced together in the workshops. I was very fortunate to have had support from the Howard Hughes Medical Institute and the National Institutes of Health for the duration of this program.

The teachers learned to use computer technology, and we gained valuable insights into what was wrong with the educational courseware then on the market. In connection with the workshops, each year the teachers previewed software with the intent of incorporating it into their curriculum, and I bought it for them, using grant money. To their surprise, the teachers found that 95 percent of the available software was not suitable for their curriculum—it was often little more than textbooks converted to the computer screen. What they wanted instead were word processing, spreadsheet, and graphics or drawing programs. The lack of usable software in the life sciences was particularly notable. In the latter years of the program, we ran special workshops in collaboration with the TELab for teachers who wanted to develop their own courseware. Approximately 10 percent of the teachers returned for the courseware development workshops. This confirmed for us that while everyone can be enabled to use the technology at some level, only a fraction of the enabled have the interest or aptitude to become developers of educational courseware. This holds true within the university setting as well as without, which is why the collaborative team approach to development is so successful.

< 152 >

Some of the greatest successes I have had in development of computer models for teaching, particularly for the first year Modern Biology class, have come from the students themselves. In one instance, a student developed a tutorial on proteins, based on the facts presented in class and information found in the textbook. While it was a bit rough around the edges scientifically, he used his abilities as a computer science major to develop quickly (he did it in one night) a tutorial for a concept that was difficult for him and others in the class to grasp. Tools that enable students to actively participate in their own learning by using their own talents are an exciting extension of education.

Another student project involved visualizing the three-dimensional structure of the DNA molecule. The student combined his abilities in computer programming and his experience from an engineering design class he was taking. He used the coordinates of DNA available in an online database to develop a physical three-dimensional model of DNA using stereolithography that is used for engineering prototyping. I still use his model in class today, not only to help students visualize the structure of DNA— it is far better than a two-dimensional textbook drawing—but also to demonstrate how skills in one discipline can help solve a learning problem in another, for individual students as well as multidisciplinary teams. The computer made it possible to bring biological processes and structures to life. These examples also illustrate how today's students treat the computer as just another natural part of their lives.

Another benchmark for the advancement of computation in the life sciences at Carnegie Mellon was the success of Susan Henry, then department head of Biological Sciences, in competing for support from the Howard Hughes Medical Institute. This funding successfully launched a number of initiatives related to computational biology and chemistry. In addition to the science teacher's workshops already described, the funding supported a joint, state-of-the-art computer lab—involving the Pittsburgh Supercomputing Center and the Departments of both Biological Sciences and Chemistry—for instruction of Carnegie Mellon students in computational biology and chemistry. Also with this support, Robert Murphy, a colleague whose research is in cell biology and computational biology, developed a nested set of Computational Biology courses that set the stage for the department's strategic move toward greater programmatic links with the School of Computer Science. In collaboration with Computer Science, a Computational Biology undergraduate curricu-

< 153 >

lum was developed, quickly followed by a master's program in Computational Biology.

The department, as a result of strategic planning designed to take advantage of interfaces with other university strengths, also identified computational biology as one of two areas for expansion of its faculty and recruited computational biologists Dannie Durand and Russell Schwartz. In Dannie's first two years, she has run a Computational Molecular Biology Symposium that, in addition to educating the department as to the breadth of possibilities in this new field, has brought together a wide ranging set of faculty from across the campus. Together with Murphy, Durand and Schwartz now have the task of defining this new field. (At this stage, if you were to ask five people for a definition of computational biology, you would probably get five different answers.)

Computers have also moved us to the next stage of teaching and learning in biology. While developing the department's website, Peter Berget developed a number of animated modules. These demonstrated molecular biological processes, and were designed for use in his first year Modern Biology course and the junior level Molecular Biology of Prokaryotes. We were also fortunate in the early stages of this courseware development to have our own software designer, Tom Manderfield. He facilitated development of a number of small animations for a variety of courses across the curriculum, and his presence provided additional encouragement to many members of the faculty to place their own materials on the department website to support their courses.

The development of modules that can be used for multiple courses at different levels is the premise of the most recent Hughes initiative being led in Biological Sciences by Gordon Rule and William McClure. The development of these materials continues to use the expertise of the TELab in a team approach. For example, Rule, McClure, and I developed tutorial modules, in collaboration with the TELab personnel, to teach the elements of membrane structure and protein translation. These were developed for use first in Modern Biology and then, as review, with specific advanced level additions, for the sophomore level biochemistry course. These tutorial modules will then reside in a kiosk on the Internet for access by our students throughout their educational careers.

We have been fortunate to have the encouragement and the funding to develop course materials. The fraction of enabled faculty has grown, and a few, such as Will McClure, have developed

< 154 >

nationally recognized educational materials. Together with Gordon Rule, he has transformed the approach to teaching biochemistry through the introduction of web-based, problem-based, molecular models that are used not only at Carnegie Mellon, but throughout the nation. In parallel with these developmental activities, studies have been undertaken to measure the impact of this work on learning. Parallel and integrated assessment studies are guiding the future development and implementation of this type of interactive distance modality for teaching and learning.

Cognitive psychology and biology have been brought together, utilizing the expertise and experience of John Anderson from Psychology and Albert Corbett at the Human Computer Interaction Institute (HCII). The cognitive tutor in algebra that they developed is widely used in public schools across the country. Building on this collaborative approach, Elizabeth Jones from Biological Sciences is leading a team composed of Ken Koedinger, Albert Corbett and Ben MacLaren—all from HCII—and Linda Kauffman from Biological Sciences to construct an "intelligent" tutor in genetics, based on the successful algebra tutor. This project combines the power of artificial intelligence with the science of genetics to help solve real problems.

We have found that the tools we use in teaching, whether they come from courses in computational molecular biology or introductory biochemistry, also translate well to the research lab. Thus the students not only acquire knowledge and skills by using the tools, but also learn to use the tools to advance their own research. And one of the strengths of our educational programs in the biological sciences has always been our ability to bring the research laboratory into the classroom. Today's student comes to the university with a computer and from the first day experiences its applications in molecular modeling, library searching, problem solving and data analysis. That same student in the research lab freely uses the Internet as a resource to perform literature searches.

Using programs to which they are exposed in their first year at Carnegie Mellon, students are able to find the coordinates of a particular protein and build a virtual three-dimensional model of the protein they are studying. Having examined the protein structure, the student is able to hypothesize how the structure and function of the protein are related and to devise tests of their hypotheses by changing the sequence of specific amino acids. The altered protein sequence is remodeled using an energy minimi-

< 155 >

zation program that is found on the Internet. Another database search yields the DNA sequence of the gene for the protein, and the student designs DNA sequences to accomplish the proposed amino acid changes in the protein.

The DNA sequence is then sent by e-mail to a lab that inputs the sequence into an instrument for automated DNA synthesis. The synthesized DNA is shipped to the student who performs the mutagenesis of the natural DNA and clones the altered DNA into a host that synthesizes the altered protein in the lab. The student observes any changes in the function of the protein to test the original hypothesis. This is just one example of how the computer is now a tool facilitating both student's and researcher's ability to do science, and the future is both bright and exciting for both.

So how should we gauge the impact of computing on the future of biology at Carnegie Mellon? The university's strategic planning process, brought to a successful close by President Jared Cohon, identified both biotechnology and information technology as two major future thrusts for the university. The planning process, which had broad faculty participation, fostered new collaborations for faculty in these two fields, and encouraged a number of efforts to explore answers to this question. Elizabeth Jones, head of Biological Sciences, initiated a seminar series to bring computer scientists to Mellon Institute to help us understand what computer scientists are doing that impacts us. Reciprocally, Jonathan Minden, from Biological Sciences, conducted a course to help university faculty and administrators understand molecular biology and biotechnology. Interactions between the two fields are continuing to develop.

Computing approaches in the life sciences move across disciplinary boundaries. Projects using computational approaches to biological imaging can be found not just in Biological Sciences, the NMR Center and the STC—all in the Mellon College of Science—but in the Departments of Psychology and Statistics in the College of Humanities and Social Sciences, and Electrical and Computing Engineering in the College of Engineering (CIT). Modeling of complex biological systems is being conducted in Mathematical Sciences, Chemistry, and Civil and Environmental Engineering, as well as in Biological Sciences. The availability of the yeast, drosophila, and human genomes has expanded virtually every research effort in biology.

Exploring and utilizing that vast wealth of information will fuel research in molecular genetics, cell and developmental biol-

< 156 >

ogy, structural biology, and proteomics. Carnegie Mellon is training a new generation of scientists to do research at the interface of computer science and biology, and the university's innovative researchers are helping to extend and enrich both of these fields. The changes that have taken place during my three decades at this university appear huge and radical, as I described them, but they may be just the harbinger of even more dramatic developments to come.

< 157 >

DESIGN, MAKING, AND A NEW CULTURE OF INQUIRY

Richard Buchanan

Richard Buchanan is Professor of Design in the School of Design at Carnegie Mellon. His research addresses issues of interaction design, verbal and visual communication, communication planning and design, and product development. He received a Ph.D. from the University of Chicago in 1973, and has been at Carnegie Mellon for 12 years.

When I was a student at the University of Chicago in the early 1970s, the eminent philosopher Richard McKeon came to class one day with a news clipping. This had never happened before in all the time that I had studied with him, so I listened carefully to understand what had attracted his attention. What he read was a story about the creation of a new university, formed from the union of the Carnegie Institute of Technology and the Mellon Institute of Science. The new institution would be called Carnegie Mellon University, and it would explore new problems in areas such as technology, cognitive psychology, decision making, and information processing. It would build on existing strengths in engineering, the natural sciences, cognitive psychology, economics and industrial administration, and the visual and performing arts. Thus, it would have some of the traditional disciplines found in other universities. However, it would also emphasize interdisciplinary collaboration and encourage the creation and develop-

< 159 >

ment of new disciplines that would likely emerge from such collaborations in areas such as computer science, information and decision sciences, and design. In essence, Carnegie Mellon would cultivate the new sciences of the artificial, the domain that was articulated by Herbert A. Simon in the Compton Lectures, delivered at MIT in 1968 and soon afterward published as *The Sciences of the Artificial*.[1]

At the time, I had little understanding of what the "sciences of the artificial" meant, except as a possible, if somewhat unusual, translation of "poetics" in the Greek tradition established by Aristotle. For Aristotle, "poetics" meant the productive sciences or the science of human-made things; he used the word as the title of his famous treatise on tragedy, which provides the primary example of his method of productive science. The leap of imagination from a study of the literary and dramatic form of tragedy to a study of technology, decision making, and human behavior was suggestive and, at the same time, puzzling. I did not know that the sciences of the artificial, whatever they are today or will become in the evolving intellectual environment of Carnegie Mellon, initially represented Simon's theory of design. Even more puzzling was the idea that "poetics" or the "sciences of the artificial" could form the basis for a new kind of university that would explore interdisciplinary connections among established disciplines of human learning and a variety of newly emerging disciplines focused on new problems of inquiry.

After reading the news clipping, McKeon paused and seemed to look briefly into the distance. He had already written his provocative and visionary paper, "The Uses of Rhetoric in a Technological Age," as we knew from the course in which we were enrolled.[2] The title of the course was somewhat misleading if one did not understand the direction of McKeon's genius. Called simply "Creativity: Poetic and Rhetoric," it was a course on discovery and innovation in inquiry. When he turned back to the class, McKeon commented that the new institution was clearly a "neoteric" university. It was a university devoted to inquiry into the new problems and the new learning of our time, as Chicago had been at its founding and continues to be to the present.[3] Almost as an afterthought, he added a comment that only later would become personally significant for me. The new institution, he remarked, would play an important role in higher education by the next century because it would both reflect and contribute toward some of the most significant changes taking place in our culture. Few of us understood precisely what McKeon meant,

< 160 >

but I wrote "Carnegie Mellon—1968" in the margin of my notebook and placed beside it a small question mark.

The question mark grew larger and larger in my mind over the years as I watched confusion and uncertainty of purpose settle over many established disciplines and institutions in the United States and abroad. However, I did not associate it again with Carnegie Mellon for many years. At first, the issue in my mind concerned the relationship between the old learning and the new learning in the disciplines of the humanities. Educated in philosophy and rhetoric, with the distinctive interdisciplinary orientation that characterized the Chicago "committees" of the 1950s, 1960s and 1970s, I did not find the traditional established disciplines entirely satisfying as locations for pursuing the kind of intellectual questions that were taking shape in my mind. Disciplines form over hot spots of intellectual inquiry, centered on the problems that human beings find significant in their experience and environment. In this sense, they are like ocean atolls that form over hot spots of geological activity that lie far beneath the surface of the earth. However, like the hot spots beneath the ocean that move on and lead to the creation of new atolls, the hot spots of inquiry also move on in human culture, creating new ferment and leading to new disciplines and organizations of learning. I was certainly interested in many theoretical issues in philosophy, the humanities, and the social and natural sciences, but I was also interested in practical matters. And, as I gradually learned, I was deeply interested in the problems of "making"—how human beings make the world around them, beginning with literature and the fine arts, but extending much further in human culture. For me, the emerging field of design—with special professional disciplines in areas such as graphic design and industrial design—was hospitable and perhaps ideal for exploring the connections among theory, practice, and production that attracted me. I found a place in the new field and felt the freedom of pursuing questions that seemed to cross and connect a variety of other disciplines.

I soon learned, however, that new disciplines, unless they merely add incremental extensions to established disciplines, do not fare well within traditional institutions—whether those institutions are art schools, technical institutes, liberal arts colleges, or large research universities. Established disciplines are jealous guardians of new ventures, often seeking to reduce new forms of inquiry to their own ideas and methods. Cultural change comes slowly in colleges and universities. New disciplines that challenge

< 161 >

the traditional organization of learning face high walls that frequently block communication and understanding, and stand in the way of administrative, financial, and political support.

The problem is one of entrapment in success. It is a serious problem for established universities that seek to lead in inquiry and education by moving on to new problems and new challenges. How can such an institution balance its devotion to the old learning that was once the basis of its success with the new learning that is needed to address new problems in the changing circumstances of society and intellectual culture? It would be too simple to suggest that established universities are entirely "paleoteric"—solely devoted to the old learning—and that new universities are entirely "neoteric"—solely devoted to the new learning of our time. The old learning and the new learning are often closely related in a strong, purposeful university. Those who are devoted to traditional disciplines speak of the extension and application of ideas to new areas of subject matter. In turn, those who are devoted to exploring new problems in new disciplinary forms are often quite mindful of earlier ideas and the struggle to establish what are now regarded as traditional disciplines, studying them for insights that may bear on the solution of present problems. Yet, there is typically a dominant spirit in each institution that leads one to think of it as either paleoteric or neoteric. I think of Carnegie Mellon as a university that is neoteric in spirit, though it, too, now faces the challenge of balancing old accomplishments with new ideas and intellectual ventures.

DISCOVERING DESIGN AT CARNEGIE MELLON

I came to Carnegie Mellon as a visiting professor in the fall of 1991 and returned the following year as Head of the Department of Design, now known as the School of Design. I returned because the department offered a hospitable environment for new ideas and possessed an excellent faculty and student body with the courage to rethink the future of their discipline in the context of a changing world. I also came because the university was open to thoughtful and well considered arguments for change, and because the various colleges and departments of the university were willing to provide the kind of interdisciplinary cooperation that I felt was needed to advance the theory and practice of design in the contemporary world. I admit, however, that there was another reason. I remembered Richard McKeon's prediction about

< 162 >

Carnegie Mellon, and I wondered if he was as prophetic in this matter as he had been in so many others. For me, the evidence came in three forms: a personal encounter with a distinguished colleague, work on developing a new design curriculum and related design research, and broader observations on the liberal arts and the place of design in the culture of the university.

The first evidence came during my term as a visiting professor. Colleagues from the Department of English invited Herbert Simon to join me in presenting public seminars in successive weeks on our respective work and its relationship to rhetoric. I remember Professor Simon sitting in the first row of seats as I began my presentation on what I saw as an emerging relationship between design and rhetoric. It was late in the afternoon and few undergraduate students were in the building, but some raucous noise broke out in the hallway. Simon virtually leaped from his chair and went into the corridor, sternly telling a small group of startled students that there was a seminar in progress and that they should be quiet.

I continued reading my presentation—I seldom read a formal text to audiences, preferring a more spontaneous style of delivery, but on this occasion I decided I would—until I reached the section of my paper where I dealt directly with Simon's *The Sciences of the Artificial*.[4] At that point I put my paper down and spoke directly to him, discussing what I found to be a conflation of poetic science and rhetoric in the book. I argued that this led to a weakness in the proposed method of decision making, since it reduced invention to memory and neglected the role of "topics" in shaping radically "indeterminate" situations, situations such as those in design where "things may be other than they are" by human choice. Simon listened carefully but asked no questions in the discussion period following the talk.

Students told me later that he was uncharacteristically quiet, since he was known to respond vigorously when he was dissatisfied with a speaker. However, he simply came over afterward and invited me to visit him in his office when I had an opportunity. We subsequently talked for two hours or more, covering a wide range of topics that included some of our philosophical differences, his experience teaching in an architecture program early in his career, and his experiences with Rudolph Carnap and Richard McKeon at Chicago, where he had been a student of the former, as I was a much younger student of the latter.

Later, when I attended Simon's seminar, I asked only one question in the discussion period. I asked whether his approach

< 163 >

to science and logic, with its special reliance on empirical data, rested on any philosophical assumptions that he cared to share. I expected this question merely to open the way for some general remarks on the philosophical foundations of his work. However, his quick reply was a loud and firm "No." He remarked that reliance on empirical evidence was adherence to truth and reality and required no assumptions. Clearly—and to me, quite ironically—he did not regard his views on the nature of empirical evidence and its role in scientific investigation to involve any assumptions or to be open to alternative views or methods of exploration, at least in the context of that meeting. I, too, have a serious regard for empirical evidence, but I have also found that philosophical assumptions strongly influence what we consider empirical evidence to be and how we interpret it. I include this anecdote because it was, for me, an introduction to the battle of the liberal arts that I would later join at Carnegie Mellon, where logic, rhetoric, dialectic, and even grammar were interacting to shape a new environment for inquiry. I will comment more on this later.

Shortly after my arrival as Head, the Design faculty began a process of discussion and planning that quickly led to a restructuring of the undergraduate curriculum. The goal was to reorient our programs toward what we believed would be the future of our field, based on a study of current problems in design and strategic trends in industry and society. What emerged was, in the words of the distinguished national accreditation team that visited and reviewed our new direction, "the most clearly thought out and interdisciplinary program (produced with the greatest faculty unanimity) we have seen." I will provide a brief sketch of this curriculum for two reasons. First, the curriculum is based on a different vision of design than that represented in Simon's theory of the sciences of the artificial. It is based on the logic of inquiry rather than the logic of empiricism, and it incorporates aspects of rhetoric that encourage invention and pluralism in the study and practice of design. It does not ignore Simon's insights, but it places his approach in a humanistic context with other reasonable alternatives. Second, the ideas behind the curriculum have implications for how specialized studies may relate in new ways to general studies and how educators may approach liberal education in a neoteric institution. This is partly a reflection of "project-based" education. Projects are a core feature of design education and have been from the earliest days of the field. This is an emerging feature of education in many disciplines at Carnegie Mellon and at other institu-

< 164 >

tions as well, so there is good reason to consider how project-based education is addressed in the field of design.

The new curriculum is based on a humanistic vision of design. For this reason it contrasts sharply with visions of design that are based on engineering, the fine arts, or an area of the behavioral and social sciences such as cognitive psychology. The goal is to prepare students for professional life or further study in a world of increasing complexity, where knowledge from many sources must be integrated in order to support a high quality of interaction in the lives of the human beings that we seek to serve. We teach design as an integrative discipline that allows students to synthesize the insights afforded by aesthetics and the fine arts, engineering and the natural sciences, and the social and behavioral sciences. We believe this leads to *informed* intuition among our students, and to a new kind of professional designer.

We began by considering the goal of design education, reflected in the titles of our two undergraduate programs. The term "Graphic Design" is a somewhat outdated expression with roots in the medium of print. It was replaced as a program title with "Communication Design," because the designers of texts and images now work—and will work more in the future—in a wider variety of media in order to accomplish the goals of communication. In addition to print, text, and image, they will work with sound, time, and motion—sometimes in film, video, or the kinetics and dynamics of the digital medium. They will explore new ways of presenting information in visual display and persuasive argumentation. We did not change the term "Industrial Design" as the title of our other undergraduate program, since it remains a current reflection of three-dimensional creation. However, we did change the curricular content to reflect new materials, production methods, conceptual and physical tools, and, perhaps most significant, the increasing importance of the social sciences and research in this branch of professional design practice. In addition, we placed greater stress on the emerging practices of "new product development," involving interdisciplinary collaboration among designers, engineers, and marketing experts. In general, the curriculum was conceived to prepare students for entry-level professional work and, in a clear departure from many other design schools, to prepare students for leadership and citizenship, emphasizing the whole person and what that person could become in society.

Coherence in the curriculum comes from our perspective on inquiry and student development. It is based on the sequence of

< 165 >

student experience as he or she encounters new subject matter and content. Each stage is an adjustment of subject matters and methods to the condition and degree of development of the individual student, with a long-term view toward what is needed in each successive level and, ultimately, what we believe will be needed by graduates.

We distinguish three stages of understanding and mastery for student development and personal growth. The first stage is a one-year period of *discovery*. Students develop sensitivity in perception and expression; explore materials, methods, and techniques; acquire fundamental skills; expand awareness of the social and cultural context of design; learn some of the central concepts that distinguish design from fine art; and learn some of the fundamental similarities and differences among the design professions. It is useful to note, however, that the core studio course of this stage significantly revises the "foundation" or "preliminary course" of the Bauhaus, the school that provides the model for programs of design education. Instead of teaching materials, tools, and techniques as the primary subject matter, the new studio focuses on projects and problems that are situated within the experience and motivation of students. In essence, this "first-year course" turns away from the grammatical approach of the old "foundation" course, toward a rhetorical engagement with purpose and action, encouraging invention and creativity. In this course, the grammar of design is introduced as needed rather than providing a sequence of formal exercises that a student must follow. The second stage is a two-year period of *concentration and development*. Students pursue a set of required and elective courses that deepen their skills and understanding in their chosen field of design—either Communication Design or Industrial Design. In this period students also begin to work on practical projects for corporate or industrial sponsors or not-for-profit agencies, gaining concrete experience of design in realistic, client-focused situations. Finally, the third stage is a period of *integration and advanced study*. Students focus on special projects in both individual and team settings, pursue special topics of advanced study, and often work in collaborative research projects in design or in other areas of the university.

In addition to the sequence of the curriculum, we also distinguish four elements that represent the kinds of experience and knowledge that we believe are essential in undergraduate design education. All of these elements are represented at each stage of the curriculum, with content and methods that are suited to

< 166 >

student growth. The first element is *studio experience*, with an emphasis on practice, creation, and synthesis. This is where students gain practical knowledge of how products are conceived, planned, and made in the form of models, prototypes, or other kinds of concrete realization. The second element is what we call *ideas and methods of design practice*, with an emphasis on investigation. Courses in this area are a mixture of studios, laboratory studios, and seminars. They help the student gain understanding and mastery of some of the central ideas and methods of contemporary design practice. The third element is *design studies*, encompassing design history, theory, and criticism, with an emphasis on reflection. The distinguished designer Paul Rand first proposed this element at Carnegie Mellon when he visited the campus in the 1970s. He urged the faculty to create a sequence of courses to help students gain an understanding of the principles of design. This element has evolved significantly over the years, reflecting our recognition of the importance of pluralism and the philosophy of culture in new design thinking. The purpose of this element now is to help students understand the cultural and intellectual foundations of design, the place of design in society and business, and the qualities of effective thinking and communication that are essential for reflection and practice.

In my view, this element is an exploration of the liberal arts in a context imposed specifically by the field of design. It seeks to provide the core disciplines of reflection that enable students to profit from exploring other courses in the liberal arts and sciences in the rest of the university. The fourth element is *general education*, with an emphasis on breadth of understanding. To be effective in the contemporary world, designers need a wide base of knowledge. They must be familiar with the basic concepts and methods of the natural sciences and engineering, the social and behavioral sciences, and the fine arts and humanities. Fully one third of the design curriculum at Carnegie Mellon is devoted to general education and the liberal arts and sciences, with courses taken throughout the university.

As we began implementing the revised undergraduate curriculum, our attention turned toward development of a graduate program. By the 1990s, design education in the United States was established at the master's level, but it was still not as common as in other fields. In the pragmatic culture of the United States, combined with the youthful nature of design as a profession, many students entered professional practice directly from an undergraduate education. However, we recognized that certain

< 167 >

areas of emerging design practice would benefit from, and perhaps ultimately require, graduate study. So, we began planning a graduate master's program that would be relevant to new problems. This is one of the distinguishing features of the culture of Carnegie Mellon. Instead of planning a program in an already well-established area—merely replicating work elsewhere—the faculty look for special opportunities in new areas of interest and ferment where our resources and special strengths converge. For this reason, colleagues sometimes refer to Carnegie Mellon as a "niche" institution, though this term fails to capture the innovative intention behind our exploration of new problems and disciplines.

Instead of developing traditional master's programs in graphic design or industrial design, we tried to assess emerging design practice, anticipate where the field of design was moving, and determine where we could play a useful role in new ventures. What we discovered was interaction design. Interaction design is the third great field of design to emerge in the twentieth century. It combines qualities of visual communication and information design, which are characteristic of traditional graphic design, with the qualities of the whole body experience in a physical environment, which are characteristic of industrial design. Interaction design is about people: how people relate to people, how people relate to products, and how people relate to each other through the mediating influence of products. It is a synthesis of many traditional and new elements of design thinking, organized into intelligent and emotionally satisfying experiences that meet a wide variety of human needs. Products are no longer treated simply as physical artifacts or visual symbols. Instead, they are expressions and enablers of human action and experience, situated in a social and cultural environment. For many of us, interaction design is more than a new branch of design practice. It is a new approach to design thinking in general, and a foundational critique of the entire field of design and the place of design in culture.

The idea of interaction emerged in contemporary consciousness around problems of digital media and multimedia production, but it is by no means limited to the digital realm. Interaction design is equally important for traditional analog products as well as the new digital products that increasingly surround us. This is one of the distinctive features of the approach to interaction design taken by the School of Design, and it contrasts with other approaches at Carnegie Mellon that emphasize the narrower area

< 168 >

of human-computer interaction. Our approach certainly includes mastery of design in digital media, with all of the sophistication that is required for successful professional practice. But it also encourages students to explore any area of application—whether in graphic design for the medium of print, industrial design for three-dimensional products, the design of services and activities, or environmental design for larger scale creation. Indeed, we explore the interrelation of all of these areas, because interaction design breaks down the boundaries among the old branches of traditional design practice and leads to many new and unexpected areas of application. This is evident, for example, in new applications of the concepts and methods of interaction design to human services and action programs, whether in the context of social agencies, education, governmental agencies, or businesses and corporations.

Interaction is too complex and important a theme to belong to any single discipline. Indeed, its roots may be traced throughout the twentieth century in a variety of fields. However, the development of computers and the digital medium played an important role in returning attention to how human beings interact with their environment, and this theme is explored in a wide variety of contexts at Carnegie Mellon, with the School of Design offering only one variation. The interdisciplinary nature of human interaction led the School of Design to develop one of its master's programs in cooperation with the Department of English, particularly its rhetoric program. We call this program "Communication Planning and Information Design," and it emphasizes a rhetorical and socially situated perspective on interaction. We call the other program "Interaction Design," and it emphasizes the poetics of interaction—the creative logic of shaping intelligent and emotionally satisfying experiences. Both programs are explorations of interaction design, and they share many core elements. In addition, however, Design also participated in the development of the Human-Computer Interaction Institute, along with the School of Computer Science, Psychology, and other disciplines at Carnegie Mellon.

Interaction design is only one example of how the School of Design has participated in interdisciplinary ventures at Carnegie Mellon, but it illustrates one of the cultural values of the university in such matters. The walls are typically low among departments and colleges, and individual faculty members are encouraged to take the initiative in pursuing questions that cross disciplinary boundaries. With this in mind, the School has participated

< 169 >

in ventures with engineering, business and industrial administration, and other departments and colleges. One of our greatest concerns today is to gain greater recognition throughout the university community of the importance of new product development as a powerful connecting theme for new research and educational programs. We believe that Carnegie Mellon has become one of the most important universities for exploring this emerging area of inquiry.

When I arrived at Carnegie Mellon, the provost told me that Design would probably never have a graduate program. Within a few months, the undergraduate curriculum took shape, and by the end of the year, the strength of our planning became evident. The provost then came to accept the inclusion of a graduate program. A year later, when I placed proposals for the two new master's programs on his desk, he immediately endorsed them both and asked when we would like to begin a doctoral program in design. This question was encouraging, but we decided to develop thoroughly our new master's programs before exploring doctoral education. However, a doctoral program is now established in the School of Design in a form that we believe serves both the emerging needs of the field of design and the long-term interests of the university as a whole. I know of no other institution of higher education where change can occur so quickly, provided that the arguments are well considered and the planning is thorough.

DESIGN, LIBERAL ARTS, AND THE CULTURE OF INQUIRY

After joining the university, I soon understood that the idea of design does not belong exclusively to the School of Design. Design is a shared theme among many departments and colleges of the institution. Indeed, I have never found another university where design is so widely discussed. However, I also learned that the term "design" has quite different meanings in the university, depending not only on disciplinary context but also on the philosophical assumptions held consciously or unconsciously by individuals. Exploring these differences has been one of the intellectual pleasures of my time at Carnegie Mellon, but it has also been a practical necessity. The success of arguments that explain the contribution the School of Design seeks to make in the development of the university depend partly on engaging the principles and values of those to whom the arguments are addressed.

< 170 >

The explanation I give is that the School of Design contributes a humanistic or human-centered vision of design in the contemporary world, explored through an integrative process of design thinking. This process leads to "whole" or "total" products—as opposed to the partial products that typically emerge in an academic environment—in four areas of professional design practice: communication design, industrial design, interaction design, and environmental or human systems design. These are areas of product creation that intersect with the academic interests of many other departments and colleges in the university. The School of Design offers a pathway for bringing their knowledge to expression in concrete products. In addition, the School offers an interdisciplinary opportunity for students who major in other disciplines to gain experience in making real products under the significant constraints and demands of studio production.

Over time, however, I became interested in how diverse individuals at Carnegie Mellon are able to work together in a productive manner without the degree of intellectual conflict that one sometimes finds in other institutions. I was interested in how they are able to communicate without the excessive influence of ideology. This led me to reflect on the liberal arts at Carnegie Mellon and how they shape the culture of inquiry, ultimately affecting what we mean by the sciences of the artificial.

By "liberal arts," I do not mean the arts and sciences that have developed and proliferated in Western culture since the Renaissance based on increasingly refined distinctions of subject matter. This is usually what is meant by the liberal arts in most colleges and universities, although specialization and the expansion of factual knowledge has rendered the arts and sciences ineffective in serving the function of integrated understanding that once qualified them as liberal arts. Nor do I mean the liberal arts of the trivium and the quadrivium—the arts of words and the mathematical arts of things—that once provided the organization of learning and knowledge in the Middle Ages.[5] While traces of these arts operate quietly in the background of universities, they tend to reinforce the tensions and divisions that exist between the sciences and the humanities in our time. Instead, I mean the new liberal arts of communication, reasoning, and intellectual inquiry that are emerging in contemporary culture around new problems of expression and experience.

Whatever names we give them, the new liberal arts are suited to our time because they relate what we *say* about the world to what we *do* in the world, and to what we *make* as products of

< 171 >

inquiry. The new liberal arts serve to overcome the specialization of factual knowledge in the arts and sciences, as well as the division between words and other forms of symbolic representation employed in understanding our experience of the world. They offer the opportunity for an integrated understanding of thinking, doing, and making. I believe these arts are still in the process of formation, but they lie at the core of Carnegie Mellon, contributing to the neoteric quality of the institution and forming its distinguishing character and culture among other universities. I will refer to them as logic, dialectic, grammar, and rhetoric, but I do not mean the old arts of words based in the trivium. To me, they are newly emerging arts of communication and inquiry, merging words and things in human experience.[6]

My early encounter with Herbert Simon suggested that one specific form of logical reasoning—the logic of empiricism—played a central role in the university. However, I soon discovered that another form of logic is perhaps stronger in the community, and that a third form of logic is also present and influential. The first form of logic may be characterized as a system of rules of operation and criteria of empirical evidence and prediction. Meanings are established wholly on the empirical elements of which they are composed and on the operations by which they are defined. Some people believe that this form of logic is quintessentially "scientific," but it is a form of reasoning that one may find as often in the social sciences and the humanities as in the natural sciences or engineering. It is no more scientific than other forms of reasoning.

The second form of logic is the logic of inquiry. In inquiry, logic is characterized by distinguishing the general forms of argument from the concrete forms of reasoning that human beings employ in different situations to address special problems. It is the form of logic explored by John Dewey, among others in the twentieth century. It is also the form of logic focused explicitly on "problem solving," since it examines concrete situations and seeks to find the instances of more general reasoning that occur in special problematic situations. In the culture of Carnegie Mellon, "problem solving" became a central theme from an early time and is still employed as a general phrase to describe what is characteristic of this university. The phrase comes from the logic of inquiry, but it has become a shared theme of the university as a whole, expressed sometimes in the idea of "liberal professional" education and sometimes in the research mission of the institution.[7]

< 172 >

This form of logic is explored in many disciplines at Carnegie Mellon, including the humanities and the visual and performing arts. Of course, creative artists today seldom characterize their work in terms of logic or even artistic logic. They prefer a term like "poetics" or, more often, some other term more closely associated in contemporary culture with their own specific art form, perhaps fearing that to use a term such as "logic" will suggest a reduction of art to science. Nonetheless, as Dewey has argued and as many artistic movements explain in their declarations, artists think and reason as intently and as clearly in their own forms and media as any scientist in his or her medium of inquiry. In the School of Design, the logic of inquiry is the form of logic most often explored by my colleagues, where they carefully analyze problems and seek the most likely and effective solution or a variety of reasonable solutions.

The logic of empiricism and the logic of inquiry are seldom distinguished explicitly in ordinary conversations within the university community, but they account for some of the contrasting insights that have emerged in the development of disciplines and lines of research around themes such as design. However, a third form of logic also operates in the university community. This is a logic based on the examination of different languages— natural and artificial—and what those languages signify. At Carnegie Mellon, this frequently means constructing languages and interpreting them in concrete applications such as computer programming. This form of logic is closely related to the intellectual discipline of grammar, but it is most often developed and expressed in its logical aspect within the university. This form of logic, too, is seldom explicitly distinguished in ordinary conversation. Instead of being disruptive, the interplay of these three forms of logic has been productive because of a shared focus on the problems of making and designing.

In contrast to the full and varied development of logic as a mode of inquiry at Carnegie Mellon, there is little representation of either idealist or materialist forms of dialectic. This truncation is typical of American culture in general, because these forms of dialectic, as intellectual arts, have never played a central role in our intellectual life. This is in strong contrast to the central role that they play in many European countries, Asia, the Middle East, Africa, and South America. However, there is another form of dialectic that does play an important role in the intellectual life of Carnegie Mellon. It is found, first, in the gradual sifting of opinions through the give and take of private conversation about re-

< 173 >

search and education—such as my private conversations with Herbert Simon. It is found, second, in our public discussions of the vision and mission of the university, where we seek to articulate a coherent account of the remarkable diversity among us and shape our collective plans for the future. This form of dialectic is perhaps best described as pragmatic and skeptical, since it does not depend on an ideological foundation in philosophical idealism or materialism. Its roots lie in the tradition of American pragmatism, the philosophy formally developed by Pierce, James, and Dewey—and developed in a new way by Richard McKeon, a former student of Dewey at Columbia. And its roots also lie in the tradition of rhetorical debate that has shaped American social and political practice from an early period. Because this form of dialectic does not reflect, in itself, a formal ideology but, rather, a shared commitment to community process and communication, it tends to be conducive to pluralism and diversity of opinions.

One of the functions of dialectic is to clarify shared principles through conversation and discussion. At Carnegie Mellon, the process of skeptical and pragmatic dialectic has yielded two principles that, taken together, characterize the university and its culture. The first is a time-honored commonplace of inquiry that, by itself, does not significantly distinguish the institution from many others in the United States. It is a community belief that theory should be tested by how it is applied and by the results that follow from its application. What is perhaps distinctive at Carnegie Mellon is the expression of this principle in the daily life of the institution. One's first impression is that theory is not a subject of intense discussion among faculty and students and may not be highly valued in the workings of the community. What I have found, instead, is that theory is highly valued but does not have the privileged position that it appears to have in other institutions. Theory is found more often in close discussions of practical and productive problems than in broad formulations. In essence, theory is seldom isolated from practical development and testing in application.

This principle has advantages and disadvantages. One disadvantage is that theory is sometimes neglected in the haste to act. The formation of compelling theory takes time and nurturing, and sometimes events move so fast in the university that theory receives too little attention. This is a serious disadvantage that must be overcome through personal determination and vision, often with less surrounding support than one may wish. In contrast, the advantage is that philosophical or ideological dif-

< 174 >

ferences are usually accepted with more grace and less political conflict than in some other universities. I do not know whether this is because of benign neglect or serious intellectual tolerance, but the consequence is the same. The intellectual orientation is toward concrete experience, and the challenge of testing theory often prevents ideologies from dominating the intellectual life of faculty and students. In my experience, the advantage appears to be a fair compensation for the disadvantage.

The significance of the first principle at Carnegie Mellon becomes clearer when we consider the second principle that has emerged in collective discussions. The second principle is a community belief that, for the kind of university we seek to develop, there should be a creative balance among theory, practice, and production—a balance of thinking, doing, and making. This means that the testing of theory at Carnegie Mellon is located not only in the possible practices of application but specifically in the challenge of creating concrete products.

By "product" I do not mean simply the physical artifacts that we often associate with technology. It is true that this type of product has a long history at Carnegie Mellon, beginning in the origins of the campus as an institute of technology. However, other kinds of making also have a long history in the institution. The disciplines of architecture, art, design, drama, and music were established early and quickly attained national recognition and influence. For example, the first degree-granting program in industrial design in the world was established in 1934 at the Carnegie Institute of Technology, providing an influential model for other industrial design programs in the United States. Indeed, the gradual expansion of diverse forms of making in areas such as social and governmental policy, operations research in business, economic models, the languages and applications of computer science, computer hardware, robotics, information systems, and humanly shaped environments is a distinctive feature of the institution. It is surely one of the features that make the university important in contemporary culture, since what is made in the university often significantly affects what is made in society.

Explicit recognition of the second principle is recent at Carnegie Mellon. Despite a history of diverse forms of making and the articulation of a theory of design and the sciences of the artificial by Herbert Simon, general recognition of the creative balance of thinking, doing, and making in our community has emerged only within the past decade. It came through a strategic planning process that drew together what we understood of the

< 175 >

history of the institution, the emerging circumstances of society, and ideas about what the university could and should become in the future. We recognized that at Carnegie Mellon making products is the connective activity that integrates knowledge from many fields for impact on how we will ultimately lead our lives. In essence, we recognized that Carnegie Mellon could be a new kind of university, exploring the dynamic balance of theory, practice, and production—a balance that we do not find in the vision of most universities today.

The radical nature of this principle becomes evident when one considers the difficulty that universities in the past have had in incorporating the disciplines of design, making, and production within their vision.[8] The organization of knowledge following the Renaissance had little place for knowledge about the actual work of making. Making was reduced either to an application of knowledge from the sciences or dismissed as servile skill in craft. Nonetheless, making is a key factor in explaining why Carnegie Mellon is important at this time in contemporary culture. Faculty and students, as well as supporters and friends of the university, are increasingly aware of how deeply our cultural and natural environment is shaped by what human beings choose to make in and of their world—and how they consciously go about the work of making. Our society needs institutions that provide leadership in identifying and addressing problems of the human-made world, bringing to bear the knowledge gained in both old and new disciplines.

INVENTION AND THE FUTURE OF THE UNIVERSITY

While logic and dialectic play a central role in the culture of inquiry at Carnegie Mellon, I believe they do not adequately explain the innovative quality of the university. Logic provides a variety of analytical tools for inquiry, and dialectic provides a community process for articulating shared principles. But finding the important problems to solve and discovering the new forms of making that are needed to bring ideas forward in concrete embodiment depend on another liberal art that is also emerging in the culture of inquiry at Carnegie Mellon. They depend on a form of invention, practiced consciously or unconsciously as an intellectual art by individuals who seek the key issues for decision and investigation. In the past, the art of invention was formalized in the old liberal art of rhetoric and typically limited to

< 176 >

verbal invention. In the new culture of inquiry and technology, invention has a wider scope, employed in the sciences, the humanities, and the arts.[9]

The art of invention at Carnegie Mellon may be found in the issues that emerge in the work of individuals and small research teams as they pursue new problems. However, it is also evident in dialectical conversations about the future direction of the institution. One example lies in recent work on strategic planning for the university. In the latter 1990s, the evident success of Carnegie Mellon presented two alternatives for the future. Should the institution seek to remake itself in the image of older traditional universities or should it continue to explore the implications of its own unique genius as a new kind of university? As a participant in the planning committee charged with discussing the vision of the university, I believe the choice was not difficult. Although both alternatives were carefully considered, the vision that came forward was clearly a development of the unique genius of the university. It was a neoteric vision, grounded in humanism and in the circumstances and problems of emerging technological culture. Although there were several important elements of the emerging vision—issues of social diversity, new directions for research, and new relationships with the community, industry, and government—one set of issues addressed the intellectual core of the university. The issues were presented as questions for further discussion.

- *First, how can we give greater emphasis to problem finding as the creative counterpart of problem solving?*
  Focus on problem solving is a legacy of our history as an institute of technology. It led to expertise in analyzing problems and a focus on professional education. In the new circumstances of contemporary culture, we need to explore problem finding, since changing circumstances present so many new opportunities for the exploration of learning and research.

- *Second, how can we reinvent the organization and distribution of subject matters that all students should study if they are to be successful in the future?*
  The traditional disciplines of the arts and sciences remain important, but the old divisions tend to work against integrated learning and action. We need to explore new ways of presenting subject matters so that their interconnections become productive of new understanding.

< 177 >

- *Third, how can we articulate a new vision of the liberal arts suited to a technological culture so that our students can communicate clearly, reason effectively in addressing new problems, and prepare for life-long inquiry?*

  We need to reach a new community understanding of the liberal arts, recognizing the pathways that are already evident in our teaching—pathways that promote interdisciplinary understanding, action, and creative production. We also need to understand that technology is not simply the physical artifacts of our culture. Technology—combining the ancient words for art and reason, "techne" and "logos"—is how we use the "art of science" or the "science of art" to create the human-made world of communications, artifacts, human interactions, and the large systems that provide their environment. This will expand our understanding of the sciences of the artificial in ways that are appropriate for the complexity of contemporary culture.

- *Fourth, how can we give greater emphasis to educating for leadership and the development of the whole person?*

  In the past, we have emphasized education for the professions and sometimes neglected the broader framework of humanistic values that lies behind science, technology, and other professional pathways pursued by our students. We need to recognize that our students can and should play leadership roles in integrating knowledge, and we need to be explicit in how we develop the qualities of leadership and responsible action, affirming the place of human beings in the future development of technology.

These are emergent issues in the culture of Carnegie Mellon, and the way that we address them will significantly determine the character and importance of the institution in the future. The implementation of a well-conceived plan of action will complete our transition from an institute of technology to a new kind of university. However, the effort will not be easy. It will lead the university community beyond the early foundational idea of a "liberal professional education" and beyond the initial formulation of Herbert Simon's "sciences of the artificial." It will lead us to a deeper understanding of design and technology in contemporary culture and the dimensions of the new learning of our time.

The issues we must address at Carnegie Mellon are also emergent issues at an increasing number of other institutions, reflecting

< 178 >

deep problems in contemporary culture as well as the challenge of balancing old accomplishments with new intellectual ventures. At Harvard, for example, a new president has begun a conversation about the nature of liberal education in an age of technology. The question is whether the university can reorganize education to prepare students for the new circumstances they will face in the twenty-first century. The outcome is uncertain. Resistance among many faculty members is reported to be strong, perhaps because of entrapment in past success, or less experience of the problems of making in our culture, or less recognition of the new meanings of "technology" that are transforming learning and knowledge. In contrast, Carnegie Mellon appears to be well positioned to lead the exploration of these issues. After all, the issues we face are design issues, in the broadest sense of "design" at Carnegie Mellon. They are issues in the design of the university, itself. By a combination of chance, circumstances, and deliberate planning, the university is now positioned at the nexus of some of the most significant problems of a new culture of inquiry and learning. After a decade at this university, I believe I have begun to understand what Richard McKeon foresaw about the future of Carnegie Mellon when he spoke to his class so many years ago.

Notes

[1] Simon, Herbert A. *The Sciences of the Artificial.* Cambridge: MIT Press, 1969.

[2] McKeon, Richard. "The Uses of Rhetoric in a Technological Age: Architectonic Productive Arts," in Backman, Mark (ed.) *Rhetoric: Essays in Invention and Discovery.* Woodbridge, CT: Ox Bow, 1987.

[3] As Dean of Humanities, Richard McKeon was one of the central architects of the "Hutchins College" at the University of Chicago. This was one of the great experiments in general or liberal education of the twentieth century.

[4] Buchanan, Richard. "Wicked Problems in Design Thinking," in *The Idea of Design*, Margolin, V. and Buchanan, R. Cambridge: MIT Press, 1995.

[5] Buchanan, Scott. *Poetry and Mathematics.* Philadelphia: J. B. Lippincott, 1957. Also, *The Doctrine of Signatures: A Defence of Theory in Medicine.* New York: Harcourt, Brace and Company, 1938. The latter includes a discussion of the liberal arts in the emerging field of medical research in the 1930s. Scott Buchanan (no relation to the author of this essay) played a central role in the development of the liberal arts program at St. John's College, another of the great experiments in liberal education in the twentieth century.

[6] Schwab, Joseph J. "Eros and Education: A Discussion of One Aspect of Discussion," in Westbury, Ian and Wilkof, Neil J. (eds.) *Science, Curriculum, and*

< 179 >

Liberal Education: Selected Essays, Chicago: University of Chicago Press, 1978. "The 'intellectual' arts and skills with which the liberal curriculum is concerned are not then intellectual as to subject matter, and thus exclusive of other subject matters, but intellectual as to quality. They are the arts and skills which confer cogency upon situations and actions whether these be scientific, social, or humanistic, general and abstract or particular and concrete."

[7] Doherty, Robert Ernest. *The Development of Professional Education; The Principles Which Have Guided the Reconstruction of Education at Carnegie Institute of Technology, 1936–1950*. Pittsburgh: Carnegie Institute of Technology, 1950. This document presents the "Doherty Plan" for liberal professional education at the Carnegie Institute of Technology.

[8] Buchanan, Richard. "Design Research and the New Learning," *Design Issues*. Vol. XVII, No. 4, Fall, 2001.

[9] Buchanan, Richard. "Design and the New Rhetoric: Productive Arts in the Philosophy of Culture," *Philosophy and Rhetoric*. Volume 34, No. 3, August, 2001.

< 180 >

Architecture, the Workplace, and Environmental Policy

Volker Hartkopf and Vivian Loftness

Volker Hartkopf is Professor of Architecture in the School of Architecture at Carnegie Mellon. He has been involved in a variety of research and action projects designed to improve the efficiency and inhabitability of a built environment, and in efforts to reduce the negative environmental impact of such construction. Professor Hartkopf received his Dr. Ing., (Ph.D.) from the University of Stuttgart, Germany, in 1989, and has been at Carnegie Mellon for 31 years.

Vivian Loftness is Professor of Architecture and Head of the School of Architecture at Carnegie Mellon. Her research deals with the performance of a range of building types (from museums to high-tech offices), and the innovative building delivery processes necessary for improving quality in building performance. Professor Loftness received her Master's degree in Architecture from MIT in 1975, and has been at Carnegie Mellon for 22 years.

Introduction

Carnegie Mellon's architecture program, created in 1912, is one of America's oldest. Yet it has remained innovative in its curriculum and outreach, integrating new technologies, seeking appli-

< 181 >

cations for its know-how, and fostering new ways of collaborating with industry. Part of its success over the decades can be attributed to the semi-autonomous centers and consortiums it has created, each with its own budget and fund-raising strategies. No centers have been more successful than those designed to foster collaboration with the building industry. The goal of such collaboration is to make the workplace more healthy, comfortable, productive, and energy-efficient. To achieve this, we have been pursuing a long-term plan to re-shape current practice through a focus on basic and applied studies in building performance and diagnostics. We believe that this effort by architects at Carnegie Mellon will contribute significantly to producing a more sustainable environment—and environmental policy—for America.

As the world's environmental ministers met recently to debate the Kyoto agreement, America argued that reducing carbon dioxide emissions would reduce the quality of life. We would argue that just the opposite is true. The built environment is a major factor in global environmental quality. The building sector consumes almost 40% of all US energy used to heat, cool, light, and ventilate buildings; it consumes as much as 40% of the wood harvested, 25% of raw material used, and 40% of our landfill. The built environment—from material manufacturing to land-use policy—is also the major factor in greenhouse gas production and outdoor air quality, producing 40–50% of SO_2, NO_2 and CO_2. Inasmuch as buildings are such a significant factor in the health and productivity of Americans, why, we ask, is there almost no federal or industrial research on the built environment?

Carnegie Mellon's National Science Foundation (NSF) Center for Building Performance and Diagnostics (CBPD) and an industry-university-government consortium, ABSIC, have been addressing these issues now for two decades. We have joined a number of leading institutions here and abroad in demonstrating the technical, economic, and social feasibility of creating buildings that use as little as one-tenth the resources of US average practices, while substantially improving the quality of life in those buildings. In our view, these studies and collaborative opportunities offer a way to make a major US contribution to meeting the Kyoto agreement targets by improving the quality of our own built environment and developing a worldwide market for the building industry.

< 182 >

The Scale of the Opportunity

We have found that commercial buildings often do not offer adequate levels of thermal, air and visual quality; indeed the newest buildings, by standardizing deep floor plans with sealed facades, offer limited access to daylight, natural ventilation, and natural heating and cooling opportunities. They often run 24/7/365 without any individual controls. At the same time, sick building complaints and outbreaks of asthma and allergies are at the highest levels ever. Best environmental practices for building design and renovation, however, ensure direct benefits from the natural environment—daylight for lighting, passive solar heating, natural ventilation, and dynamic shading, for example—while creating healthier indoor conditions and ensuring higher individual and organizational productivity. At ten percent of the conditioning energy, a ten percent increase in productivity and health have been measured, easily outweighing both development and implementation costs.

The Robert L. Preger Intelligent Workplace at Carnegie Mellon, for example, uses 0.2w/sq.ft for lighting as compared to 2w/sq.ft for standard practice. During regular office hours, no lighting is required in work areas because of daylighting. At night, individually ballasted, high performance light fixtures with individual controls ensure that lighting quality fully supports individual productivity and health while energy consumption is at a minimum. The importance of replacing electricity use for lighting with more effective daylighting/electric lighting systems is amplified by inefficiencies in power generation. Typical central power plants produce electricity with a 25–40% efficiency. More than 10% of the electricity generated is lost in transmission. As little as 20% of the delivered electricity is transformed into light, leaving us with a 6–8% overall efficiency. The waste heat generated instead of light becomes coolingloads, thus making further demands on power generation. Given 10,000 footcandles of daylight for 50 footcandles of lighting requirements on the worksurface, this is a very inefficient use of an inefficient electric power generation system.

Lighting in buildings is but one illustration of a long overdue need to address regional building strategies for environmental responsibility. Just as building design and renovation is a major opportunity, land use and infrastructure engineering also offers major opportunities to reduce environmental loading and resource inefficiencies. Innovations in distributed combined power,

< 183 >

cooling, and heating technology could dramatically improve power generation efficiency by using rejected heat for process, space conditioning and water heating. Energy-effective smart building practices could decrease the 40% of the nation's energy use in buildings to less than 10%, while dramatically improving our quality of life. A national program enabling institutions of higher learning to further develop, integrate and demonstrate these technologies would open the door to a more desirable future and to constructive leadership in the evolving built environment worldwide.

OBJECTIVES, GOALS, AND RIGHTS

The focus of the CBPD is on predicting building performance in a realistic occupied setting, advocating a team decision-making process for the design and delivery of integrated building systems, and performing in-depth analysis of interactions between different building performance descriptors and building systems. To meet the long-term research goals of the Center and the Architecture M.S./Ph.D. program, the ABSIC consortium pursues research, demonstrations, and development towards improving the quality and performance of commercial buildings and building systems. In the past twelve years, over twenty building industries and eight government agencies have participated in this partnership for research, development, demonstration, and education. The partnership pursues the following eight strategic objectives:

1. To identify international developments in new office design, organizational approaches, and developments in integrated components and systems through in-depth field studies with transdisciplinary teams, summarized in executive summaries.
2. To generate concepts for new products and integrated assemblies towards the long-term performance of advanced buildings, through collective efforts of consortium members and the CBPD.
3. To improve the process for the delivery of high performance commercial buildings, developing building performance quality assurance design processes and tools (including guidelines, simulation, field evaluation, and life cycle tools), and seeking opportunities to integrate improved processes and tools in ongoing projects in the US and abroad.

< 184 >

4. To develop a highly innovative demonstration laboratory with an evolution of advanced products and advanced product integration into high performance systems for educational and research purposes. The Robert L. Preger Intelligent Workplace of the Center for Building Performance and Diagnostics is this laboratory, and provides ongoing performance monitoring and feedback to sponsors.
5. To support state-of-the-art demonstration projects with innovative products and product integration, and to assist the industry to penetrate the building delivery process with high performance components and systems,
6. To improve graduate and undergraduate educational programs and texts on Systems Integration for Building Performance for professional design/engineering programs throughout the US, and to direct M.S. research and Ph.D. theses that significantly increase the professional knowledge base.
7. To increase communication on advances in building performance and innovations in product and systems integration for performance.
8. To develop Intelligent Workplace approaches to retrofitting existing buildings: engineering and refreshing building shell, core, service, and furnishings to support organizational and technological change with high occupant and management benefit.

In 1992 the Center for Building Performance and Diagnostics was established as the first National Science Foundation Industry-University Collaborative Research Center focused on buildings. The NSF/IUCRC Program develops highly leveraged industry/university research centers focused on industrially relevant fundamental research topics. Since its inception, the Center and the Intelligent Workplace have received numerous awards including the American Institute of Architects National Honor Award for the Robert L. Preger Intelligent Workplace, the 1999 Business Week/Architectural Record Awards, and the AIA Earth Day 2000 Top Ten, sponsored by the Pennsylvania Department of Environmental Protection.

Environmental sustainability should be only one major goal for the building industry, however. The Center has identified four goals to ensure a balanced improvement in the built environment:

- Individual comfort, health and productivity
- Organizational flexibility and effectiveness

< 185 >

- Technological adaptability
- Environmental sustainability

In an effort to address all four of these goals, it is necessary to move beyond least-cost yet code-compliant buildings, or even "high tech" buildings, to the creation of truly motivational buildings and communities. Motivational buildings provide environmental performance at a level that consistently and reliably ensures health, comfort, security, and financial effectiveness, while supporting high levels of productivity with continuing organizational and technological change. In contrast to present practice, motivational buildings rely on guarantees that every building occupant, at their individual workstation, will be supplied with critical services:

- Fresh air and air quality
- Temperature control and thermal quality
- Lighting control and visual quality
- Privacy and interaction and acoustic and spatial quality
- Connectivity and multiple data, power, and voice connections
- Ergonomic and healthy furniture and settings
- Access to the natural environment

By ensuring these seven mandates over time, intelligent buildings can provide productive environments that attract the best workforce, offer personalized infrastructure and control, and support continuous change in organizational and technological configurations through infrastructure flexibility.

The question remains, however, as to what innovations and changes are required in the various building subsystems and disciplines—from structure to enclosure, mechanical, lighting, networking and interior systems. The CBPD has repeatedly made clear that the dynamic reconfigurations of space and technology and function typical in buildings today cannot be accommodated through existing infrastructures: neither the "blanket systems" for uniform open-plan configurations nor the idiosyncratic systems for unique configurations. To avoid frequent environmental quality failures and near-term obsolescence, it is critical to invest in user-based infrastructures that are modular, reconfigurable and expandable for all key services. This includes ventilation, air, thermal conditioning, lighting, and data/voice/power networks. Indeed, what are needed are flexible infrastructures capable of

< 186 >

changing both location and density of services. We advocate Flexible Grid/Flexible Density/Flexible Closure Systems as a constellation of building subsystems permitting each individual to set—under reasonable limits—his or her optimal working environment.

A Living Laboratory of High-Performance Flexible Infrastructures

Not since the General Services Administration "Peach Book" effort in the late 1960s and the California School Construction System Development, have so many diverse industries and university researchers pursued such a collective performance agenda. The Robert L. Preger Intelligent Workplace at the CBPD is a leader at this frontier, providing a living laboratory of component and subsystem innovations and serving as a testing ground for the next generation of critical interfaces. Although individual performance-simulation labs do exist for lighting, acoustics, and thermal, and individual performance-demonstration projects exist for energy, air quality and component innovations, there has long been a need for a fully reconfigurable office laboratory to test a variety of component innovations and their interfaces against a spectrum of performance agendas in an occupied setting. The School of Architecture at Carnegie Mellon University has taken the position that future architects should be accountable for the measurable performance of the buildings they design. This accountability demands that architectural education provide hands-on knowledge about thermal, air quality, visual, acoustic, and spatial performance, as well as long-term building integrity. To this end, the Intelligent Workplace plays a vital role in the education of our students.

The Intelligent Workplace is located on the roof of Margaret Morrison Carnegie Hall, one of the university's historic Hornbostel buildings dating from 1906. The 7000-square-foot facility, dedicated in 1997, demonstrates innovations in each building subsystem—including structure, enclosure, heating, ventilation and air conditioning, lighting, interior systems, and telecommunications. Here we demonstrate a wide range of innovations in materials, components and assemblies for environmental quality and conservation, and the relationships these have to the individual worker.

< 187 >

The first commitment to a healthier workplace and environmental consciousness in the Intelligent Workplace is the move away from large, deep floor plans with minimum window area (1 window per 10 people) to a window for every workstation. The increased periphery maximizes environmental contact, and the viability of daylighting and natural ventilation, at the same time that it eliminates internal, high-density spaces. A corollary commitment to worker health is the provision of direct access to the outdoors through open doorways and windows—to bring in the outdoors and to provide outside meeting and relaxation areas.

The Intelligent Workplace demonstrates the only US installation of a fully plug-and-play Gartner™ façade. The façade is a 100% recycled aluminum, metric, pre-manufactured and green assembly. An innovation that may fully justify the return to highly articulated buildings is the use of airflow windows or water flow mullions to offset perimeter losses by reusing excess internal heat gain from the building's machines, lights, and people, simultaneously allowing for increased glass exposure. The move to highly articulated buildings, once common in the pre-air-conditioning era for ventilation, requires a parallel commitment to layered, dynamic, enclosure design. The Workplace demonstrates the use of the highest performance glass commercially available, and will test and demonstrate further innovations as they arise. A high visible light transmission glass offers visible transmission of over 60 percent to clearly access views while providing low solar heat transmission of less than 40 percent. The low-e glass coatings and argon-gas -filled air spaces also increase the thermal resistance of the double-glazed assembly to the equivalent of a quadruple-pane window.

A major area of our research includes the reintroduction of daylighting and natural ventilation. There is little utilization of daylight in most offices today, due predominantly to deep buildings and reflective facades. Yet daylighting can amply provide for ambient lighting needs as well as task requirements, given appropriate window configurations. The Intelligent Workplace will continue research and development regarding light shelves and light redirection devices, exploring industry developments such as holographic and fiber optic daylight redistribution.

The Workplace is also a test bed for comparing air- and water-based thermal conditioning systems decoupled from the delivery of breathing air, for maximum thermal, air quality, and energy performance. One half of the facility is dedicated to a high-performance all-air system, and the other half to a combined air

< 188 >

and water system. In the all-air system, a desiccant air handler with variable speed fans and an array of changeable filters feeds 100% outside air (with 70% heat/cool recovery from return air) to personal environmental conditioning systems at each workstation. These Johnson Controls PEM™s, developed with contribution from the Center, allow each worker to control temperature, air speed, and direction, as well as the quantities of conditioned outside air and local filtration.

The north half of the facility demonstrates the use of displacement ventilation for breathing air combined with water-based radiant systems for cooling and heating. The side-by-side demonstration of two different strategies allows the Center to compare the performance of different international approaches. Displacement ventilation feeds 100% filtered and conditioned outside air to continuous perimeter diffusers. The high volume, low velocity air slides across the floor and rises wherever a heat source exists to bring breathing air directly to the occupant. In combination with LTG radiant ceilings and 'paddle-coil' Coolwave™ ceiling elements, the lab studies may reveal that the air-water north zone outperforms the all-air southern zone for comfort and energy performance.

A critical healthy building strategy in both the air- and water-based systems is the decision to separate ventilation from thermal conditioning demands. Constant volumes of no less than 20 cfm of outside, filtered air should be provided to each individual regardless of the need to cool or heat. Decoupling ventilation from thermal conditioning also enables the widespread use of operable windows and doors for thermal conditioning and ventilation whenever the climate conditions are benign, or internal thermal or pollution loads are beyond the norm. In this "mixed-mode conditioning", the decoupled system allows for maximum air quality, thermal quality, and energy effectiveness.

In the Workplace, there is also a commitment to the design of a flexible-grid, flexible-density, flexible-closure conditioning system (see Hartkopf, Loftness et al. 1996). This implies that the occupant and furniture locations and densities can change continuously while still accessing the key services of heating/cooling, air, light, and networks. The workstations can also migrate from open plan to closed (flexible closure) with assurance of appropriate environmental conditions, because the occupants can relocate the diffusers.

The flexible systems incorporate split ambient and task thermal conditioning for which ambient temperatures are set at a wide

< 189 >

temperature band of 60° to 80°F, while individuals set task temperature requirements. Once split ambient and task conditions are supported, it is possible to use occupancy sensors to decrease task temperatures to an energy minimum whenever the space is unoccupied. Similar to the benefits of separating task and ambient lighting, split task and ambient thermal conditioning offers significant energy savings as well as greatly improved individual health and well-being through control of both thermal comfort and air quality. The Workplace demonstrates a strong commitment to "Green Architecture" by separating ambient and task conditioning, providing user controls, and demonstrating the widespread use of operable windows for passive thermal conditioning and ventilation, with light redirection devices for natural lighting.

As in the case of mechanical systems, the electrical lighting systems in high-performance workplaces must provide flexibility and dynamic controls to accommodate the wide variety of tasks in the modern office, while maximizing energy effectiveness and daylight usage. The Workplace demonstrates a relocatable, individually dimmable lighting system which is a major shift away from the uniform, high level lighting in the ceiling. Lighting is accomplished with indirect Zumtobel LaTrave™ luminaires that have T-5 fluorescent fixtures with electronic ballasts supporting daylight-based dimming. While daylighting provides for both ambient and task lighting during the work day, each workstation has dimming control of two or more high-efficiency fixtures at night. External light redirection louvers reduce glare at the windows and increase light levels away from the windows. The internal perforated blinds from Huppe™ provide an additional level of glare control by diffusing and redirecting the light.

In the past, large office buildings relied on central building cores for the manageable distribution of traditional needs for power, voice, and data. However, demands on office *connectivity* have changed drastically in the past decade, and even workgroups of 30–35 people require significant access to vertical and horizontal plenums for data, power, and voice—and with continual demands for modification and expansion. The Workplace addresses this challenge by introducing distributed satellite closets with the capability to run connections from individual workstations to the panels, allowing unlimited power, voice, data, and inter connectivity to supply individual needs. These satellite closets house the following equipment for voice, power, and data needs: racks for data connections, local area networks, gateways, repeaters, and

< 190 >

file servers; patch panels for voice and video connections; panels for power distribution to feed data peripherals, lights, and appliances; and environmental controllers for thermal, light, air quality, fire, life safety, and energy management. The AMP Access Floor Workstation Module™ provides the data, power and voice interface for building occupants. These modular floor boxes with interchangeable outlets fully support today's constant layout and activity changes. The combination of these modular boxes with raised floors and connections to satellite closets offers maximum connectivity with effective wire management over the long term.

Although the design of building massing, enclosures, and flexible infrastructures are major determinants of building performance over time, interior design decisions will also contribute significantly to the goals of individual health and productivity, organizational effectiveness, technological adaptability and environmental sustainability. The Intelligent Workplace demonstrates a special commitment to environmentally benign, flexible, space-defining systems while trying to improve ergonomic and technological support for individual and collaborative work. It also demonstrates renewable and healthier materials for floors, fabrics, paints, and adhesives. Competitive solutions to stacking storage walls, walls on wheels, and post-beam & infill systems help to define spaces and support work materials. Ergonomic chairs, keyboard supports and work surfaces support individual reconfiguration for maximum ergonomic support. More than 70% of musculo-skeletal disorders could be avoided with appropriate ergonomic furniture. Furniture or space-defining systems must be designed for environmental sustainability and for organizational change. The use of drywall, cubes with panel-hung worksurfaces, even pre-wired panels result in a rigidity of layout and supporting infrastructures that compromises individual and organizational effectiveness in the near term. We demonstrate that there are better and more desirable alternatives.

BROADER APPLICABILITY OF THE IDEAS OF THE INTELLIGENT WORKPLACE

A university setting should be neither market- nor politics-driven, while of course sensitive to both market mechanisms and policy. Within a university environment, free to work along a number of frontiers, the Robert L. Preger Intelligent Workplace supports, tests, and evaluates products, policies, and designs in a real work-

< 191 >

place setting while keeping abreast of all advances in technology. Applying the concepts of the Workplace, the Consortium, in turn, has consulted on many major building projects and workplace labs in the US and around the world, including the Pennsylvania Department of Environmental Protection Region III Headquarters, the Soffer Tech Building in Pittsburgh, the Beijing Energy Demonstration Project, the General Services Administration Adaptable Workplace Lab in Washington, DC, the EDF Laboratory of Design for Cognition in France, and the Owens Corning headquarters in Ohio, among others.

In addition, the Center for Building Performance is actively developing strategies to impact the building delivery process. Limited by first-cost decision-making, the development of a life-cycle tool identifying the cost-benefits of advanced building technologies is central to the commercialization of higher performance building solutions. In a web-based tool called BIDS (Building Investment Decision Support™), the Center is developing life-cycle justifications for high performance building systems with user-customized recalculations of world-wide case studies. Life-cycle justifications have been identified in ten areas to date:

- First-cost reductions
- energy/operation . . . maintenance
- individual productivity
- organizational productivity
- health
- attraction/retention
- organizational renewal/churn
- technological renewal
- tax/insurance/code
- salvage/waste

Building on the Intelligent Workplace literally and figuratively, the next phase of intelligent-workplace research is the development and demonstration of the "Building as Power Plant." Its purpose is to integrate advanced, energy-effective systems, such that most or all of the building's energy needs are met on site in ways that maximize the use of renewable energies. This initiative particularly emphasizes systems integration in order to reduce first costs, increase efficiency and performance, and maximize return on investment. The use of innovative and sustainable energy systems for buildings will be technologically and economically feasible only if buildings are inherently "intelligent"; that is, they must minimize their energy needs from the beginning.

< 192 >

The Center proposes to realize and demonstrate this idea by completing the second wing of Margaret Morrison Carnegie Hall on the campus at Carnegie Mellon. The new wing will provide a unique opportunity for multidisciplinary collaboration in research and development. The retrofit of Margaret Morrison Hall will also provide an opportunity for a major renovation to incorporate intelligent environmental and lighting systems that can be integrated with advanced energy systems. A primary focus will be on technological innovation, rather than market viability. We believe the results of this effort will support implementation of advanced energy-efficient and integrated building systems in the public and private sectors informing and influencing global as well as national energy and environmental policy.

References

Hartkopf, V., Loftness, V. et al. (2000) *The Intelligent Workplace Decision Tool CD.* Carnegie Mellon University and the Advanced Building Systems Integration Consortium, The Center for Building Performance and Diagnostics. Carnegie Mellon University, Pittsburgh.

Hartkopf, V., Loftness, V. (1995) *Interior Environmental Control System for an Intelligent Building,* ABSTRC, pp. 1–24. Carnegie Mellon University, Pittsburgh.

Hartkopf, V., Loftness, V., Mahdavi, A., Lee, S., Shankavaram, J. and, K. J. Tu (1995) "The Relationship of Environmental Quality in Buildings to Productivity, Energy Effectiveness, Comfort and Health: How Much Proof do we Need?" Carnegie Mellon University, Pittsburgh, PA.

Loftness, V., Hartkopf, V., Aziz, A. and S. Lee. (2000) "The Adaptable Workplace Laboratory," ABSIC Report, Carnegie Mellon University, Pittsburgh, PA.

Slatin, P. (1992) "The Intelligent Penthouse: Workplace Laboratory," *Architectural Record.* June.

Acknowledgments

The work outlined here is the result of a team of faculty and researchers in the Center for Building Performance including Volker Hartkopf, Vivian Loftness, Stephen Lee, Ardeshir Mahdavi, Azizan Aziz, and Rohini Brahme, as well as a long list of graduate students from around the world. The research of the Center has been supported by the Advanced Building Systems Integration Consortium for over 14 years, with members that include the following:

CORPORATE MEMBERS

AMP Incorporated	Bricsnet
ArmstrongWorld Industries Inc.	BP Solar

< 193 >

Consolidated Edison of New York, Inc.
Electricité de France
Johnson Controls Inc.
Siemens Energy & Automation, Inc.
Steelcase Inc.

Teknion
LTG Aktiengesellschaft
Thyssen Krupp AG
United Technologies / Carrier
Zumtobel Staff Lighting, Inc.

GOVERNMENTAL MEMBERS

National Science Foundation
US Department of Defense
US Department of Energy
US Department of State
US Environmental Protection Agency

US General Services Administration
Dutch Government Buildings Agency
Public Works and Government
Services Canada

UNIVERSITY MEMBER

Carnegie Mellon University

PAST MEMBERS

American Bridge Company / Continental Engineering Corporation
Bank of America
Bechtel Corporation
Bell of Pennsylvania
Duquesne Light Company

Interface Inc.
LG-Honeywell Co., Ltd.
PPG Industries
Westinghouse Electric Corporation /
The Knoll Group

CORRESPONDING MEMBERS

Bayer USA
Bosse Design
Grahl Industries, Inc.
Hüppe Form
ICC Technologies

Josef Gartner & Co.
Mahle GmbH
Mori Biru
Nucor
Osram / Sylvania

< 194 >

TECHNOLOGY AND PUBLIC POLICY

M. Granger Morgan

Granger Morgan is Professor and Head of the Department of Engineering and Public Policy at Carnegie Mellon, where he is also Lord Chair Professor in Engineering. He also has appointments in the Department of Electrical and Computer Engineering and the Heinz School of Public Policy and Management. His research addresses problems in science, technology, and public policy, and especially the development and demonstration of methods to characterize and treat uncertainty in quantitative policy analysis. He received his Ph.D. from the University of California-San Diego in 1969, and has been at Carnegie Mellon for 29 years.

Over the past four decades a number of technically based academic programs have been created to address problems in public policy in which matters of science and engineering are of central importance. This chapter begins with a general discussion of the growth of such programs. It then discusses a number of key obstacles that have complicated such growth, and prevented the creation of programs at many universities. The chapter concludes with a description of the Department of Engineering and Public Policy (EPP), an unusual department in the College of Engineering (CIT) at Carnegie Mellon University. The history of the department is outlined, the institutional arrangements which allow it to function are described, and the academic and research pro-

< 195 >

gram are briefly summarized. The focus is on what makes our Department distinctive and innovative.

Introduction

Like business schools, professional schools of public policy have become commonplace. Leading examples include the Lyndon B. Johnson School of Public Affairs at the University of Texas, Austin; the Goldman School of Public Policy at the University of California at Berkeley; the John F. Kennedy School of Government at Harvard University; and the H. John Heinz III School of Public Policy and Management at Carnegie Mellon University. Business schools and policy schools are built on the proposition that there is a core of analytical and management skills that provide graduates with the foundations to succeed across a wide range of positions in their field.

While it is true that an MBA is good preparation for many management jobs, it is also true that success in a number of management jobs in highly technical industrial sectors requires a deep knowledge of the core technologies of the industry. It is not an accident that Raytheon, Hewlett Packard, Microsoft, and Qualcomm were founded and built by first-rate technical people. The same holds true in public policy. There are many policy problems that can be readily addressed by treating the technical dimensions, if any, as a "black box." Indeed, such a strategy can be beneficial because it minimizes the risk of getting bogged down in irrelevant technical detail. However, as in business, there is an important subset of public policy problems in which reasonable solutions can only be developed if one understands and deals in detail with the technical substance of the problem. As the world becomes more and more dependent on technology, the portion of policy problems that fall in this latter category continues to grow.

Harvey Brooks has long argued that such problems can be usefully divided into two categories, which he terms "science for policy" and "policy for science." The first brings scientific and technical knowledge to bear on solving society's policy problems—how best to control the risks of pollution, how to allocate scarce resources such as the electromagnetic spectrum, how to choose the best weapon systems. The second involves the development of social policy for the management and control of the scientific and technical enterprise—how much to fund the Na-

< 196 >

tional Science Foundation (NSF) and the National Institute of Health (NIH), how to manage the National Labs, and how to support the education of new scientists and engineers.

While they do a great job of preparing deep and narrowly educated experts, schools of engineering and science are not readily able to produce graduates who have the mix of skills needed to address problems in science, technology and public policy. Over the past century, many senior technical people have migrated into these roles, rendering valuable service, especially in addressing issues of "policy for science." But the fields of policy analysis, decision science, economics, political science, and behavioral social science all offer valuable insights and analytical techniques that most such senior technical people never acquire. Indeed, even after years in the policy arena, many such people continue to display a combination of ignorance and disdain for these fields, and the powerful insights and analytical tools they can offer.

A number of universities have recognized this problem and attempted to build programs that could produce graduates who combine substantial technical knowledge and a broader set of policy analysis and social science skills. In the late 1960s and the 1970s, the NSF and the Alfred P. Sloan Foundation made a series of grants designed to support the creation of such programs.[1] Most lasted only as long as the soft money continued. A few, such as the programs at Carnegie Mellon and at MIT, have survived and prospered. Some, such as the Department of Technology and Human Affairs[2] at Washington University in St. Louis, founded by chemical engineer Robert Morgan,[3] prospered for a couple of decades and then died as new academic management, with other priorities, replaced the original founders. Some, like the program built at Cornell by chemist Frank Long and physicist Raymond Bowers, started out with a heavy focus on technical issues and then evolved into a program on social studies of science and technology. Later faculty appointments did not include scientists or engineers.

Today the leading US academic programs that address issues in the area of technology and public policy from a technical perspective are at Carnegie Mellon and MIT. Stanford's Department of Management Science and Engineering (MS&E), the result of a merger of three departments, including the Department of Engineering Economic Systems (EES), founded by engineer William Linville, continues to do a small amount of public sector work, but is now largely focused on technology and management

< 197 >

problems in the private sector.[4] A number of programs address technology and policy problems in the area of energy and the environment, including the Energy and Resources Group at UC Berkeley, a group in the Department of Environmental Engineering at North Carolina State, and a set of programs at Princeton. There are also a number of programs in systems engineering, such as the one at the University of Virginia, which has worked extensively in risk analysis and management. Listings of these programs are maintained by the American Association for the Advancement of Science (AAAS) (2000) and the Peterson's Guides (2000).

Outside the US the strongest technically based programs are at the two Technical Universities at Delft and Eindhoven in the Netherlands. Programs at Sussex, Manchester and Cambridge in the UK do some policy work that is technically based, and there are small islands of activity in several other European universities. At the Instituto Superior Technico in Lisbon, Manuel Heitor has been working for several years to build an engineering-based program. Several universities in the developing world, such as Catholic University in Santiago, Chile, IIT Bombay in India, and Tsinghua University in Beijing, show signs of growing technically based policy activities.

WHY AREN'T THERE MORE PROGRAMS?

Given the large and growing importance of technology in today's world, why are there so few technically based programs addressing issues of public policy? There are at least four basic reasons:

1. Promotion and tenure processes, which apply traditional disciplinary criteria to the evaluation of junior faculty and give existing tenured faculty great power (if not always an outright veto), seriously impede most universities' ability to build interdisciplinary programs in traditional schools of science and engineering.
2. Traditionally educated scientists and engineers frequently display a combination of arrogant ignorance and disdain toward the social and policy sciences. Faculty from science and engineering who engage in technically based policy research are routinely made to feel inferior or second class, even when their work is outstanding.
3. There are very few people who combine deep technical skills with a first-rate modern understanding of policy analysis and

< 198 >

applied social science. Thus, even when a university has openings for such faculty, they can be extremely difficult to find.

4. When evaluating proposals, funding agencies typically give little attention to past success in performing interdisciplinary research when they evaluate responses to requests for proposals (RFPs) which call for new interdisciplinary work. Thus, it is hard for university groups to build the sustained interdisciplinary relationships that are essential to creation of a successful academic program.

Business schools, schools of public policy, schools of public health, and others have solved their own equivalent versions of these problems by creating an entire academic environment that is problem-focused, and in many cases, more tolerant of interdisciplinary activity. Such a strategy is far less attractive in the area of technology and public policy. If the quality of the technical content of the work is to remain high, and the academic program is to provide a significant technical "value-added" component to its students, the program needs to maintain close working ties with traditional technical disciplines. The group based in a professional school that has come closest to succeeding with such a strategy is the Program on Science and International Affairs at Harvard's Kennedy School. Staffed by a number of first-rate technical people, including Harvey Brooks and Lewis Branscomb (both now emeritus), Bill Clark, Ashton Carter and John Holdren, this program does excellent, often rather general and high-level work. But on the educational front, it provides its graduate students with little or no additional technical knowledge, relying instead on whatever technical background they happened to have when they joined the program. It also maintains a cadre of technically trained post docs.

Even in institutions that have built stable academic programs, promotion and tenure continue to pose problems. Until recently, MIT found it safest to staff at the senior level with people who had already built established interdisciplinary records. The Department of Engineering and Public Policy (EPP) at Carnegie Mellon has achieved by far the most successful solution to the problem of promoting and tenuring faculty who work on interdisciplinary problems. Carnegie Mellon has a built a 30-year track record of successfully promoting and tenuring such people. But that said, it remains the case that EPP faculty who mainly do technical work, with some policy relevance and interests, typically

< 199 >

receive much higher evaluations in the tenure and promotion deliberations of the engineering college than do faculty who attempt to fully integrate their technical and policy interests. Further, as new faculty join the traditional departments of the engineering college, EPP must engage in a continuing program of education and acculturation to assure continued support from traditional discipline-oriented department heads and faculty. In contrast, traditional established engineering departments do not have to do this.

Faculty recruiting is a serious problem. Often Carnegie Mellon's EPP has been forced to hire promising young faculty who have outstanding technical credentials, but only stated policy interests, and then work to grow their policy dimensions over time. This strategy has been surprisingly successful, but clearly is slow and carries risks. For many years the Technology and Policy program at MIT, which was built by Richard De Neufville, relied on non-tenure track staff to do most of the core teaching. With the creation of the new Engineering Systems Division at MIT, a number of interdisciplinary faculty openings have been created and this problem is now slowly being addressed.

There are a number of programs such as the Congressional and Executive Branch Fellows programs run by professional societies, the Washington Internship for Students of Engineering (WISE) summer internship program, the Fellows programs at the National Research Council (NRC), and staff opportunities at places like the now defunct Office of Technology Assessment (OTA), which one would think might be a source of faculty candidates. However, remarkably few of the people who have passed through these programs have developed serious policy *research* interests and moved to academic jobs. Significantly larger numbers have moved into jobs as policy analysts and practitioners.

As in all fields, occasionally programs have hired established people from one another. EPP hired Marvin Sirbu from the Sloan School at MIT while he was still fairly junior. MIT hired Greg McRae from Carnegie Mellon's EPP after he had been promoted to full professor. Harvard recently hired John Holdren to a chaired position in the Kennedy School after a long and successful career as the founding leader of the Energy and Resources Group at UC Berkeley.

While government agencies and funding organizations frequently decry the lack of technically skilled interdisciplinary educational and research activities in universities, they do relatively little to improve the situation. With rare exceptions, there are no

< 200 >

funding programs for institution building, or to support the development and demonstration of new analysis tools and methods. Such work must be bootstrapped under other venues. There are now a number of programs, run by agencies such as the Environmental Protection Agency, the Department of Energy, and the NSF, which provide fellowship support that can include graduate students with technology/policy interests, although most provide resources that fall significantly short of full support in private universities such as Carnegie Mellon and MIT.

But perhaps the biggest problem with government funding programs is their consistent failure to recognize that successful interdisciplinary research is not something that can simply be turned on and off at will. Building a successful interdisciplinary research teams takes years of sustained collaboration on multiple problems. Participants must get to the point where they understand one another's disciplinary perspectives and analytical approaches and have some familiarity with relevant literatures. This is a process that must be nurtured through repeated collaborations over time. With few exceptions, there are not state or federal funding agencies, or private foundations, prepared to make such sustained investments. Indeed, there are instances in which funding officers avoid supporting qualified existing groups in favor of untried teams that talk a good line. This dual failure by funding agencies to recognize the diagnostic importance of past track record, and the importance of building and sustaining institutional infrastructure, remains a serious problem for the field.

EPP AT CARNEGIE MELLON

The Carnegie Institute of Technology (CIT) houses five traditional departments: chemical, civil and environmental, electrical and computer, mechanical, and materials science and engineering. In addition, for approximately 30 years, it has also been home to the very non-traditional Department of Engineering and Public Policy (EPP). EPP was originally established as an undergraduate educational program, designed to add additional dimensions and skills to the education of students who planned conventional engineering careers. Beginning in the late 1970s, a research-oriented doctoral program was added.

< 201 >

In order to understand EPP, as with virtually all technology/ policy programs, one must first understand its broader institutional setting. Indeed, it is Carnegie Mellon's unique institutional setting that has made EPP possible. Carnegie Mellon was founded at the turn of the century by Andrew Carnegie as the Carnegie technical schools. In establishing the schools, Carnegie was not setting out to create a major research institution, but rather a high-quality vocational school for the sons and daughters of Pittsburgh mill workers. By the period between the two world wars, it had grown into a good regional engineering school, with a reputation for educating students in the practical solution of problems drawn from the real world. Since such problems typically did not fit neatly into traditional academic disciplines, engineering at "Carnegie Tech" took on a distinctly interdisciplinary character.

Carnegie Mellon's emergence as a major US research university occurred in the period following the Second World War.[5] During the postwar period, the University undertook two very important institutional innovations (See Simon, pp. 1–13). First, it built a new business school, the Graduate School of Industrial Administration (GSIA), by assembling an interdisciplinary team of quantitatively oriented faculty. Following the institutional tradition of doing empirical work on real world problems, faculty in GSIA, which included Herb Simon, James March, and Richard Cyert, revolutionized modern social science, developing the Carnegie Behavioral School of Social Science (Bower 1968). In addition, GSIA pioneered modern quantitative approaches to business education that are now widely used in business schools around the world.

The development of computer science was the second key institutional innovation during the postwar period. At most universities, computer science grew out of mathematics and electrical engineering. At Carnegie Mellon, it also grew out of GSIA and psychology. That broad interdisciplinary background, combined with many years of strong funding by the Advanced Research Projects Agency of the Department of Defense (NRC 1999) led to the creation of one of the strongest computer science units anywhere in the world.

By the time Richard Cyert became President of Carnegie Mellon in 1972, the institution had clearly decided that it wanted to be a leading research university. But how does a small private

< 202 >

university, with modest resources, "play with the big boys?" Clearly good ideas are necessary, but they are not sufficient. Once others with larger resources understand those good ideas, they may easily surge ahead. Cyert recognized that the University needed to look for areas in which it could not only establish, but also maintain, a competitive advantage. With strong interdisciplinary research traditions already established in engineering, GSIA, and computer science, addressing problems at the boundaries between traditional disciplines, something that most universities find very difficult to do in a stable way, emerged as an obvious area for comparative advantage.

In this environment, in the late 1960s and early 1970s, a group of faculty in the Engineering College decided that, while undergraduate engineering education was doing a fine job of providing technical skills for engineers in the modern world, engineers should also have an understanding of the relationship of their technology to the broader society. Thanks to the efforts of Rod Williams, Herb Toor, Bob Dunlap, Bill Gouse, and others, this concern led to the creation of a set of undergraduate double-major degree programs with all five of the traditional engineering departments. These double-major undergraduate programs provided the undergraduate curricular structure for what would shortly become the Department of Engineering and Public Policy.

FACULTY ARRANGEMENTS

In most universities, interdisciplinary joint appointments between academic departments are a recipe for disaster, especially for untenured faculty. However, because of Carnegie Mellon's unique institutional environment, it has been possible to build EPP largely with true 50/50 joint appointments with all five of the traditional engineering departments, and with four different social science units in three other colleges.

There are currently 24 tenure-track faculty in EPP. Fourteen tenure-track faculty are funded by EPP. Twelve hold joint appointments with one of the other five traditional engineering departments or with one of four social science units in three other colleges (Humanities & Social Sciences, the Heinz School, and GSIA). Eleven, called "affiliated faculty," do not receive salaries from EPP, but in all other respects are equivalent to jointly appointed faculty (e.g., senior-affiliated faculty vote on tenure, etc.). Twenty (54%) of the tenure-track faculty in EPP are tenured. There are

< 203 >

currently 12 research-track and special faculty, and 22 adjunct and part-time faculty in EPP.

The Undergraduate Program

The Department now offers double-major B.S. degree programs with each of the five traditional engineering departments and with the School of Computer Science. These joint-degree programs are now chosen by about ten percent of all undergraduate engineering students at Carnegie Mellon. They all lead to fully accredited engineering degrees that prepare students for traditional engineering careers. EPP double-major engineers are not educated to be a different kind of engineer. Rather, their education is intended to help them to become better, more socially responsible engineers in the traditional engineering fields. In addition to these double-major degrees, the Department also offers a minor in "Technology and Public Policy" for students outside of engineering and computer science.

All the undergraduate degree programs in Engineering and Public Policy combine a strong foundation in mathematics and physical sciences, and the development of engineering skills in a specific engineering field, with a rigorous preparation in the analysis of social and political problems. The curricula include subject matter which is not part of traditional engineering or social science curricula, but which contains elements of each. This is accomplished through Engineering and Public Policy technical elective courses, social analysis elective courses, and through participation by each student in two interdisciplinary problem-solving projects. Problems for these contexts are drawn from local, state, and national situations and have dealt with topics like industrial automation and robotics, environmental control, telecommunication and computer technologies, product safety, and energy systems.

To make the double major work, EPP takes over all of the technical and non-technical elective courses in the traditional engineering major and shapes them to meet the needs of the second degree. Table 1 provides a general illustration of how this works. The double-major degree is completed in the same four years as the traditional single major, but in some cases requires a few more units, and typically involves a more demanding set of courses. Four of the technical electives in a traditional major get replaced by EPP technical electives. Humanities, Social Science

< 204 >

and Fine Arts electives are replaced by Social Analysis electives. Two EPP project courses and two Probability and Statistics courses are worked into restricted elective slots.

Table 1   Comparison of the traditional Carnegie Mellon undergraduate engineering curriculum with the non-traditional EPP double-major undergraduate program

TRADITIONAL MAJOR	EPP DOUBLE MAJOR
• Common freshman year • Required engineering or computer science (CS) courses • Free electives • Restricted electives • Technical electives • Humanities, social science, and fine arts electives	• Common freshman year • Required engineering or computer science (CS) courses • 4 EPP technical electives • 2 courses in probability and statistics & 2 EPP project courses • EPP technical electives • 6 social analysis electives, including microeconomics and decision analysis

---

PROJECT COURSES

"Project courses" are an important part of the Department's undergraduate program. The typical project course involves about 25 students, half of whom are junior or senior engineering students in EPP and half of whom are a mixture of first year master's students in the Heinz School and undergraduate policy majors in the Department of Social and Decision Sciences. Projects address some real world problem in technology and public policy, usually with an outside client for whom the work is being done. Students start the semester with a vaguely defined problem area and various background materials, which they must use to define and shape a workable problem, and then undertake the necessary analysis to get the problem solved. There are usually two faculty advisors, one from engineering and one from social sciences, together with one or two student managers. Over the first couple of weeks of a project, the students work on developing a thorough understanding of the subject and defining the focus of the work they will do. About a third of the way into the semester, students make a first formal presentation at which they present their proposed research to an outside review panel of experts who represent different expertise and points of view in the problem field.

< 205 >

The review panel assists the students by providing critical comments on the way in which they have structured the problem and by suggesting various resources and information sources. About two thirds of the way through the semester, students make a second presentation to the project review committee at which they present a progress report and receive steering suggestions from the review panel. At the end of the semester, the students prepare a final written project report and make a final verbal presentation of their findings and conclusions to the review panel. Of course, it's impossible for 25 students to work a single problem all together, and for this reason, much of the work in project courses gets done in smaller working groups of four to eight students, each making a different and valued contribution to the group as a whole.

Project courses serve several important educational functions. First, they are the one place where students get an opportunity to put together the various technical and social analysis components of their education and gain hands-on experience working on real world problems. Second, project courses provide valuable opportunity for students to develop and refine their verbal skills, which turn out, in the real world of daily engineering practice, to be every bit as important for success as the more traditional mathematical and quantitative analytical skills.

Project courses are very demanding, and it is not at all unusual for students to complain about them while they are going through the experience. However, in three extensive surveys of all EPP undergraduate alumni we have done over the past 20 years, the consistent message we have received is that "project courses were the single most valuable educational experience that I had in my four years at Carnegie Mellon."

The majority of the double-major graduates in Engineering and Public Policy pursue conventional engineering careers, using the additional dimension in their background to improve the quality, sensitivity, and social responsiveness of their work and the work of their colleagues. Many who begin in conventional engineering careers later migrate into positions with responsibilities which make special use of their EPP education. A number of graduates elect careers with local, state, or national government or with policy research and consulting firms. Some choose to continue their formal education, doing graduate work in an engineering discipline, in the social sciences, law, or in an interdisciplinary program.

To date, EPP has graduated 555 double-major B.S. students and has a current double-major enrollment of 71. Approximately

< 206 >

80 percent of double majors go into traditional engineering careers. Five students are also currently enrolled in the newly created Minor in Technology and Public Policy for non-engineering students.

THE GRADUATE PROGRAM

The graduate program in Engineering and Public Policy has a different goal. It educates technically skilled men and women at the doctoral level to be leaders in policy-focused research. With a strong doctoral focus, the department admits terminal M.S. students only in special circumstances. The focus is on policy problems in which the technical details matter—where technology cannot be treated as a "black box." Policy-focused research differs from policy analysis in three important ways: it takes a longer-term perspective; it takes a more fundamental view; and it may focus on the development of theory and of analytical tools and techniques, as well as on solving specific problems.

Perhaps the quickest way to understand more fully EPP's graduate program is to look at a few of the titles of the slightly over 100 doctoral dissertations the Department has now granted. Titles of theses, 1998–2001, are listed in the Appendix.

The Ph.D. in EPP requires a rigorous program of courses and research accomplishment. The courses include a series of core classes on fundamental approaches and methods for engineering and public policy; required classes in statistics and economics; electives in engineering, sciences and mathematics; and electives in the social sciences. Research experience begins very early in the academic program, leading to a research paper of journal quality after the third semester. This paper is the first part of the qualifying exam process and is followed by development of subsequent papers and, finally, the doctoral thesis.

The qualifying exams, which occur at the end of a student's third semester, include both a research paper and a take-home exam. After the research paper has been developed, written and submitted by the student, an oral presentation and subsequent question-and-answer session with the faculty follow. Questions can relate directly to the analysis presented in the paper or to more general disciplinary knowledge and skills. The exam is taken over a five day period and asks students to analyze and evaluate a real life problem with engineering, science, social science and policy content. In a given five day period, all students receive the

< 207 >

same problem and the faculty do a "blind grading" of reports that the students produce.

To date, the Department has graduated just over 100 Ph.D.s and has a current graduate enrollment of 44. Doctoral graduates go to policy-oriented research careers in universities (45%), industry (25%), government and national laboratories (15%), and consulting firms and "think tanks" (15%).

RESEARCH IN EPP

Research focuses on that sub-set of public and private sector policy problems in which the technical details are important. In choosing this focus, the Department makes no statement about the relative importance of such problems. It simply argues that its particular comparative advantage lies in addressing such problems.

Most research in EPP currently falls in one of four areas: (1) problems in energy and environmental systems; (2) problems in risk analysis and communication; (3) policy problems involving information and communication technologies; and (4) problems in technology policy, including issues in technological innovation, green design, industrial automation, productivity, and engineering education for the technical workforce. Within the context of these four focal areas, the Department also addresses issues in technology and economic development, focusing in particular on India and China. It frequently undertakes the development of new software tools for the support of policy analysis and research. And from time to time, it undertakes work on issues in arms control and defense policy.

The research style in the Department has always involved collaboration among groups of faculty and students. Recent years have seen a growth in the scale of these collaborations, and the establishment of several formal research centers. They include the Center for Integrated Study of the Human Dimensions of Global Change; the Green Design Initiative; the Center for Energy and Environmental Studies; the Center for the Study and Improvement of Regulation; and the Brownfields Center. There is also a center-like set of activities in Internet commerce, the telephone, etc.; a similar set of activities in risk analysis, ranking, and communication; and a set of activities involving energy and information systems in India. Details on many of these activities can be found under the research portion of the EPP web page at http://www.epp.cmu.edu/.

< 208 >

Conclusion

The past four decades have witnessed the emergence of a group of technically based academic programs that address problems in public policy in which issues of science and engineering are of central importance. Carnegie Mellon is a leader in this group. Creating such programs within the disciplinary framework of traditional science and engineering schools has posed great, in some cases insurmountable, difficulties. While strong, well-established programs now exist at a few leading institutions in the US and The Netherlands, their number remains limited. This is unfortunate. Given the large and growing role of technology in today's world, the need for such programs, the research they perform, and the graduates they produce will continue to grow.

Notes

[1] Prior to this, IBM made a large gift to Harvard in the early '60s to create a program in Technology and Society under the leadership of Emmanuel Mesthene (Harvard 1972). The program, which involved only modest technical content, was terminated in 1972 and the remaining funds used for professional endowment.

[2] Later called the Department of Engineering and Policy. This department developed undergraduate programs and M.S. and Ph.D. programs quite similar to those of the Department of Engineering and Public Policy at Carnegie Mellon. Unlike the Carnegie Mellon program, it did not operate with joint faculty appointments with traditional departments, since that would have posed insurmountable promotion and tenure problems.

[3] Robert Morgan and the author of this chapter, M. Granger Morgan, are not related.

[4] In its early years, EES at Stanford did a large amount of public sector work, pioneering the practical application of decision and other systems-analytic tools. The early death of Bill Linville, and Ron Howard's growing involvement with Libertarian Philosophy, which led him to argue that much analysis done for the public sector is unethical, contributed to a reduction in the quantity and scope of public sector work in that department. Today, Department Head, Marie-Elisabeth Paté-Cornell, is one of the few remaining MS&E faculty members with strong public sector research interests.

[5] The name change occurred in 1967, when Carnegie Tech was merged with the Mellon Institute, an industrial research laboratory.

References

AAAS Guide to Graduate Education in Science, Engineering, and Public Policy, Directorate for Science and Policy Programs, American Association for the

< 209 >

Advancement of Science. Originally published as a booklet in 1985, the current fourth edition is maintained online at http://www.aaas.org/SPP/ESPP/SEPP/index.htm

Bower, J. L. (1968) "Descriptive Decision Theory for the 'Administrative' Viewpoint," Chapter 3 in Bauer, R.A. and Gergen, K.J. (eds)

The Study of Policy Formation, R.A. Bauer and K.J. Gergen. Free Press.

Harvard University Program on Technology and Society: 1964–1972 — A final review. (1972) Cambridge, MA: Harvard University.

National Research Council. (1999) *Funding a Resolution: Government support for computing research*, Committee on Innovations in Computing and Communications, Computer Sciences and Telecommunications Board.

Peterson's Guide to Graduate Programs in Engineering & Applied Science. (2000) Section 15, "Management of Engineering and Technology," pp. 1247–1296.

Appendix

Titles of Ph.D. Theses Completed in Carnegie Mellon's
Department of Engineering and Public Policy 1998–2001

John Chung-I Chuang, "Economies of Scale in Information Dissemination over the Internet"

James C. Corbett, "An Assessment of Air Pollution and Environmental Impacts from International Maritime Transportation Including Engineering Controls and Policy Alternatives"

James N. Follin, "Environmental Risks, Decision Making, and Public Perception: A case study involving environmental impact statements"

Vasiliki Hartonas-Garmhausen, "Formal Verification of Computer Systems"

Hiroshi Hayakawa, "Automobile Risk Perceptions and Insurance Decisions: A Japan-US comparison during deregulation"

Charles D. Linville, "Mathematical and Computational Techniques for Research Prioritization with an Application to Global Climate Change Research"

Heather L. MacLean, "Life Cycle Models of Conventional and Alternative-Fueled Automobiles"

Kara Morgan, "The Development and Evaluation of a Risk Ranking Method"

Kathy Notarianni, "The Role of Uncertainty in Improving Fire Protection Regulation"

Donna M. Riley, "Human Factors in Exposure Analysis for Consumer Paint Stripper Use"

< 210 >

John Shultz, "The Risk of Accidents and Spills at Offshore Production Platforms: A statistical analysis of risk factors and the development of predictive models"

Neil A. Stiber, "Decision-Making Tools for Environmental Cleanup and Redevelopment"

Neil D. Strachan, "The Adoption and Supply of a Distributed Energy Technology"

Guodong Sun, "An Integrated Study of China's Air Pollution Management: Effectiveness, Efficiency, and Governance"

Margaret R. Taylor, "The Influence of Government Actions on Innovative Activities in the Development of Environmental Technologies to Control Sulfur Dioxide Emissions from Stationary Sources"

Daniel Teitelbaum, "Technological Change and Pollution Control: An adaptive agent-based analysis"

Rahul Tongia, "Issues in Electric Power in India: Challenges and Opportunities"

Qiong Wang, "Pricing of Integrated-Services Networks"

James Jason West, "Studies in Natural and Human System Response Relevant to Global Environmental Change"

Hung-Yao Yeh, "Designing Wireless Local Loops Using Low Tier Technology: An approach to providing basic telecommunications service in less developed countries"

< 211 >

THE GREENING OF THE UNIVERSITY

David A. Dzombak and Cliff I. Davidson

David Dzombak is Professor of Civil and Environmental Engineering at Carnegie Mellon. The emphasis of his research and teaching is on water and soil quality engineering. Professor Dzombak received his Ph.D. from MIT in 1986, and has been at Carnegie Mellon for 16 years.

Cliff Davidson is Professor of Civil and Environmental Engineering and Engineering and Public Policy at Carnegie Mellon. His research and teaching interests are in the area of air quality engineering. Professor Davidson received his Ph.D. from the California Institute of Technology in 1977, and has been at Carnegie Mellon for 26 years.

Until recently, we had not realized the extent to which human activities could disturb and permanently change natural systems, and we had not thought about the ways in which these changes could affect future generations of people. Thus, education programs prior to the 1970s had little information covering human impact on the environment. Following conventional perspective, resources were viewed as infinite, and natural systems were viewed as completely resilient to abuse. We now know, however, that many of the day to day activities of people around the world are not sustainable. The rising global population, the desire of people worldwide for a better standard of living, and the finite resources of the earth indicate that we simply cannot maintain

< 213 >

the status quo. Either we will voluntarily change lifestyles in the coming decades, or future generations will face major shortages, disruptions, and reduced quality of life.

Universities must play a critical role in efforts to make the transition to sustainable lifestyles and economic systems. Indeed, higher education is vital both for conducting research on how to make this transition and for informing people that the transition is necessary. Both of these tasks require great amounts of information about the environment and our relationship with it. In this chapter, we explore ways in which universities can assist efforts to promote sustainability in society. We begin by examining briefly the background of a few current environmental problems that serve as examples of unsustainable practices. We then consider roles that universities can play in developing environmental education programs that can help society avoid such practices, pointing out work at Carnegie Mellon as an example. Next, we consider roles of universities in conducting research to develop solutions to current problems and approaches to avoid future problems, again referring to work at Carnegie Mellon. We then examine how some universities are moving beyond traditional curriculum and research avenues for environmental education. Finally, we conclude with a summary of our main observations about the evolution of environmental education and research in universities, and the important role that universities have for bringing about a more widely distributed sense of responsibility for the environment and effective approaches for its protection.

SOME CURRENT ENVIRONMENTAL PROBLEMS

Understanding the sustainability dilemma requires us to look backwards to a time when people were largely unaware of or unconcerned about environmental damage. The Industrial Revolution, beginning in the mid-1800s, was such a time: efforts were focused on industrial development, with little thought given to conservation of resources or minimizing environmental impact. Pittsburgh offers an excellent example of this mindset, with the rise of glass, iron, and steel production undeterred by huge amounts of smoke from its factories, the use of rivers as sewers, and widespread scarring of the land by mining activities.

Industry prospered and people demanded better products. For example, tetraethyl lead was introduced as a gasoline addi-

< 214 >

tive in 1922, in response to public pressure for faster cars. Chlorofluorocarbons (CFCs) were developed for use as refrigerants and other applications in the 1930s. DDT and other pesticides were found to mitigate substantially insect infestations of agricultural crops and insect-transmitted disease, leading to greater crop yields and prevention of disease epidemics. Although these chemicals were then widely praised as solutions to societal problems, in actuality they created far more sinister problems than they solved. Let us consider the history of each of these chemicals as examples of what can happen if we are ignorant of environmental effects, or if we ignore the information we have.

Leaded Gasoline

As more and more families became first time automobile owners in the years following World War I, there was greater pressure for cars that would go faster. The limiting factor was engine "knock"—and the automakers were searching for a way to solve the problem. Thomas Midgely, Jr., an employee of General Motors, discovered that tetraethyl lead added to gasoline essentially eliminated engine knock. Ethyl Corporation was formed and leaded gasoline went on sale soon after.

Yet public health officials as well as tetraethyl lead manufacturers knew that lead was toxic. After months of warnings, an accident at a tetraethyl lead manufacturing plant in New Jersey in 1924 poisoned virtually all workers in the plant. The accident made news headlines. Plant owners argued that careless workers caused the poisonings, and that lead would not pose a risk if it were handled carefully. Doctors and public health scientists, on the other hand, argued that lead should be removed from gasoline: not only were there occupational exposures to workers in the manufacturing plants, but the poisonings suggested the danger of annually emitting thousands of kilograms of lead in vehicle exhaust to the atmosphere. After some debate, leaded gasoline was banned in several states. The arguments continued, however, and pressure from the automotive industry and from the public ultimately forced these states to rescind their laws and allow leaded gasoline once again (Nriagu 1999).

Worldwide consumption of leaded gasoline rose rapidly, unchecked, during the next several decades. Then in the 1960s, Clair Patterson of the California Institute of Technology made a startling discovery: emissions from the use of leaded gasoline as well as other lead sources had elevated the amounts of lead in the natural environment by factors of 100 or more. This included

< 215 >

remote areas of the world's oceans, where lead concentrations in fish had increased dramatically, and Greenland, where snow that had fallen fell hundreds of years ago, nearly perfectly preserved in the Ice Sheet, had only a tiny fraction of the lead found in recent snow (Murozumi et al. 1969). This was followed by Herbert Needleman's discovery, in Boston in the late 1970s, that children exposed to lead even at modest levels were suffering from neurological disorders (Needleman et al. 1979). After more than fifty years of leaded gasoline use and widespread health and ecosystem effects, lead was finally removed from gasoline in the US. Several other countries have now banned leaded gasoline, although it remains in use in much of the developing world.

CFCs

Environmental problems caused by chlorofluorocarbons (CFCs) were unknown for many years. When first discovered, these chemical compounds were found to have many outstanding characteristics: they were excellent refrigerants, they could be used as propellants for aerosols, they were non-flammable, non-corrosive, and non-toxic, and they did not degrade over long time periods. Who could ask for a better combination of properties? Their production increased rapidly over the next several decades. They soon became a textbook example of how chemicals manufactured by industry, as opposed to chemicals found in nature, could contribute to the betterment of society in a major way.

The acclaim for CFCs ended in the 1970s when American scientists Sherwood Rowland and Mario Molina discovered that the long lifetimes of these chemicals cause a troubling side effect. After leaking out of refrigerators, freezers, and air conditioners, CFCs survive the slow natural transport from the earth's surface up to the stratosphere (Rowland 1989). Once in the stratosphere, CFC molecules contribute chlorine atoms that destroy ozone molecules. The process is remarkably efficient, with one CFC molecule destroying thousands of ozone molecules. Thus even a tiny concentration of CFCs can have a major effect on stratospheric ozone.

The ozone in the stratosphere serves as a protective layer that prevents harmful ultraviolet radiation from reaching the earth's surface. If allowed to pass through the stratosphere, this radiation can cause skin cancer and cataracts. It was hypothesized that if allowed to continue, the destruction of the ozone layer by CFCs could lead to significant increases in these health problems. In fact, data collected by the British Antarctic Survey in the early

< 216 >

1980s showed that massive amounts of ozone destruction had occurred by that time over Antarctica and other high-latitude areas of the Southern Hemisphere (Farman et al. 1985). Later work showed that significant destruction of the ozone layer had occurred over the Arctic region as well. Fortunately, countries around the world responded to the results of research pointing to destruction of atmospheric ozone, and replacements for CFCs were found. International treaties such as the Montreal Protocol now prevent manufacturing of CFCs and propose chemicals that are less harmful to the ozone layer as substitutes. In 1995, Rowland and Molina, along with Paul Crutzen of Germany, were awarded the Nobel Prize in Chemistry for identifying the role of CFCs in stratospheric ozone depletion.

DDT

The organic chemical DDT (dichloro-diphenyl-trichloro-ethane), originally synthesized in 1874 by a German chemist, was discovered to have powerful insecticidal properties in 1939 by Swiss entomologist Paul Müller. The Swiss firm for whom he worked began production of the compound for insecticidal use, and it immediately was put to many beneficial uses for people. It was used by the US Army to treat soldiers afflicted by lice infestation; it was used to halt a typhus epidemic in Italy in 1943–44; and it was employed across the world to combat malaria, yellow fever, and typhus (Lowrance 1976). In the space of just a few years, millions of lives were saved throughout the world. In 1948 Paul Müller was awarded the Nobel Prize in Medicine for the discovery of the insecticidal properties of DDT.

Production and use of the compound expanded greatly in the 1950s and 1960s. As use of DDT became widespread, negative effects associated with its use became evident. It was observed by the public that spraying of elm trees to control Dutch elm disease resulted in high mortality rates for robins and other birds. This prompted scientific study of the effects of DDT on birds and other organisms, and of the fate and transport of DDT in the environment. A variety of worrisome effects were identified: direct toxicity to Coho salmon, robins, and other animals; reproductive failure in speckled sea trout; reduced reproduction rates in birds of prey due to thinner egg shells; and a host of other effects. Further, it was discovered that DDT is very persistent in the environment, that is, very resistant to degradation, and that it tends to accumulate in plant and animal tissues and thus be passed up the food chain. Animals higher up in the food chain, such as fish,

< 217 >

birds of prey, and humans, were found to have the highest concentrations of DDT, acquired through accumulation in tissue of DDT transferred from food sources.

These findings and those from studies of other long-lived pesticides in the environment were made widely known to the public in Rachel Carson's famous 1962 book *Silent Spring*. This book prompted widespread public concern about pesticide use, which resulted in new regulations and eventually a ban on DDT production and use. DDT use restrictions and bans were implemented in the United States, Canada, and most European countries in the early 1970s. While DDT is now banned in other countries as well, and is regarded as a "pesticide of last resort" by the World Health Organization, its use continues in many parts of the world and there is resistance by some countries to a worldwide ban.

Progress was made in addressing these problems over periods of decades by huge efforts in research, education, and policy development. The successes provide evidence that serious environmental problems can indeed be controlled. But many more environmental problems remain unsolved despite continued efforts. Mineral resource extraction activities continue to have very large, long-term impacts on water quality and ecosystems. Many contaminated water discharges contain toxic chemicals that can persist in the environment, such as in the sediments of rivers and lakes. These discharges continue in many areas of the US and elsewhere because of the lack of resources or lack of will to provide the necessary control technology. Global warming due to carbon dioxide and other greenhouse gases continues, with only token efforts thus far to reduce emissions. Depletion of nonrenewable resources, such as fossil fuels and scarce minerals, has not been curtailed despite knowledge that our current rate of usage cannot continue indefinitely. These are very important issues that are intertwined with the health of our economy and quality of life. They will only be addressed effectively with the widespread interest and involvement of educated citizenry.

Universities have a critical role to play in developing appreciation among students for the relationship of environmental quality with human prosperity, quality of life, and morality, and in developing solutions to the increasingly complex environmental challenges faced by society. In the following sections we discuss the evolution of environmental education and research in universities, and how both are changing to help society step up to the environmental challenges that confront us.

< 218 >

Evolution of Environmental Education:
Innovation at Carnegie Mellon

It is of interest that the history of environmental education mirrors the history of environmental controls. Industrial development began without concern for the environment. When problems were finally recognized, their solutions began as "end of pipe" treatments: electrostatic precipitators to capture particles in industrial exhaust gases, chemical treatment of wastewaters before the effluent reached natural bodies of water, and catalytic converters to destroy poisonous gases created in the internal combustion engine. Pollution control with these techniques is seen as an "add-on" since the basic processes that produced the pollutants in the first place are not altered. Such controls are inherently inefficient, requiring additional resources to prevent pollutants from reaching the environment.

Within the past decade, the concept of environmentally sustainable practices or "green design" has been recognized as a significant improvement over end of pipe emission treatment methods. If new industrial processes and products can be developed that minimize the generation of pollutants, there is no need for inefficient and expensive control devices. In fact, research has shown that processes producing less pollution are, in many cases, cheaper to use and require less material as inputs (Graedel and Allenby 1995). Achieving success in green design requires careful consideration of all of the environmental effects associated with a process or a product, such as extraction of the raw materials, transportation of materials to the plant, packaging, transportation of the product to the consumer, use of the product, and ultimate disposal. Thus environmental concerns must be considered at each step of a product's life cycle.

Education, including that in technology related fields, began without concern for environmental damage. When courses in environmental science and environmental engineering were finally developed, their place in the curriculum was *after* the mainstream courses—a course in water pollution, a course in waste disposal—that could be taken as an elective, or an "add-on." With little attempt to integrate environmental issues in the core of the curriculum, such as in design courses, students got the impression that environmental issues should be considered as separate topics, not during the central design phase of a project.

In contrast to past curricula, it is now becoming recognized that environmental issues should be integrated with traditional

< 219 >

courses in engineering, science, design, architecture, and numerous other disciplines (Collett and Karakashian 1996). There are several advantages to this integrated approach.

- First, students are made to realize that key decisions need to account for environmental constraints—as well as traditional constraints like safety, economics, and performance—right from the start, dispelling the notion of considering environmental consequences "after the fact." For example, in designing a product, it is far cheaper to determine how environmental damage can be minimized while the product is still in the initial concept phase rather than waiting until the basic design is determined. Students no longer think about environmental factors in isolation, but rather as vital components in decision making.
- The second advantage of the integrated approach is that students learn to appreciate environmental constraints early in their college years rather than discovering at the end of their degree program that such constraints exist. Exposing students early to value-laden issues such as environmental preservation helps them consider what is important to them. When combined with information on the role of ethics in personal and professional lives, students can be made aware of the ethical implications of environmental decision making—and the ethical implications of ignoring environmental issues.
- Third, exposure to environmental issues in several courses with different perspectives can help students to make connections among their various learning experiences. One of the challenges of learning material in separate courses is that the material is usually viewed in a narrow context. Students often report how difficult it is to use knowledge and skills acquired in one course and apply it in another. With environmental issues as a common thread in several courses, even if it is merely a minor component, the students can gain a perspective on the material that would not be possible with conventional environmental courses. This can make learning more efficient and interesting.
- Finally, adapting courses to include environmental issues early in the curriculum enables these vital concepts to reach a much greater number of students. The increasing severity of environmental problems demands that universities help in their solution, both by training environmental specialists and by training non-specialists who have at least a minimum

< 220 >

awareness of these problems. Including environmental components in core courses in many disciplines will help both endeavors: such courses can serve as recruitment vehicles for the environmental majors, and they can help non-majors to improve their communication with environmental specialists.

Interestingly enough, Aldo Leopold recognized the need for integrated environmental education in his 1949 classic, *A Sand County Almanac*. In his impassioned discussion of the need for a "land ethic," he stated: "One of the requisites for an ecological comprehension of land is an understanding of ecology. . . . An understanding of ecology does not necessarily originate in courses bearing ecological labels; it is quite as likely to be labeled geography, botany, agronomy, history, or economics."

Although the advantages of integrated environmental education are compelling, there are formidable challenges present in making such changes in university curricula. Faculty generally teach their courses somewhat autonomously; there is little incentive for them to change, especially to teach material that is outside their training. A major effort is needed to communicate why such a change is necessary. Furthermore, most universities were traditionally oriented toward helping with economic development—educating workers, training professionals, and conducting research to help build economic infrastructure. And despite the emergence of environmental programs on many campuses, the main orientation of most universities toward economic development has not changed. This in part reflects the financing of universities—from government agencies and industries that value economic development. Professor David Orr of Oberlin College promotes the idea that current environmental problems are first and foremost "a crisis in education," and argues that universities should reorient their programs to help solve the problems (Orr 1992). It is not surprising that Aldo Leopold noted in 1949: "Much higher education seems deliberately to avoid ecological concepts."

Despite the challenges of integrating environmental knowledge into existing courses, Carnegie Mellon, through its Environment Across the Curriculum initiative (EAC), is attempting such a task. Learning activities on environmental topics are being put together for use in various engineering, science, and liberal arts courses across campus. The idea is that a course in chemistry can present basic concepts in the discipline using chemical reactions of atmospheric pollutants or water pollutants as an example. A course in history can discuss the environmental impli-

< 221 >

cations of lifestyles and societal decisions in times past. A course in design can consider environmental damage as one of the constraints in the evaluation process. The EAC initiative is being implemented through the use of "modules," or short written pieces covering specific environmental case studies (Rubin, 2001).

Evolution of Environmental Research: Contributions by Carnegie Mellon

Reflecting the industrial orientation of Carnegie Institute of Technology, the forerunner of Carnegie Mellon University, and the limited societal interest in environmental protection, environmental research was minimal in the first 60 years of the University's history. There was a curriculum in sanitary engineering focused on municipal wastewater and solid waste disposal from the opening of Carnegie Tech in 1905 into the 1920s, but this activity was eventually replaced by a focus on water resources development in the 1930s and 1940s. With rising public awareness of environmental impact and the need for pollution control in the 1960s, research efforts in environmental engineering were initiated at Carnegie Mellon in the College of Engineering.

Environmental research at Carnegie Mellon in the 1960s and 1970s focused on air and water pollution control in the steel industry, in coal-fired electric power production, and in coal mining—industries of great importance to Western Pennsylvania but involving significant environmental impact. These efforts were all focused on development or improvement of technologies for treating and thus controlling emissions to the environment from the existing processes. Consistent with the governmental regulations and state of practice at the time, the aim of the treatment was not to eliminate environmental pollution, but to reduce it to levels considered acceptable.

As progress in development and implementation of emission treatment technology advanced, researchers and practitioners began to identify and think about a number of important issues related to pollution control, including:

- consequences of treatment system deployment, e.g., the generation of solid wastes in water and air discharge treatment systems, resulting in increased land disposal and transfer of the pollution from water or air to land;

< 222 >

- the need to weigh benefits and costs in making decisions about what level of treatment to deploy, and the critical role of the public in determining the appropriate balance;
- the need for improved scientific understanding of the transport, reactions, and impact of contaminants in the environment, to assist in evaluation of risks and societal costs of contaminants in the environment;
- the need for computer modeling of contaminant fate and transport in the environment, to assist in evaluation of risks and benefits of control; and
- the need for risk assessment to assist in determining the appropriate balance of benefits and costs.

This growing recognition of the technical and social complexity of environmental issues led the environmental research community across the US to look at environmental pollution control more broadly. The interdisciplinary culture at Carnegie Mellon facilitated the rapid development in the 1970s of new initiatives in assessment of cross-media environmental impact, risk assessment, and environmental engineering science.

The work on cross-media environmental impact represents well Carnegie Mellon's contributions in the evolving environmental research agenda of the 1970s. Faculty from several engineering departments studied total environmental impacts of coal conversion processes for different kinds of environmental control strategies. In evaluating optional strategies for control of gaseous sulfur emissions from coal gasification processes, for example, they discovered that control of sulfur emissions from the coal gasification process beyond a certain point would be offset by sulfur dioxide emissions from the power plant supplying the electricity for the pollution control equipment. In addition, they found that water pollution control regulations under consideration at the time would result in significant air pollution and solid waste problems. Their analyses pointed to problems with the way that environmental regulations and regulatory agencies were organized at the time, namely with divisions focused on only one environmental medium and without consideration of total environmental impact.

Environmental research at Carnegie Mellon expanded in the 1980s to encompass fate, transport, and treatment of pollutants in the environment, and environmental policy development and analysis. Air quality research included study of the transport and

< 223 >

health effects of particulates in air, the long range (global) transport of particle-associated air pollutants, indoor air quality, and linking local, regional, and global scale air quality models. Driven by growing public interest in problems of land pollution associated with abandoned waste disposal sites, water quality research focused on investigation of the fate, transport, and treatment of contaminants in groundwater and soil systems. Policy-related research included significant work on the science and tools of risk assessment, the new foundation for environmental decision making. This research was conducted in the context of applications such as risk from industrial air emissions and from electromagnetic fields near electric power transmission lines. There was also research in the 1980s on the development of tools and approaches for integrated assessment of the complex environmental problem of acid rain. This work led to the development of strategies for mitigation of acid rain. The environmental policy research of the 1980s, continuing into the 1990s, involved true collaborations of social scientists and engineers, and earned Carnegie Mellon recognition as a leader in methods for integrating social analysis in environmental decision making.

With the emergence in the 1990s of interest in development of environmentally sustainable practices for mankind, new research programs were established with the aim of prevention of environmental contamination through greater consideration of waste generation and energy consumption in design of buildings, processes, and products. Research was undertaken to identify and develop green design practices through a wide variety of activities. These range in scale from molecular research focused on development of environmentally benign oxidation processes, to component scale research related to materials selection in product design, to system scale research in green chemical/energy production process design and green building design, to community scale research on urban infrastructure design. Collectively, these efforts are described as the Green Design Initiative.

Energy is clearly a key issue in any consideration of sustainable practices. Carnegie Mellon has made, and continues to make, significant contributions in the study of environmental impacts of energy production, redesign of energy production processes to minimize such impacts, energy policy, energy use in buildings, and energy efficient technologies and systems for buildings and production plants. Research conducted in the College of Engineering has focused on fossil-fueled energy production processes, and has addressed advanced control technologies, pro-

< 224 >

cess optimization for waste minimization, alternative fuels, and other topics. The Center for Building Performance and Diagnostics (School of Architecture) has conducted path-breaking work on use of advanced technologies and system integration for energy conservation and design of sustainable buildings.

Environmental research at Carnegie Mellon, which has occurred mostly in the College of Engineering, has evolved with changes in national attitudes toward environmental protection. It began in the 1960s with a focus on control technology, to be applied "at the end of the pipe" of existing processes by environmental engineering specialists. By the 1990s the research agenda was moving toward pollution prevention, with involvement of engineers, scientists, and managers. This evolution has reflected our continually improving understanding of the complexity of causes of environmental degradation, and the distributed responsibility for prevention of environmental degradation.

PUBLIC INTEREST AND INVOLVEMENT IN ENVIRONMENTAL PROTECTION

New laws, agencies, and regulations have improved environmental quality markedly in the US since 1970, but the programs have been inefficient and have not always focused on the issues most in need of attention. A large reason for the inefficiency has been the public's lack of basic understanding of the issues and risks. In the United States and other democracies, public policies cannot stray far from what people accept and judge to be sound. For issues such as assistance to farmers or the amount of the minimum wage, Americans are generally knowledgeable and arrive at reasonably considered opinions, but the same is not true for environmental policies. A great deal of research at Carnegie Mellon and elsewhere has shown that the public does not think about environmental issues in the same way as scientists, that emotions run high, and that people do not feel confident in their judgments.

The limited ability of the public to evaluate environmental issues is becoming increasingly problematic because the importance of public participation for effective environmental decision making is now very clear. For example, a 1996 report by the National Research Council on the use of risk analysis in societal decision making calls for citizens to define the terms of risk analysis, in order that risk evaluation processes can be designed in the

< 225 >

way people want and will defend. If motivated, informed, and effective public participation is to be achieved, educated citizens must first understand environmental issues enough to care.

THE CAMPUS AS A MODEL ENVIRONMENTALLY SUSTAINABLE COMMUNITY

Exposure of large numbers of students to environmental issues and the personal role and stake that they have in these issues is difficult to achieve solely with curricular and research programs. Few students have the interest or opportunity to experience environmental research. Only limited coverage of environmental topics is possible in most courses except for those focused on environmental engineering, science, or policy. Further, the success of an environment across the curriculum program is dependent on the willingness, competence, and enthusiasm of a critical mass of faculty in an institution. This is difficult to maintain. As emphasized in a forward looking study by the National Science Board (2000), more widespread environmental education will require greater use of informal education methods such as science centers, zoos, aquariums, television, and other vehicles.

Carnegie Mellon and some other universities have recognized the opportunity to provide informal environmental education and to help lead society toward sustainable practices through implementation of sustainable living practices as a campus community (Keniry 1995, Dzombak et al. 1998). Campus green practices programs aim to encompass operation, design work, and research in the academic units and in facilities management, as well as student organizations and other grassroots efforts. Such programs provide credibility for the green practices and management techniques being developed and promoted by universities. These programs also provide opportunities for green design research and education efforts to use the campus as an experimental or demonstration site. Most important, these programs provide a means of universal environmental education for the students, staff, and faculty. Environmental education and research was included as a strategic area of focus in Carnegie Mellon's 1998 Strategic Plan (Dzombak et al. 1998), and an aggressive green practices program was identified as a key component of our environmental education and research efforts.

Green practice reforms are being explored in three general areas at Carnegie Mellon: campus life, facility infrastructure, and

< 226 >

transportation. Campus life opportunities pertain to the daily life of community members on campus, such as practices in dining services, recycling, and procurement. Widespread communication of green practices that have been implemented, and the need for community member cooperation and support of initiatives, are important parts of the campus life efforts. Facility infrastructure refers to buildings, grounds, and their management, including energy, water, and chemical use. Development of an energy management plan, implementation of green building design principles, and use of environmentally sensitive, low maintenance landscaping are examples of relevant infrastructure development and maintenance practices. Transportation pertains to all the travel activities of the campus community, including commuting, professional travel, and use of fleet vehicles on campus. There are significant opportunities for lessening environmental impact in all these areas, e.g., through use of public transportation, van pools, and vehicles that do not use gasoline as a fuel.

A committee comprising faculty, staff, administration, and student representatives leads the green practices program at Carnegie Mellon. There is strong commitment to and involvement in the program by the senior management of the University. The program aims to influence the campus community broadly and to provide environmental education to future generations of students at Carnegie Mellon, regardless of their field of study.

Conclusions and the Path Forward

The world's population faces serious regional and global environmental challenges in the 21st century. Most of these problems relate to inefficient and unsustainable resource use and economic development. The University has a critical role to play in leading society toward sustainable practices. All educated people must realize that human activities have the potential to jeopardize the planet's life support systems, and we must develop a shared responsibility for protecting the earth's resources. Because addressing environmental challenges requires widespread public recognition and support, progress will only be achieved through an educated citizenry. Specialists alone cannot move societies. The University needs to provide environmental education in some form to all students, in the same way that some basic concepts in the humanities (e.g., the importance of lessons of history, eco-

< 227 >

nomic systems, and cultural differences) are viewed as important in the higher education of any person. What is needed is the greening of the University.

There has been continually increasing environmental awareness over the past half century, but simultaneously there have been changes in society that increasingly disconnect people from the environment. The advent of the information age and its emphasis on virtual environments represents a powerful new force. Many educated people will have even fewer opportunities for interaction with the environment in the future than was the case in the past. There is a danger in this for us all. Telling in this regard were the remarks of Carnegie Mellon's Herbert Simon, Nobel Laureate and the Father of Artificial Intelligence, on the occasion of the opening of a new computer science building named in his honor: "We're not observers of the future. We're actors. Our task is to design a sustainable and acceptable world and bring it about. We must find a way for living at peace with all of nature and limit the total demands on the planet's resources. We must give up the false pride that views us as separate from nature." Universities are well positioned to meet this challenge. We must step up to the task.

References

Carson, R.L. (1962) *Silent Spring*. New York: Houghton Mifflin.

Collett, J., and S. Karakashian, eds. (1996) *Greening the College Curriculum*. Washington, DC: Island Press.

Dzombak, D., Collins, T., Davidson, C., Florida, R., Lave, L., Loftness, V., Minkley, N., and Tarr, J. (1998) "Strategy for Environmental Research and Education at Carnegie Mellon," Final Report to President Jared L. Cohon.

Farman, J.C., Gardiner, B.G., and Shanklin, J.D. (1985) "Large Losses of Total Ozone in Antarctica Reveal Seasonal ClOx/NOx Interaction," *Nature*. Volume 315, pp. 207–210.

Graedel, T.E. and Allenby, B.R. (1995) *Industrial Ecology*. Prentice Hall, Englewood Cliffs, New Jersey.

Keniry, J. (1995) *Ecodemia*. National Wildlife Federation, Washington, DC.

Lowrance, W.W. (1976) "DDT: An Archetypal Modern Problem," in *Of Acceptable Risk: Science and the Determination of Safety*. Los Altos, CA: W. Kaufmann, Inc. pp. 155–173.

Leopold, A. (1949) *A Sand County Almanac*, New York, New York: Oxford University Press.

< 228 >

Murozumi, M., Chow, T.J., and Patterson, C.C. (1969) "Chemical Concentrations of Pollutant Lead Aerosols, Terrestrial Dusts, and Sea Salt in Greenland and Antarctic Snow Strata," *Geochimica et Cosmochimica Acta*. Volume 33, pp. 1247–1294.

National Research Council (1996) "Understanding Risk: Informing Decisions in a Democratic Society," National Academy Press, Washington, DC.

National Science Board (2000) "Environmental Science and Engineering for the 21st Century," Report NSB 00–22, National Science Foundation.

Needleman, H.L., Gunnoe, C., Leviton, A., Reed, R., Peresie, H., Maher, C. and Barrett, P. (1979) "Deficits in Psychological and Classroom Performance of Children with Elevated Dentine Lead Levels." *New England Journal of Medicine*. Volume 300, pp. 689–695.

Nriagu, J.O. (1999) "Automotive Lead Pollution: Clair Patterson's Role in Stopping It," in Davidson, C.I. (Ed.) *Clean Hands: Clair Patterson's Crusade Against Environmental Lead Pollution*. Commack, NY: Nova Science Publishers. pp. 79–92.

Orr, D.W., *Ecological Literacy: Education and the Transition to a Postmodern World*, State University of New York Press, Albany, NY, 1992.

Rowland, F.S. (1989) "Chlorofluorocarbons and the Depletion of Stratospheric Ozone." *American Scientist*.Volume 77, pp. 36–45.

Rubin, E.S. (2001) *Introduction to Engineering and the Environment*. New York, New York: McGraw Hill.

Simon, H.A. (2000) Remarks presented at "earthware: a good world in 2050 . . . will computers help or hinder?", a symposium highlighting the opening of Newell-Simon Hall, *Carnegie Mellon News*, Vol. 8, No. 4, p. 12.

< 229 >

THE CAMPUS: CENTERED, DISTRIBUTED, AND VIRTUAL

Ömer Akin

Ömer Akin is Professor of Architecture in the School of Architecture at Carnegie Mellon. His main research interests are in the areas of design, cognition, and computation. Professor Akin earned his Ph.D. from Carnegie Mellon in 1979, and has been on the faculty for 24 years.

Today we are in the midst of the electronic revolution, palpably so at Carnegie Mellon. Increasingly, more of the information we generate is in electronic form. Also increasingly, more of the information generated in the past is being re-encoded in this form. Communication through electronics is pervading all channels: telephone, TV, Internet, buildings and everyday artifacts. This has led to new and better tools for processing information accurately and in real time. Carnegie Mellon is a prime exemplar of the information-rich and information-processing university.

All of this means that fundamental changes are taking place in the structures that accommodate the functions of the university. In order to communicate, we no longer need to be in the same space with others or even at the same time in different places (e-mail). We no longer have to go to the library to obtain the contents of publications (e-collections). We no longer have to commute to hold conferences (e-conferences). We no longer have to

< 231 >

search distributed sources to find comprehensive and accurate information (the Internet). Increasingly, we can do things from the comfort of our office or study without having to go to specific locations. Thus, the electronic revolution is already transforming the physical structure of the campus. How far will this go is a question we will address next, and first from a historical perspective.

The university campus, the single most important, physical organizing concept of an institution of higher learning, has evolved over several centuries. The campus provides an important indicator of the behavioral and functional aspects of the university. As the university of the future emerges, the campus will experience equally important transformations both accommodating and foretelling academic advances.

The campus is the primary physical manifestation of an institution of higher learning. It provides a setting for the university that enables appropriate activities of teaching, learning, research, and artistic exhibition and performance to take place. This setting is often critical in determining the extent to which these goals can succeed. At a minimum, the campus is a reflection, if not an instigator, of the quality of academic life. We can usually find evidence of research capabilities by observing the setup of laboratory space and equipment. We may gauge the importance placed on teaching through the physical conditions of classrooms and faculty offices. Quality of life on campus can be surmised from the facilities allocated to recreation and outdoor life. The physical structure of the campus, then, is an important factor in the evolution of the university. So, let us begin by going through a brief history of the campus with an eye to the ways in which the functional needs of the university have been met.

The History of the Campus

The concept of the campus dates back to Carolingian monasteries and Muslim *medrese* of the eight h and ninth centuries. In these religious settings, associated with libraries and archives, resided scribes and scholars. In early medieval times, the critical factor for an academic function was the collection of information in one location, under the patronage of royalty and in the service of organized religion. In terms of physical facilities, this amounted to individual rooms or buildings. Obviously this is a far cry from our current notion of a campus.

< 232 >

The earliest advancement in the facilities of academic institutions came during the urbanization of Europe in the 12th and 13th centuries, paralleling other institutional advancements. The first "university" was born in Bologna. This was an international, democratic institution with no campus but a lively, youthful, urban existence in rented and borrowed facilities. This gave the institution an integrated urban life and freedom from facility caretakership. Private residences served as meeting places. Public halls accommodated large lectures. Rented "halls" or "hostels" were run under the "dictum of Masters." Students lodged with townsfolk.

In later versions of the university, for example at the Sorbonne in Paris as well as the *medrese* in Al-Azhar Mosque in Cairo, the role of the library became more central. In 1379, the first campus quadrangle was conceived in the New College at Oxford, marking the beginning of the integrated collection of academic buildings around open spaces, which has remained in currency until our day. During the Renaissance, the university flourished through academies of higher learning in the West, especially in Italy, and the *kulliye* incorporated the *medrese* into the royal mosque of the Ottomans (Kostof 1985).

New World colonization since the 17th century, principally in North America, has brought to us many innovations in architecture and planning, and these have affected the design and physical structure of the campus. In 1650 we see the establishment of Harvard University in a small town near Boston named Cambridge in intentional reference to the peer institution located in England.

Thomas Jefferson created one of the most influential designs in the history of campus planning, in 1817–1826. Using one of the primary planning strategies of the day, Jefferson allocated the departments of the university to pavilions arranged along both sides of an axis marked at one end by the rotunda, containing the library. This design at once acknowledged the architectural center of the university in its library and articulated the new form of the university as a collection of many disciplines. These components were integrated into the structure of the quadrangle. The strength of this design identified the idea of the university with a planned physical campus—a model that continues to inspire architects, designers and planners. In the 19th century, the United States federal government seeded the development of land-grant institutions, which provided the new nation with dozens of newly designed campuses.

< 233 >

The campus quad in its many guises and compound agglomerations helps structure small and large, rural and urban, new and old universities all over the world. As the university has developed into the universal home for an immense variety of teaching and research activities, the quad has become its single most effective planning element. The quad is composed of the universal modules (buildings) from which one can create the entire campus. These modules can be individually defined to represent academic units while their composition is endowed with essential properties governing the functions of the entire quad. One of these properties, and a critical one, is the coordination between a campus plan and scheduling of classes.

In the cost-conscious contemporary university, a central activity is to coordinate the serving of the largest number of students by the smallest number of faculty, without sacrificing quality. An important vehicle for this is to schedule classes so that faculty can deliver their courses and students can attend their selection of subjects without time conflicts. Furthermore, faculty and students need to move efficiently from classroom to classroom. This makes "campus travel distance" a determining design criterion (Akin 1972). In other words, the most remote classrooms on a campus cannot be farther than the ten-minute walking distance, which is the typical break time between classes.

This tends to make the typical campus flat, in order to eliminate vertical travel time, and relatively small, within the ten-minute walking distance diameter. One way of avoiding these constraints is to have longer breaks between classes, but this is inefficient use of time. Another option is to have mentors or "masters" run one-on-one meetings with students instead of formal classes, as is the case in the traditional English college. Today, for obvious reasons, very few universities can afford to do this. A third option is to create a conglomeration of multiple campuses, as is the case at many public universities in the United States. This tends to work against achieving closer integration between different academic disciplines. Due to these disadvantages, the "ideal" campus tends to adhere to strict restrictions of spatial size.

In summary, the typical campus concept that has emerged during the past few centuries of evolution is a location-driven, relatively flat, conglomeration of specialized buildings, arranged around quads over relatively small expanses of land. Multiple quads can be appended together to accommodate larger institu-

< 234 >

tional agendas or to disaggregate functional specializations such as the residential, recreational and academic.

FUNCTION OF THE CAMPUS

The central function of the campus is to accommodate those activities that are indispensable for a university. Arguably, these indispensable functions are *acquisition* and *dissemination* of knowledge. This implies a variety of concerted efforts between faculty and students as well as within faculty and student groups, such as laboratory research, projects, lectures, discussions, seminars, and other academic meetings. Supporting this set of activities is the raison d'être of any university. Once a campus comes into existence, other behaviors emerge almost spontaneously and mostly out of necessity. The inhabitants of the campus engage in residential functions, social interaction, the maintenance of their physical well-being, and, most importantly, creation and sustenance of an academic ethos. In most cases, the functions of a campus go further and end up being equivalent to those of a small "community." Typically this includes a police force for security, building crews for construction, maintenance crews for landscaping, clerical staff for administration, medical staff for health care, and a small fleet of vehicles for local transportation. It is virtually impossible to distinguish these functions from those of a small town or neighborhood.

These functions are neither simple nor static. They belong to a growing and evolving set. The dynamism is not solely due to the evolving purposes of a university campus but also to its growing and evolving physical structure. In the early academies, where meetings were held in rented or borrowed space, security, maintenance, and even administrative responsibilities were minimal or non-existent. When ownership became a normal function of an institution of higher learning, so did the responsibilities of real estate maintenance. Still, campuses in Europe, the Middle East, and the Far East existed only in the context of major urban settings. For most support facilities such as lodging, food and entertainment, academics relied on the functions of the city.

Even today there are many urban campuses, both in the United States and elsewhere, that rely on public amenities for most support functions. In fact, due to the emergence of modern forms of commercial enterprise, some of the traditional functions such as sale of food, merchandise, and textbooks can be sourced

< 235 >

out to independent vendors. In the case of the self-contained campus (urban or rural), the trend is in the reverse direction. More and more activities are included in the campus setting, making it a true microcosm of a normal community. Bilkent University, located near Ankara, Turkey, has taken this trend further than any other example I know. It houses, both physically and administratively, several factories, hotels and one of the largest, and most successful suburban shopping malls in Turkey. These commercial sources of revenue are clearly too tempting for the university administration to pass up.

It is this kind of symbiosis between the function, structure, and behavior of the campus that makes it difficult to characterize in normative terms. Each historical period brings with it a context that flavors this relationship differently. The medieval campus was a creature of necessity, created from a ragtag combination of urban structures to serve the emerging purposes of academia. Thus it was urban, distributed, and heterogeneous. The university of the 17th and 18th centuries was also urban but it was by and large self-sufficient, with a diverse set of functions housed in an increasingly homogenized physical setting. The most recent campus design concepts of the 19th and 20th centuries, particularly in the United States, have gone a long way in making the self-sufficient campus model context-independent. One can find this model in the suburbs as one would in the heart of an urban area, with equal likelihood. The functions of the contemporary campus are so diverse and substantial that they have established the space and design of the campus as the most characteristic representation of the modern university.

STRUCTURE OF THE NEW CAMPUS

The principal purposes of the campus setting are the collection and concentration of information. The university had emerged in the collection of books and the concentration of scholars in mosques, monasteries, and palaces. As the university matured so did its physical campus. Early on, ownership of a collection of buildings in an urban setting sufficed. It provided adequate control for the scheduling of relevant academic activities. The urban setting provided all of life's amenities not present in academic buildings. Supported in these buildings and extending the diverse set of life's functions into the realm of learning and discovery, the university functioned.

< 236 >

Next came the need to create an integral environment. First in the urban, then in the suburban setting, the "integrated campus" became synonymous with the ethos and ethics of learning and research. This ushered in diversity of building types, ranging from the dormitory to the fraternity house and from the library to the laboratory.

Today, mostly owing to historical circumstance, we find a range of different models for the integrated campus setting. Some are integrated with urban environments, playing town-and-gown games with municipal and commercial properties and interests. Others are independent, suburban college "towns" constituting the essential draw for all of their inhabitants. Yet others started as suburban campuses, which due to rapid growth or encroachment of urban sprawl, find themselves nestled in urban contexts as they continue to maintain an independent, integrated campus setting. Carnegie Mellon has the advantages of an urban setting such as easy access through public transportation to major concert halls and theaters, but it has the sequestered feel of a suburban campus, protected by a beautiful adjoining public park and walking access to privileged residential neighborhoods.

Throughout this evolution, the governing factor for the physical campus has been the concentration of information or knowledge at a physical location. Concentrations of faculty, who, today, have become the true repository of information, play the role that the medieval library used to play. This indicates a trend for the campus that is increasingly determined by the location of the faculty. The concept of the virtual university, which in fact had been played out decades ago through the examples of the Open University and the Free University, illustrates this best. It is certainly possible to create a conduit between the knowledge possessed by the faculty and students who seek it. In this case the campus is nonphysical. Even the faculty can be remotely located.

The new arrangement of distributed information, faculty and students, brought together only through the Internet or an equivalent electronic physical structure raises the possibility of the distributed campus, or no campus at all. In this model the conduit performs the functions of the campus, minimizing the maintenance of auxiliary structures that are necessary in a campus environment. For example, the duplication of residential facilities, at home and at the dorm, eating facilities, at the dining room and at the cafeteria, can be eliminated. This helps cut costs. The cost of education, which has skyrocketed during the second half of the 20th century, can now be brought down again. Ironically, this has

< 237 >

the prospect of bringing the campus setting full circle to its medieval origins: a distributed campus with little or no physical infrastructure.

Let us assume that the new campus provides the newest and best forms of electronic storage retrieval and communication of information to support the traditional functions of the university. What kinds of new behaviors would we expect to see in such a setting and how would the existing behaviors be affected by all of this? Let us speculate for a moment without heed for caution or convention.

The Internet can support many functions that have traditionally been delegated to the classroom. Class notes can be downloaded. Exercises and homework assignments can be submitted and evaluated electronically. Faculty-student interaction can be managed by software. Students can collaborate and exchange ideas through e-boards and e-mail. Laboratory experiments can be simulated. Designs can be developed, submitted and reviewed on computer-assisted design (CAD) platforms. Management games can be played to understand marketplace force.

Most administrative functions of the university are also now done electronically. Student testing, application, enrollment, registration, grading, transcript requests, payroll, benefits, reimbursements, purchases, and many other administrative functions have already been automated. The list can be easily expanded. Conference calls made between administrators, faculty, students, and parents can replace face-to-face meetings. Strategic plans can be debated and negotiated online. The "electronic town hall" hype perpetrated by politicians can become the reality of the high-tech faculty senate.

All of these are developments that can provide options for the campus community to function in the collective while spending increasingly more time in individual, personal spaces. Of course there are other location-specific innovations that can change campus design without isolating the occupants of the campus in individual cells. New technology in robotics and intelligent buildings can endow spaces with e-intelligence. Sensors can detect human dialogue and assist in managing the conference process just as they can temperature, daylight, or acoustic levels of a conference room, adjusting the environment to suit occupants' needs. The million-dollar question, as far as this chapter is concerned, is whether these changes will transform the university campus as we know it or fizzle out, as did the "paperless office."

< 238 >

There is no question that new technology changes old behaviors, but often in ways contrary to pundits' predictions. It is indeed the case that the "paperless office" prediction never materialized. However, today's office is a far cry from the electric typewriter-driven office of the '60s and the '70s. More people write their own text than hand it over to someone else to type. This has dramatically changed the quality, speed, and form of communication. Today, there is just as much, if not more, paper as back then, but the ratio of information to paper is probably a better indicator of the word processor's impact. We have online access to much more information, more accurately and quickly than we ever had on paper. Modification of data in existing documentation is considerably easier.

In other words, technology causes change and improves productivity. However, these changes do not come in the form of one-to-one substitutes for older forms of technology, and their precise effects are unpredictable. With these cautions in mind, I will stick my neck out and make some predictions about the campus of the future.

Campus facilities

Let us accept the prediction that more of what we do manually and collectively will be done electronically. However, not all face-to-face interactions will disappear. In fact, the quality of interactions may well be enhanced and intensified, while the quantity goes down. This is analogous to the widespread use of the personal motor vehicle, which did not stop us from taking walks. But now we take more walks recreationally than we do to buy groceries and household goods.

We will do more teaching electronically. Course materials will be distributed through websites. Assignments will be collected and evaluated electronically. Course material in content and in form will become standard in more cases. Routine student interactions will be relegated to the Web. In fact, all routine tasks of teaching are likely to be handled electronically. Lectures, in turn, will cede ground to recitations, seminars, and in-class discussions. These functional and behavioral changes will have important impacts on the structure of the future campus.

We will need fewer large, auditorium-type classroom spaces and more seminar, recitation, and meeting spaces. These spaces will have to be constructed with a lot of technical sophistication.

< 239 >

Cabling, electronic input-output, and large electronic display surfaces will become standard. Spaces will become smarter, participating in the regulation of environmental conditions and managing information capture and dissemination.

We will need more humanely designed, user-responsive computer clusters and hubs. Today these spaces are arranged in the most utilitarian manner with no regard for occupant interaction. In order to encourage interaction and collaboration between users in these spaces, social clustering will once again become a design consideration.

We will be able to do more research online. In researching specific knowledge areas and writing papers, location in relation to the library building will not be nearly as critical as it used to be. Course preparation is in a similar boat. Gathering the most recent materials for lectures and exercises will increasingly become an activity that can be limited to the scanner, the keyboard, and the monitor. This will place greater emphasis on livable, comfortable and technically sophisticated individual spaces (i.e., faculty, staff, and student offices—yes, students will need offices as well) and smaller, collective ones (i.e., libraries, laboratories, and classrooms). The simulated laboratory is not likely to overtake the manual one; but the management of space and equipment in the traditional library will improve, and space needs will diminish for printed material storage.

We will do more electronic informing, selecting, and negotiating. For example, for students, early stages of job search and placement will be done through websites. For faculty and staff, senate meetings—where attendance is always limited and the debate limitless—will benefit from the electronic town hall meetings. Many such functions will be consolidated into information management centers administered centrally and accessed locally.

This will affect the distribution of space in relation to the organizational chart of the institution. Instead of keeping departments in separate clusters for ease of face-to-face communication, other criteria will play a greater role in the spatial distribution of staff. For example, specialists in different departments (accountants, secretaries, and directors) may be grouped together and away from their individual departments.

This consolidation of functions will also have an important impact on the physical structure of the campus. Administrative spaces will become less specialized by application area (departments) and more by specialization domain (skill). Economies realized through the clustering of personnel will translate into less

< 240 >

administrative staff and space. An undesirable effect of this may be greater hierarchical clustering.

Social and recreation spaces will become more critical. Meetings will be called only when necessary (one would wish) since routine interactions can be satisfied in the distributed milieu. Thus when called, meetings will need more amenities such as those for easy information access and sophisticated communication. Diminished need for meetings will lead to fewer but better equipped meeting rooms (quality over quantity).

With the ubiquitous computer, hardware and software maintenance facilities will become ubiquitous as well. This, at a minimum, is a new space need. Ideally these facilities and the personnel they support will become an integral part of central as well as distributed units of the university. An important agenda item for this part of the organization will be how to deal with obsolescence of technology and even techno-fatigue. The concept of maintenance will include recycling of material as well as reconditioning of people affected by technology. There can be a close connection between this and recreation, sports and entertainment facilities on a campus. This will affect how designers consider such spaces.

Social interaction will gain greater importance. Longer hours before the computer can be balanced with more face-to-face interaction at other times. Recreation in the form of sports and entertainment will become even more important for the well-being of members of the academic community. This will counteract the disconnection created by the long hours spent in the office. Greater awareness of healthful self-maintenance will also spur on this trend.

From all of this, a new model of the university emerges where the types of facilities that support the central mission of knowledge acquisition and dissemination will be mingled with those of socialization and recreation. Instead of specializing buildings into discrete and homogeneous functions like the library, laboratory and the lecture hall, we will need to create hybrid units that resemble the early English college model. The universal module of the campus—buildings—will become diversified facilities to support all kinds of behaviors: work, entertainment, sports, dining, studying, and residential life.

Faculty, staff and students will be free to organize their academic responsibilities through electronic media rather than spatially. This will provide opportunities for them to affiliate their location with those parts of the campus environment that they

< 241 >

find conducive to their personal growth. A faculty office may be located along the park adjoining the campus. There may be adjoining student offices for those who share career similarities with the faculty, while staff members who work with the faculty and the students may choose to be closer to the gym.

Campus planning

Things will also be different from a larger, planning perspective. The historical campus had a physical order that can best be described as a "location-bound information-centric" arrangement. The electronic revolution suggests a physical setting that is information-centric, but not *necessarily location-bound. This is a fundamental change for the physical constitution of a campus. In location-bound settings, occupants are obligated to reside at designated locations in order to access appropriate information. In non-location-bound settings, they can access appropriate information from any location (ideally) or from a number of different locations (realistically). This can change the physical constitution of the entire campus plan.*

In the locally bound campus we have observed the critical role of the ten-minute walking distance as a determinant of horizontal sprawl and institutional scale. In the non-locally-bound campus the spatial contiguity constraint can be replaced by the temporal. One can be at different locations, but a conference call or an electronic class meeting still requires co-temporality. Then the design of the future campus will reflect the order of the temporal and not the spatial. Direct communication will require time synchrony, but not spatial contiguity—a modality match, not face-to-face interaction. All of these considerations suggest new design principles that take advantage of other resources in the context of the campus such as natural beauty, residential stock, commercial strip, and so on.

There are important infrastructure implications as well. As buildings become smarter, they will be capable of using less energy, if not generating surplus energy. As a result, some of the infrastructure constraints keeping them in close proximity, like steam and electrical lines, will no longer be there. While telecommunication cabling will become more important, wireless technologies, like those widely used at Carnegie Mellon, will overcome this constraint as well. This also will help release proximity constraints between buildings and allow the campus to become more integrated with its physical context.

In conclusion, with greater diversity in academic units and less need for intra-building commuting, the age of "wider" and

< 242 >

"taller" campus facilities may be dawning. This means that campuses may be spread over greater areas than the ten-minute walking distance diameter and in buildings taller than the walk-up (five to six stories), without sacrificing either human social interaction or collaboration among those in different disciplines. The time of "situated" campus design, integrated with its larger context, seems to have arrived.

References

Akin, Ö. (1973) "Contextual fittingness of everyday activity encounters" in Preiser, Wolfgang F. E. (ed.) *Environmental Design Research*. Stroudsburg, PA: Dowden Hutchinson & Ross, Inc., Volume 1, 123–137.

Kostoff, S. (1985) *The History of Architecture, Settings and Rituals*. New York: Oxford University Press.

Wilson, R. G. (ed.) (1993) *Thomas Jefferson's Academical Village: The Creation of an Architectural Masterpiece* / Bayly Art Museum of the University of Virginia, Charlottesville, VA: University Press of Virginia.

< 243 >

APPLIED ETHICS IN A DIGITAL AGE

Robert Cavalier

Robert Cavalier is Senior Lecturer in Philosophy at Carnegie Mellon, and is affiliated with the Center for the Advancement of Applied Ethics on campus. He is a winner of the Elliott Dunlap Smith Award for Distinguished Teaching and Educational Service and is known for his work in ethics education and interactive multimedia. Professor Cavalier earned his Ph.D. from Duquesne University in 1978, and has been at Carnegie Mellon for 16 years.

The history of ethics in Western Philosophy begins auspiciously with the interest of Socrates in matters pertaining to human affairs. His questions about goodness and justice set into motion a narrative about the methods of answering the "practical" question—What ought I to do?—that continues to this day. Part of any introductory course in ethics will no doubt touch upon the main figures in this conversation, covering Plato and Aristotle, Augustine and Aquinas, Hume and Kant, Bentham, Mill and others up to the turn of the 20th century. Once we reach G.E. Moore's *Principia Ethica* (1903), however, a change in approach to the study of ethics in Anglo-American universities takes hold. The study of ethics no longer focuses on the nature of moral character and the incentives to be moral, nor has an interest in establishing a foundational normative theory leading to policy- or action-guides. Moore argued that we first need to clear up the meaning of our

< 245 >

words and understand better the conceptual scope and limits of the language of morals itself. This meta-ethical approach to ethics is achieved through the "analytic turn" in ethics. And this approach to ethics becomes the dominant approach for both scholars and teachers throughout most of the 20th century. It is reflected in the books and articles of the time, including textbooks containing excerpts from ongoing debates in scholarly journals.

During the 1960s and 1970s a change of direction again occurs. The change is occasioned by, for instance, crises arising in America's hospital wards. An unexpected confluence of advances in medical technology and a growing patients' rights movement brought about cases in which it was no longer clear whether keeping a terminally ill patient alive through medical devices was really preserving the person's life or prolonging the person's death. People of good will had sincere disagreements over what ought to be done, and ethical guidance was sought. With the establishment of the Hastings Center (1969) and Georgetown's Kennedy Institute of Ethics (1971), the turn in applied ethics began, as professional philosophers sought to address these concrete issues. But as these philosophers soon discovered, applied ethics involves more than the straightforward application of ethical theory. If meta-ethics is a reflection upon the scope and limits of ethics itself (e.g., analyses of ethical relativism) and if normative ethics seeks general theories that provide substantial action guides (like the anthologized versions of Kant's Categorical Imperative or Bentham's Principle of Utility), applied ethics focuses on domain-specific areas like medicine, business, and engineering. Ethical analyses in these domains require a level of detail not available to the general theorist.

Organizing topics in the area of medical ethics along principles such as respect for patient autonomy and the professional duties of a doctor to help and not harm a patient constitute one manner in which applied ethics approaches a particular discipline. These principles can constitute the rationale for a professional code of conduct as well as provide guidelines for approaching particular cases.

Now, in order to appreciate the move of applied ethics into the digital age, we need to appreciate the "computational turn" occurring across the disciplines. We also need to appreciate Carnegie Mellon's educational computing environment itself. Since the emergence of educational computing, from the visionary work of Patrick Suppes at Stanford in the 1970s through the pioneering efforts of EDUCOM award winners in the 1980s and

< 246 >

the new web-based course applications of today, there has been an ever increasing computational turn in both teaching and research.

In 1983, Carnegie Mellon initiated a major commitment to support both a computing infrastructure across the campus and a venue for educational computing. The infrastructure was created by the Andrew Project, and the first efforts in educational technology were coordinated through the InterUniversity Consortium for Educational Computing (ICEC). The consortium consisted of a number of first and second tier universities with flagship centers at Dartmouth, Stanford, Brown, and, of course, Carnegie Mellon.

By the late 1980s, Carnegie Mellon's Center for Design of Educational Computing (CDEC) produced and worked on a number of major software programs in areas such as physics, aesthetics, history, and ethics. As specialized educational computing centers dissolved into discipline- and department-based initiatives, general support for educational computing focused on instructional technology's classroom infrastructure as well as college and university-based resources. The latter includes the TElab and the newly introduced Office of Technology for Education. All in all, Carnegie Mellon provides a world-class environment for educational computing. As such, it exhibits leadership in the computational turn that is occurring across the disciplines.

This turn is both broad and deep. In my own discipline of philosophy, for instance, traditional areas such as logic, epistemology, and ethics have witnessed new trends and seen new opportunities. In logic, the 19th- and 20th-century evolution of symbolic logic now dovetails with work in computer science, and the teaching of logic incorporates graphically rich programs like Turing's World and intelligent tutors like CMU Proof Tutor. The area of epistemology has been heavily impacted by the project of artificial intelligence. Clark Glymour's introductory philosophy book, *Thinking Things Through*, illustrates this turn in a rigorous way, as does his co-editing of *Android Epistemology*. Things have advanced to the point where those wishing to specialize in epistemology must now be familiar with articles on neural networking and with aspects of Bayesian statistical analysis. There is a need to reconfigure the undergraduate philosophy curriculum in order to bring in more training in the social decision sciences. At Carnegie Mellon we are addressing this need through the development of a web-based course in causal reasoning (see Glymour and Scheines, pp. 259–269).

< 247 >

Taken as a whole, the Department of Philosophy embodies this computational turn in teaching and research. And it is certainly not alone as a department here at Carnegie Mellon. In what follows, I will first look a little deeper at this computational turn from the perspective of the area of applied ethics[1] and then I will explore the broader impact of educational computing on new curricular initiatives before returning again to the area of applied ethics.

To begin with, work at Carnegie Mellon's Center for the Advancement of Applied Ethics (CAAE) dovetails with renewed interest in case-based moral reasoning. In 1988 Jonsen and Toulmin published *The Abuse of Casuistry*, a book that rekindled interest in the philosophical tradition of case-based moral reasoning. There are three main theses in their book. First, they argue that the emphasis on general theoretical moral principles, and the belief that an algorithmic application of those principles to each and every 'species' of moral action is possible, has distorted both our sense of ethics and our ability to deal convincingly with difficult moral choices. Second, they recognize that while there exists a clear and unambiguous set of moral paradigms (prototypical cases of good and evil; *prima facie* duties arising from such cases), there also exists a host of historically contingent cases in which such paradigms come into conflict or are marginally and ambiguously applicable. These two points provide a way for avoiding the dual trappings of moral absolutism and ethical relativism. Finally, they argue that reflection upon the tradition of "casuistry" and its background sources in the ethics of Aristotle and the rhetoric of Cicero can stimulate a fresh approach to both contemporary moral philosophy and present day discussions in applied ethics.[2]

In "Getting Down to Cases: The Revival of Casuistry in Bioethics,"[3] John Arras forcefully stresses the *pedagogical role* that case studies play in applied ethics. And certainly part of that role highlights Aristotle's concept of "practical wisdom"—the need to grasp the detailed complexity of particular circumstances in order to aim at the best human understanding of the issues at hand.[4]

At the University of Pittsburgh's Learning Research and Development Center (LRDC), Kevin Ashley and Matthew Keefer explore this element of practical wisdom in case analysis studies. Following the tradition of Kohlberg and Gilligan in Moral Psychology, they performed a number of empirical studies on how people actually reason about moral problems. In one study, students from high school and students taking a graduate course in

< 248 >

medical ethics were given a number of ethical situations and asked to analyze them. One situation describes a doctor's desire to keep a patient suffering from hypertension in the hospital a few days beyond the official coverage of her insurance company. The study, published in the 1996 proceedings of the Cognitive Science Society, showed that the "novice" group tended to discuss the case along the lines of very general rules or consequences. But many of the graduate ethics students, those exposed to cases and stories of actual hospital situations, adopted what Ashley and Keefer call "Role Specific Obligations" (RSO). This latter group exhibited a greater degree of ingenuity in brainstorming solutions (e.g., trying to find existing 'hardship' funds to pay for the patient's stay) than the less experienced group. While cases were not explicitly mentioned in their analyses, the kind of "practical wisdom" one would expect from a knowledge of many different experiences was present. This is most clearly seen in the level of sophistication contained in the RSO analyses. The study concludes: ". . . posing the hypothetical conditions pursuant to the RSO Strategy requires more expert knowledge in the relevant domain of practice . . . domain specific knowledge is a prerequisite for greater sensitivity to a dilemma's circumstances and enables greater specificity and articulation . . ."[5]

How is it that cases enter into our practical wisdom and help us analyze moral problems? One answer links rich case descriptions with *the role of narrative in human understanding*. As research in Cognitive Science reveals, we learn through stories. Stories become part of our cognitive grasp of life. This is seen in the early work of Roger Schank when he uses "scripts" to mimic human intelligence in the test case of "ordering food from a restaurant menu." Lately, Schank has added interactive multimedia and embedded his theory in learning environments.[6] Whether about learning to be a sea captain, a water company employee, or advisor to a president during a foreign policy crisis, role-based scenarios using rich case studies and much storytelling provide a powerful way to learn and quickly gain practical wisdom within specific learning domains.

Mark Johnson, in his book, *Moral Imagination: Implications of Cognitive Science for Ethics*, argues further that an important dimension of our lives can be described as having a narrative structure. Narratives help us learn "about what it means to be human, about the contingencies of life, about the kinds of lives we most want to lead, and about what is involved in trying to lead such lives . . ."[7]

< 249 >

And this is where interactive multimedia as productive art comes into play. The Ancients divided the spheres of human activity into the Theoretical, Practical and Productive (the first includes Science, the second includes Ethics, and the third includes Rhetoric and Theatre). In line with this ancient lineage, the phrase "Productive Art" has its etymological roots in the Greek terms *poeisis* and *techne*. Someone thus skilled in the "productive arts" will have the craftsmanship to create works that address, in the context of this discussion, the *poetics of life*—the drama of the lived world in all its richness and complexity.

This understanding of the productive arts informs the design and implementation of interactive multimedia at our Center. Since the late 1980s, the Center has sought to advance the field of applied ethics through the thoughtful use and development of technology. From videodiscs to CD-ROMs and web-based environments, our interactive multimedia case studies explore contemporary social issues as well as the principles of conflict resolution that can often be used to address those controversies in both private and public life. Project THEORIA: Testing Hypotheses in Ethics: Observation, Reality, Imagination, and Affect is the flagship title that guides the development of our work.[8] We seek to provide a theatre wherein to test various theories and hypotheses relating to concrete case studies. The studies themselves incorporate narrative and thick description and place a high value on reflective engagement.

One of the first multimedia programs we developed was based on a famous case in Medical Ethics. The case allowed us to explore this new medium as a pedagogical tool and also to embark upon a formal, quantitative assessment of the interactive multimedia treatment of the case itself.

The CD-ROM, *A Right to Die? The Dax Cowart Case* (Routledge 1996), investigates a burn patient's request to be allowed to die. The case relates the story of a 25-year-old man who received second- and third-degree burns over two thirds of his body. At the time that we encounter Dax in treatment, his injuries have left him severely scarred, his hands are badly deformed, and the sight in his one remaining eye is at risk. As a patient, he undergoes daily treatments in an antiseptic tank that are so painful to him that he has persistently asked the doctors to stop his treatment. Dax feels that the projected length of his treatment and the quality of life that he can expect to regain do not warrant the torment he must suffer. The doctors know that if they continue his treatment, he will live; if they stop his treatment, he will surely die. A

< 250 >

basic question posed at this point of impasse between Dax and his caregivers is: Does Dax have a right to die? And, if so, what does this mean?

Traditional approaches to this kind of case study often rely on a four- or five-paragraph case study. The study is treated as an example to be discussed within the framework of prior readings and is used to test the analytical skills of the student and to explore the relation between the general and the particular. But one pressing problem with a "case summary" is the discrepancy between its description and its reality.[9] The palpable complexity of real life situations seems to recede in the textbook overview of such cases—hence, the attempt to introduce reality into the context of case studies through the thoughtful use of interactive multimedia.

Harvard's Derek Bok once claimed that while computers may be useful in areas of data and calculation, they are ill-equipped to handle the often open-ended areas of the humanities. But shift the paradigm of "computing" away from the command screen terminal to a system that displays all kinds of information, including visually rich information, and computers might indeed address some important issues like those raised in the case of Dax Cowart. The reason lies in the ability of "multimedia" to convey "rich data" in the form of, for example, personal narratives and realistic settings. Furthermore, the *interactive* aspect of computer-mediated multimedia utilized in this program is used to engage the student's reasoning process, eliciting active reflection.

Structurally, the CD-ROM provides flexible navigation through the central, and often competing, issues of the case. In a Guided Inquiry section, users take a semi-Socratic tour of the case from the bare facts to a confrontation with doctors, patient and other principals over the issues of Medical Professionals' Obligations, Pain of Treatment, Quality of Life, and Patient's Rights and Capacities. At the end, a decision must be made as to whether Dax should be granted his request. Final sequences are determined on the basis of this recommendation.

An Archive section contains video excerpts on the principals and main issues as well as descriptions of other cases (e.g., Karen Quinlan). Recent state and federal court decisions on issues like physician-assisted suicide are also included.

To test the usefulness of this approach to the case—and its effect on the learning process—a series of formative and summative evaluation studies have been implemented. The purpose of our study was to see if learning outcomes for case studies

< 251 >

were enhanced by the use of interactive multimedia. We divided my Introduction to Ethics class into three groups: Text, Film, and CD-ROM. A stratified and controlled sample for each group was achieved through the use of student scores on previous exams and student SAT (verbal) scores. Each group was given a functionally equivalent representation of the case and allowed 1.5 hours to study it. The text group used a narrative and selected articles on the case; the film group viewed a 60-minute documentary; and the CD-ROM group was given selections from the Guided Inquiry and Archive sections of the interactive CD-ROM. The following day the students were given an in-class questionnaire dealing with the principals in the case and the issues in the case. The group that worked with interactive CD-ROM performed significantly better on the tests. (See "Learning, Media, and the Case of Dax Cowart: A Comparison of Text, Film, and Interactive Multimedia" in *Interactive Learning Environments*—Forthcoming.)

Because the study utilized those aspects of the CD-ROM that focused on *reflective engagement*, the results of the study have broader implications for interactive multimedia as such. We conclude that any similarly designed multimedia environment that provides both rich description and reflective opportunity will outperform text and film presentations of the case material. This is not to say that such environments will replace critical argument and background literature, but that they are effective tools in providing users with a concrete understanding of the case material that is being discussed.

Our recent work explores case studies in ways that take true advantage of the new medium. In line with the writings of Janet Murray (*Shakespeare on the Holodeck: The Future of Narrative in Cyberspace*) and Brenda Laurel (*Computers as Theatre*), programs like *Allwyn Hall* and *In All Respects*—described below—seek to immerse the user in a role that itself is played within the stage of human computer interaction.

The first program, *Allwyn Hall*, places the user in the role of a Resident Assistant who must manage several conflicts occurring in a student dorm (conflicts such as roommates arguing over cleaning up the room and borrowing toiletries). The second program, *In All Respects*, explores one aspect of conflict resolution (that of active listening) by placing the user in the role of a documentary film producer who must make a film dealing with the topic of racism on campus.

With these new multimedia simulations, *the* case becomes *my* case—the human-computer interaction brings the viewer,

< 252 >

through immersion and agency, into the representation of a reality. Multiple outcomes (traditionally called "flying wedges") serve to create experiences of resolving a conflict or producing a documentary. And just as flight simulators provide pilots with the critical skills necessary to get into a real plane, so too we might envision simulated case studies that enter into the practical wisdom of a person as he or she encounters the details of an interpersonal conflict or the subtleties of racial or sexual stereotyping.

But the design and development of these kinds of programs require new ways of communication and familiarity with the tools of multimedia development. These approaches to human-computer interaction will also require a new curriculum. Hence, the appearance over the past few years of Carnegie Mellon courses like "Multimedia Authoring," "Interactive Design," and "Building Virtual Worlds." Some professionals coming from this new curriculum—Murray calls them interactive designers—will become the faculty teaching these courses in the future.

As just indicated, the digital age has set into motion profound curricular changes at our Carnegie Mellon. I shall focus here on the minor in Multimedia Production and the major in Human Computer Interaction. The overall mission of the minor is to provide students with theoretical as well as technical knowledge relating to the design and development of interactive multimedia. The intellectual content of the core courses separates the minor from the purely technical aspects of a vocational curriculum. To be sure, there are tools and techniques learned and used in each course, and the final course is a capstone in which students sometimes work with faculty as clients to create Web pages and modules for CD-ROMs. And it is interesting to see how many students enter Carnegie Mellon already knowing the basics of Adobe Photoshop, Adobe Premiere, Macromedia Director, or HTML, much the way students in the early 1990s knew MS Word or Excel. But the minor in Multimedia Production emphasizes the role of the medium in a liberal arts curriculum. In this context, multimedia authoring echoes aspects of the traditional medieval *trivium*: grammar, rhetoric, and logic.[10]

The core courses for the minor come from the English and Philosophy Departments, and students from the minor appreciate the aspects of reflection and communication that form a key premise in the design of the curriculum. These courses also play a role in the Information Systems major within the College of Humanities and Social Sciences, where they form a track in Communication Design. The new major in Human Computer Inter-

< 253 >

action, on the other hand, recognizes the emerging science of its own interdisciplinary field. This is a field in which computer scientists, engineers, psychologists, social scientists, and design professionals play important roles. The main purpose of this field is to solve real problems in the design and human use of technology. To do this, students are offered courses in human behavior, design, computer science, statistics, and evaluation.

Returning to the field of Applied Ethics, we can now see how students familiar with the content of the new curriculum can contribute to the creation of multimedia case studies across the traditional curriculum. The Ethical Decision Making project,[11] for example, is designed to assist in the development and integration of models of moral reasoning used in architecture, engineering, chemistry, and business courses.

In some instances, the representation of case studies in multimedia web sites forms a central role in this integration of ethics into the curriculum. One of our Engineering and Public Policy courses uses the fatal Challenger explosion to work through moral issues relating to the decision to launch the space shuttle despite problems with its O-Rings. This is now a classic case study involving, among other things, the tensions inherent in a clash between engineering and managerial perspectives. Tragically, Carnegie Mellon alumna Judith Resnik, (Engineering 1970) was one of the astronauts on that flight.

Students at Carnegie Mellon play a key role in the design and development of the web sites for interactive multimedia cases. Such high-level participation in course materials development also creates a new relation between faculty and undergraduates, a relation that is akin to that of colleagues. In this context, Carnegie Mellon provides an apprenticeship environment for many of its students—and the impact of the new on the traditional curriculum becomes synergetic.

Future directions for the use of interactive multimedia in applied ethics are as exciting as they are speculative. Carnegie Mellon's Synthetic Interview project (see Marinelli, pp. 37–50) could be utilized to create an ethics committee environment for exploring the case of Dax Cowart. We already have archived digital videos of various ethics committee members discussing Dax's case from the perspectives of hospital policy, patients' rights, and physician responsibilities. The Synthetic Interview project would allow us to construct a natural language interface to this video database, that, in turn, would allow students to ask questions concerning, for example, Dax's right to refuse treatment. A search

< 254 >

of the program's database would call up those sequences relevant to the question. Multiple expert opinions would adumbrate the inquiry and deepen the student's appreciation of the issue at hand. Further work might include crafting an expert guide who would provide commentary and suggestions "on the fly" as the student works his or her way through the program.

Both Janet Murray and Brenda Laurel speculate about the possibility of extending human computer interaction into the realm of ethics simulations. Murray's notion of *procedural authoring* foresees the time when interactive authors will work with AI-based ideas such as Frames to create simulated scenarios in which the user interacts in real time with virtual characters possessing dispositions and values. Drawing on her analysis of Aristotle's *Poetics*, Laurel speaks of these virtual characters as 'agents' with external traits (character-based behavior) and internal traits (thought inferred from the external traits and behavior of the agents).[12] In the 1990s the OZ project at Carnegie Mellon used "interactive drama" to mean the presentation by computers of rich, highly interactive worlds, inhabited by dynamic and complex characters, and shaped by aesthetically pleasing stories. People interacting with these worlds were called "interactors."

"Highly interactive" was an important descriptor of the OZ Project. It indicates that the interactor is choosing what to do, say, and think at all times, in contrast to other interactive media such as hypertext, where the interactor is given a small number of fixed choices. In highly interactive drama, the interactor is the protagonist and determines the action.

Likewise, the term "drama" was important for the OZ project. Even though the interactor is choosing what to do, say, and think, there is a destiny, created by the author of the interactive drama. This destiny is not an exact sequence of actions and events, but is subtly shaped by the system, which embodies dramatic theory and principle in the manner suggested by Brenda Laurel.

I can imagine a time when virtual ethics cases can serve as surrogates for real world moral experience, and extended interactive dramas can stimulate the moral imagination of students in ways that become crucial for both moral development and public discourse. The classicist Martha Nussbaum, writing about the relationship between moral philosophy and literature, foreshadows this role for applied ethics in the digital age:

> Schematic philosophers' examples almost always lack
> the particularity, the emotive appeal, the absorbing

< 255 >

plottedness, the variety and indeterminacy, of good fiction; they lack, too, good fiction's way of making the reader a participant and a friend; and . . . it is precisely in virtue of these structural characteristics that fiction can play the role it does in our reflective lives. As James says, 'the picture of the exposed and entangled state is what is required.' If the examples do have these features, they will, themselves, be works of literature.[13]

Notes

[1] There are a number of ways that the digital age impacts the field of Applied Ethics. For example Larry Hinman's Ethics Updates site [ethics.acusd.edu/index.html] provides a rich resource of online materials, Teddy Seidenfeld's collaboration with Paul Kahane in medical informatics applies statistical analysis to guide control groups in clinical trials, Peter Danelison uses computer models to test Game Theory, Paul Churchland applies models of Neural Networking to an understanding of moral reasoning, Kevin Ashley explores AI models in case-based moral reasoning, and Peter Madsen develops Distance Learning modules in professional ethics.

[2] This text—and its more extreme expression in Toulmin's "The Tyranny of Principles" and Jonsen's "Of Balloons and Bicycles"—has become modified in the literature. Beauchamp and Childress, for instance, place case-based moral reasoning within their own understanding of "mid-level *prima facie* principles." [See Tom Beauchamp and James Childress, *Principles of Biomedical Ethics* 4th Ed. (New York: Oxford University Press, 1994)]. Childress suggests that we avoid false alternatives (principles *versus* cases) and try to see a dialectical relation between "principles and cases / norms and narratives." [See James Childress, "Narrative(s) Versus Norm(s): A Misplaced Debate in Bioethics" in Hilde Lindemann Nelson, ed. *Stories and Their Limits: Narrative Approaches to Bioethics* (New York: Routledge, 1997)]. There are times when radically new cases force us to formulate or expand principles and, of course, there are times when principles help us understand or articulate the moral significance of cases.

[3] Arras, John. "Getting Down to Cases: The Revival of Casuistry in Bioethics," *Journal of Medicine and Philosophy* 16 (1991): 31–33.

[4] In this regard, see Martha Nussbaum's discussion of "The Discernment of Perception: An Aristotelian Conception of Private and Public Rationality" in *Love's Knowledge: Essays on Philosophy and Literature* (Oxford and New York: Oxford University Press, 1990).

[5] See Kevin Ashley and Matthew Keefer, in "Ethical Reasoning Strategies and Their Relation to Case-Based Instruction: Some Preliminary Results," *Proceedings from the 18th Annual Conference of the Cognitive Science Society*, July 1996, 483–488.

[6] Schank, Roger. "Goal-Based Scenarios: A Radical Look at Education," *The Journal of the Learning Sciences*, 1994, 3, 429–453.

< 256 >

[7] Johnson, Mark. *Moral Imagination*. Chicago: University of Chicago Press, 1993, p. 196. See also his comment that "there is abundant empirical evidence that narrative is a fundamental mode of understanding, by means of which we make sense of all forms of human action. . . . Narrative is not just an explanatory device, but is actually constitutive of the way we experience things" (11). For Johnson, "stories are our most basic contact with rational explanation" and thus form a key role in our ability to reason well about the matters before us.

[8] See Preston Covey, "The Crucible of Experience" in Heeger and Willigenburg (eds.) *The Turn to Applied Ethics*. (Kok Oharos: The Netherlands, 1993) 55–72.

[9] See K. Danner Clouser: "Trying out one's theory on real situations, thick with details, is very different from the philosopher's typical hypothetical case, which, if not simply invented, is so highly abstracted from real circumstances that only enough details remain to defend selectively the particular point the philosopher wants to make thereby. His or her use of cases is much more to *illustrate* theory than to test it. But when *solving* the moral problem is the main point, the relentlessness of the details becomes readily apparent. There is no refuge; there is one quagmire after another; retreating to the theory is not a viable option." (Hastings Center Report, Special Supplement, 25, 6 (1993) 11.

[10] Lest we forget the 'practical' aspects of this *trivium*, consider the following from Frederick Artz: ". . . medieval rhetoric was mainly interested in teaching the pupil to write letters and to prepare documents. In an age when the ability to write was not a common accomplishment the capacity to write a good letter and to make a contract, will, or a bill of sale was of great importance." *The Mind of the Middle Ages* (Chicago: University of Chicago Press, 1980) 309. Students in the Multimedia minor are encouraged to develop their skills in a variety of practical settings.

[11] Funded in large part by Lowell Steinbrenner, Trustee and alumnus (CIT, Class of 1955).

[12] Brenda Laurel, *Computers as Theatre* (Addison-Wesley: NY, 1991) 144.

[13] Martha Nussbaum, "Form and Content, Philosophy and Literature" in *Love's Knowledge: Essays on Philosophy and Literature* (New York: Oxford University Press, 1990) 46. The quote from Henry James is from *The Art of the Novel* (Oxford: Oxford University Press, 1907) 65.

< 257 >

ACCOUNTABILITY, ACCESSIBILITY, AND COST: HOW THE WEB WILL CHANGE HIGHER EDUCATION

Clark Glymour and Richard Scheines

Clark Glymour is Alumni University Professor of Philosophy at Carnegie Mellon and former Head of the Philosophy Department. His recent research concerns the application of machine learning methods developed at Carnegie Mellon to problems in mineralogy, genetics, and psychology. Professor Glymour completed his Ph.D. at Indiana University in 1969, and has taught at Carnegie Mellon for 19 years.

Richard Scheines is Associate Professor and Associate Head of the Philosophy Department at Carnegie Mellon. His areas of specialization are in the philosophy of science and artificial intelligence. Professor Scheines received his Ph.D. from the University of Pittsburgh in 1987, and has been at Carnegie Mellon for thirteen years.

DISTANCE LEARNING AND THE FUTURE OF HIGHER EDUCATION

Distance learning over the Internet is a growing business, offering chat rooms, e-mail, video lectures and inconvenient, on-screen texts of lectures. With important exceptions (the Education Program for Gifted Youth (EPGY) at Stanford for example), distance

< 259 >

education is principally confined to delivery of technical skills courses, low-grade introductory courses, and quasi-professional graduate degrees in management, nursing, public health and the like. Perhaps sometimes correctly, critics deride the providers as diploma mills, although, for all we know, students taking similar courses on campus may learn and retain no more than do distance students. But an entirely different quality of distance education is on the horizon, and as it arrives, universities will have to change. We think the changes can and should be much for the better, that Carnegie Mellon is prepared to play a role in this process, and that underprepared minority students, slighted by poor K-12 public education, will be major beneficiaries.

Aside from language-intensive courses, and perhaps even for them, Web-based, interactive, mastery designed, automated introductory instruction will provide better instruction than the traditional lecture and recitation format, especially for underprepared students. It will increase minority access to higher education, and it has the potential to reduce the standard four- to five-year undergraduate residency to something like three years, or make graduate degrees more affordable, or both. It will give us a much deeper understanding of what students actually do when they study, and allow us to assess what they know and what they don't in a systematic, scientific way.

Will Web-based education replace the faculty? Of course not. Might it reduce the number of faculty? Not unless administrations explicitly make that a goal. Much more likely, it will change where, what, and how faculty teach. It will drive faculty who have lived on their introductory lecture notes out of the lecture halls, moving them into much smaller venues. Instead of teaching 200 students standard introductory material—yes, sometimes that can happen even at Carnegie Mellon—the same faculty will be able to tutor small groups of students on the subtleties of their subject, providing knowledge, and interaction that computers will probably never reach. That is a good thing. Perhaps most importantly, Web-based instruction will force curricular innovation; it will force us to think much more carefully about the learning process in a way we seldom have before. It will not remove the need for mentoring (see Kadane, pp. 51–62), or for campus residency for the development of many skills.

< 260 >

Facts, Anecdotes and Morals

In creating its annual ranking of American colleges and universities, *U.S. News & World Report* collects extensive data it does not publish, including percentage of faculty with doctorates, faculty salaries, expenditures per student, and much more, including drop-out rates. Here is a fact: drop-out rates are independent, or nearly independent, of all other features recorded in the database, conditional on the average predictor percentile scores of the student body on the SAT or ACT tests. These tests are indicators of how well prepared students are for universities. What these scores mean is simple: *ill-prepared students do not succeed in universities as they are now organized.*

Here is another fact: The young population of the United States is increasingly African-American, Asian and, especially, Hispanic. Minority groups will collectively soon make up a majority of the age group that traditionally receives higher education. In round numbers, consistently since 1976, when data were first collected by ethnicity, African-American students have on average scored roughly 100 points lower on the verbal SAT than white students, and 75 points lower on the math SAT; the comparable numbers for Hispanics are about 75 and 50 points lower than white students; Asian students on average score 40 points lower than whites on the verbal SAT and that much higher than whites on the math SAT. We do not have standard deviations by ethnic group, but aggregated over all students the standard deviation on the verbal test is consistently about 110, and on the math test about 120. Our point is not racial comparison, but a sociometric fact: college-age students in America are increasingly ill prepared for first-class university instruction as it is traditionally delivered. Most students who score below 1000 on the SAT are simply not going to succeed at Carnegie Mellon or other demanding institutions, and that is an increasing proportion of students. Minority students will be channeled to less rigorous institutions, and they will disproportionately select non-technical majors. That is already happening. The removal of affirmative action in the University of California system did not drive African-American and Hispanic students out of the universities; it drove them to the less distinguished, less competitive and less demanding institutions. Graduate degrees for African-Americans are largely in social services and education, and disproportionately so for Hispanics. These facts describe a real problem, but present a real opportunity. Web-based education has the poten-

< 261 >

tial to offer first-class introductory education to students who are less well prepared to succeed in first-class universities.

The first true story is this, in the voice of the first author: In 1969, for the first time, Princeton University admitted African-American undergraduates, a dozen or so, and I failed most of them in introductory mathematical logic, the first course I ever taught. Seven of the African-American freshmen were enrolled in my class, all of them smart, ambitious and brave, none of them graduates of the prep schools that fed Princeton in those days. All of them failed my course. I had taught the course in the tradition of university lecturing since the 13th century, and added the homework assignments, recitation sections, mid-term exam and final that have become stable elements in the pedagogy of American higher education. Something was badly wrong. The next year I taught the same course differently. I used a text that divided the material into many short chapters. I arranged a room with a grader to be available at regular hours throughout each week. Students could take a test on any chapter and have it immediately graded, and if they passed, they could proceed to the next chapter; otherwise they were required to wait at least two days before they could take another test on the chapter they had failed. They could repeat the process without penalty until they passed. That's called "mastery design" in educationese. Grades were based on how many chapters were mastered. I replaced the lectures with problem-solving sessions, responding to questions posed by the students. Some of the students turned the problem-solving sessions into lecture notes and sold them. I met with every one of the sixty-five students every other week. Every African-American student passed, and half of them received A grades. And students who received A grades in the second version of the course mastered substantially more material than did students who received like grades in the first version of the course.

We believe this explanation for the story. Minority students at Princeton thirty years ago were less well prepared than their white peers, and less adept at test taking. The conventional version of the course gave them comparatively little insight into their own state of knowledge of the course material, and the course moved on at a fixed pace, no matter their understanding.

Without prompts to reading, immediate correction of errors, and mastery design, traditional higher education instruction affords underprepared students no feasible way to compensate for inadequate background with the one resource in which they are rich: effort. With those added features, underprepared but ambitious students can excel.

< 262 >

There is an important afterword. At the time Princeton had inaugurated the end-of-semester student evaluation forms that are now ubiquitous. The student ratings of the second year of the course, in which all African-American students had passed, half had received As, and A- and even B- students had learned an enormous amount, were dramatically lower than the evaluations of the course from the previous year. Even though preparing and teaching the mastery version of the course required double the effort of the traditional format, half of the students wrote that the instructor had used the format so as to avoid the trouble of lectures.

A related experience took place some years later at the University of Pittsburgh, concerning an ad hoc committee to pass on the tenure of an untenured associate professor of mathematics. The professor's anomalous rank had resulted because, two years before, his research had been judged worthy of tenure but student evaluations of his teaching had been very low. Almost all of his teaching had been in sections of calculus and introductory differential equations. All sections used the same texts and similar tests. The Chairman was asked how the faculty member's students had done compared with students in other sections. The answer, which the Chairman had to look up, was that the faculty member's students were, on average, about average. The implication was clear enough. The reason the fellow had not been promoted was not because his teaching was less effective than that of other faculty, but because he was not as well liked by his students. At Princeton and at the University of Pittsburgh, learning was not what counted most.

Ken Ford, a professor of computer science at the University of West Florida, ran into trouble a few years ago when he offered one of the first courses for credit available over the Web. Students from around the country and from several foreign nations paid their tuition and attempted to enroll, but the University would not allow it. The University of Florida system requires that every enrolled student present proof of vaccination against various diseases, and many of the nonresident students had no such proof. Ford convinced the University to change its regulations, but you see the point. Some arrangements are less amusing. The California Community Colleges used to have regulations requiring courses to provide a minimum number of hours for the instructor to be in the "line of sight" of the students. Video delivery caused that requirement to be weakened, but extensive personal interaction between faculty and students is still required. Distance learning with aid as needed from human tutors is effec-

< 263 >

tively illegal in community colleges in California. The pretext is educational quality, but the community colleges do not require evidence of how much, or how little, students actually learn in any course. Evaluation forms are required, but pre-test and post-test comparisons are not. The real motive of the regulation is job protection.

The previous anecdotes suggest these morals: *students will be disappointed at unexpected formats and unexpected content, even if they benefit; institutions of higher education will block reform when they can, and they will seldom, if ever, concern themselves with gathering evidence about how well and how much students are learning and use that information in curricular and personnel judgments.*

The computer and the Web have changed expectations in thirty years. We have found the majority of students prefer Web-based delivery; blockages to reform will eventually surrender to economic and other pressures, and the process of replacing conventional course delivery with Web-based instruction will force attention to what students actually learn. For many reasons, face-to-face contact with faculty is crucial in upper division courses, whose content often varies with research trends, and mentoring at the level of recitations is critical in introductory lecture courses. Lectures are not.

Constructing a Web-Based Course

For fifteen years at Carnegie Mellon, in collaboration with Peter Spirtes, we have worked in an area of artificial intelligence and statistics that concerns causal inference. We adapted a well understood representation from computer science, Bayes Nets, or directed graphical models, and used them to give simple, pictorial representations of fundamental principles about scientific inference: recognizing alternative explanations, confounding, randomization, blinding, prediction, and predicting the outcomes of interventions. And we developed search techniques for causal relations and proofs of their adequacy under explicit assumptions. Other researchers at other universities, and at Microsoft, joined in the same project, and today the representations and algorithmic procedures we and they developed are increasingly used in data mining, and are making slow inroads into methodology in economics, biology, chemistry, and social sciences.

Four years ago, Richard Scheines, who has done extensive work on computerized instruction in logic, proposed that we

< 264 >

develop a Web-based introductory course on causal inference, using Bayes Net representations throughout, intended as a preparation for conventional introductory courses in statistics, which traditionally give short and unsystematic attention to causal questions. Joel Smith, then Dean of Information at Mira Costa Community College in California, and now Director of the Office of Technology for Education at Carnegie Mellon, joined us in a proposal to the federal government's Fund for the Improvement of Post-Secondary Education (FIPSE), which, rather to our surprise, was funded for about $350,000. And so we proceeded to create a course.

Our initial strategy was to develop the content of the course in instructional modules supported entirely by interactive Java applets. We soon discovered that Java was a moving target (it is much less so now), and enormous amounts of time were consumed in learning new variants to the language. We also discovered that for many instructional purposes other technologies were more efficient, and we therefore mixed Java with Shockwave applets. Enormous amounts of time were taken up in developing necessary tools, which by themselves provided no instruction: an applet that permits students to construct samples with a variety of properties, applets that permit them to construct causal models and investigate their statistical properties, and so forth. We tried an instructional format that proved infeasible. We hired graphics designers only to have them quit because of the difficulties of the tasks we set them. But the single largest difficulty was the difference in detail and specificity required in a course that will be learned from a computer and the detail and specificity provided in our lectures. We created a course, and gave it to a small seminar of eight freshmen at Carnegie Mellon, who quickly taught us what they did not understand. In the traditional lecture format students had not understood either, but when they performed badly on examinations we assumed, well, they weren't very bright, or weren't working very hard, or something. Now, we discovered the something was us.

The course was rewritten and reprogrammed as the eight students gave us their responses to each lesson. In the winter of 1999, with the help of Carnegie Mellon Online, the revised Web course was delivered to approximately 80 students who were randomly selected from among 120 volunteers at the University of California at San Diego (UCSD), while another 80 students received the same material through lecture/recitation format. Two teaching assistants were available for all 160 students taking the

< 265 >

course. Carnegie Mellon Online provided details of student answers to quiz questions at the end of every lesson. The database enabled us to see which topics students had difficulty with, and form an idea as to why. The course did not, however, have a mastery design. There was no significant difference in final exam scores between students taking the course on-line and students taking the course in the conventional lecture format, but the difference between scores on a test at the beginning of term and scores at the end of term on a similar test were significantly higher for the on-line group. Results from a similar experiment at UCSD in the spring quarter of 1999 were essentially the same.

The course is being rewritten again to implement a mastery design, and a further experiment took place at UCSD with the revised course in the winter and spring quarters of 2001. A more fine-grained experiment took place at the University of Pittsburgh in the spring of 2001, where researchers from the Learning Research and Development Center have been studying how students react to Web-based instruction in detail. In the meantime, more portable course administration software, independent of Carnegie Mellon Online, has been implemented.

DIFFUSION

What works in La Jolla may not work in Boyle Heights; what works in Chevy Chase may fail in Butte. UCSD and Carnegie Mellon are respectively an elite public and an elite private university, with comparatively well-prepared and comparatively prosperous students. Would similar instruction work at a community college with a large proportion of minority students? Would it work in a traditionally African-American college? Would it work in a women's college? Would it work in an undistinguished state university in a small town; would it work in a large, urban public university? And will automated instruction actually save any money?

MORALS

Comparing students in lecture and Web-based courses at UCSD and the University of Pittsburgh, we discovered that: attendance at lectures is independent of course final grade; attendance at recitations is strongly correlated with final grade, both for lecture

< 266 >

students and Web-based students—final grades increased an average of two points with every recitation attended; and among Web-based students, final grades are *very* strongly correlated (= .84) with participation in the interactive exercises distributed throughout each subject module. Students' sex is uncorrelated with final grade in both lecture and Web-based formats. We have not done studies by ethnic group.

With help from the Mellon Foundation, we plan to undertake such studies. Over the next three years we will introduce the course at 20 diverse colleges and universities, in some places in both lecture and Web-based versions, and in others only in Web-based format. We plan to attend carefully both to the costs and to student success with the format. Right now we can guess that video games and personal computers have made the format acceptable, if not preferred, for almost all American college students, that there are no material differences associated with sex, and that, provided a tutor is available for starting and for difficult spots, minority students will do better in Web-based formats than in traditional lecture courses. In three years we hope to know.

ECONOMICS

The cost of developing our Web-based course seems horrific. In addition to the FIPSE funds, about $40,000 was provided by UCSD, and the Department of Philosophy at Carnegie Mellon helped to subsidize a programmer. The cost of uncompensated faculty time, if compensated, would run to nearly $150,000. By the time the course is stable it will have effectively cost about $600,000, or more, to develop. There are, however, economies of scale. Looking back on our blind alleys, one can guess that with the present team and skills we could now develop the same course for perhaps 20 percent less. But $450,000 is a lot of money for a single semester course, and the costs of developing other courses with the same virtues—good graphics, interactivity, mastery design tailored to track and remedy the variety of misunderstandings students have—would certainly in some cases be higher. A suite of 20 such introductory courses, enough to cover many first-year curricula, might reasonably cost 10 to 15 million dollars.

Both at Carnegie Mellon and at UCSD, computer labs were made available for students, but they were little used. The students prefer to use their own computers, and about 80 percent of the computer work is done outside of the University computer

< 267 >

labs. At least with middle- and upper middle-class students, the infrastructure costs to the University client are much smaller than we expected, but with less advantaged students they will be higher. The delivery costs from Carnegie Mellon, once the course is stable, are about $20,000 per year, more or less independently of how many students are enrolled in how many universities. UCSD offered the course to 600 students in 2000–2001, and that was perfectly feasible. If UCSD alone were to use the course in this way over five years, the development costs would average $150 per student. If ten other universities do likewise, the development and operation costs per student become less than $50 per student who completes the course.

What UCSD saves through Web delivery to 600 students, at least for the purpose of hypothetical costing, is three fifths of the salary and benefits of the professors who have traditionally taught the course, and a reduction in audio-visual service and classroom costs. We might guess that the hypothetical savings in classroom costs and services approximately match the hypothetical additional costs to UCSD in computer infrastructure. Even if the course replaces the lectures of a beginning assistant professor, UCSD should save about $40,000 in salary and benefits.

The net savings to a university will therefore vary with costs of personnel for lectures, and we can guess that, all things considered, including delivery, data keeping, and amortization of development costs, savings at each client institution might range from $10,000 to $100,000 per year-long automated course. Savings in service and support are likely to be slower to appear, and classroom construction savings are likely to be long-term and to depend on the implementation of a substantial number of Web-based classes. The savings per student from courses with a smaller student audience would certainly be lower.

EFFECTS

Just suppose a suite of proven, Web-based courses were available for much of the first-year college curriculum. What would happen? That depends on whether a university or consortium of universities has monopoly ownership. (For the inconvenient-book, chat-room model of distance learning or for filmed talking heads, there will never be monopoly ownership because start-up costs are small.) Monopoly owners stand to profit from licensing arrangements with other institutions and can use the curriculum

< 268 >

in various ways to increase their applications and their enrollments of qualified minority students. The more interesting case is public ownership or, as with the Web itself and the free-ware movement, non-ownership.

UCSD now charges each in-state student about $7,000 for its first year of courses. Carnegie Mellon charges about $20,000 after scholarships. What happens if the actual delivery cost per student for a first year of courses plummets? We see three options for colleges and universities:

1. Refuse to offer such courses or to accredit them for transfer students.
2. Offer Web-based courses at the same tuition, but supplement richly with seminars and mentorship.
3. Accept such courses from transfer students and offer them at reduced fees to first-year students, making up the revenue shortfall by increased student flow-through, or increased enrollment in graduate degree programs.

The first option will be available only to elite universities that are selling social connections and name-brand credentials rather than education. Carnegie Mellon is not that kind of place. The second option is available to elite institutions, including Carnegie Mellon, but for other institutions competition should make it untenable. The third option may be in store for small, expensive but undistinguished institutions, provided that they can increase their flow-through and/or graduate or professional program enrollments. But for Carnegie Mellon, we strongly urge the second option.

CONCLUSION

Ten to fifteen million dollars or more to develop a first-class, Web-based, interactive, mastery designed introductory college curriculum sounds like a lot. The real cost is probably four times that if a reasonable variety of approaches is represented. The United States Department of Education had an annual budget in 2000 of about $38 billion dollars; its research budget alone is $66 million. The Department of Education could change the face of university education, and the access and performance of minority students, if not in a trice, then at least within the next five years. If it will not, then the evidence increasingly suggests that institutions like Carnegie Mellon should take up the burden, and the pleasure.

< 269 >

THE LIBRARY OF THE FUTURE

Gloriana St. Clair and Erika Linke

Gloriana St. Clair is University Librarian at Carnegie Mellon. Her current interests center around issues of scholarly communication in the academy, building the digital library of the future, and creating a strong library organization. Dr. St. Clair earned her Ph.D. from the University of Oklahoma in 1970, and has been at Carnegie Mellon for five years.

Erika Linke is Associate University Librarian at Carnegie Mellon. Her current interests are building library collections; copyright, intellectual property and scholarly communication; and access to information and research resources. She received her Master's degree in Library Science from the University of Minnesota in 1978, and has been at Carnegie Mellon for 19 years.

Within ten years, the total number of electronic records produced on the planet could be doubling every sixty seconds.

—Rich Lysakowski

Many experts believe the information explosion is well underway with information doubling every two to three years.

—Brian Hawkins

< 271 >

By 2047 almost all information will be in cyberspace—
including a large percentage of knowledge and creative
works. All information about physical objects, including humans, buildings, processes and organizations,
will be online. This trend is both desirable and inevitable.

—Gordon Bell and Jim Gray[1]

SCHOLARLY COMMUNICATION AND THE ACADEMIC LIBRARY

Academic libraries typically have a mission to support the knowl-
edge-based activities of their colleges and universities. In general, their collections, like those of Carnegie Mellon, reflect the
teaching and research initiatives that engage faculty and students.
Content for these collections is an aggregate of the various disciplines' scholarly communications efforts. While the library collects some materials that are created through commercial or trade
publishing venues, the majority of the collection has been refereed by discipline experts and published under their auspices.
These collecting practices inexorably tie the future of the library
to the future of the scholarly communications system.

A BROKEN SYSTEM

In May 2000, the Association of American Universities (AAU) in
conjunction with the Association for Research Libraries (ARL)
published a set of guidelines for scholars to consider in communicating their research to their colleagues. Signatories included
university administrators, discipline leaders, faculty, and librarians. They agreed that the "current system of scholarly publishing has become too costly for the academic community to sustain." New publishing models have emerged and should be used
to stem the escalation of prices and volume.[2]

The problems that compose this broken system include:

- *Skyrocketing journal prices.* Journals have gone up
  an average of 9 percent a year while inflation rose
  only 3.3 percent.[3]
- *Broken library budgets.* Between 1986 and 1999, ARL
  members spent 2.7 times more for serials and
  bought 6 percent fewer titles. http://www.arl.org/
  stats/arlstat/99intro.html

< 272 >

- *The consequent death of the scholarly monograph in the humanities.* Libraries bought 26 percent fewer monographs in 1999 than in 1986.

Daryl H. Busch, president of the American Chemical Society, summarized: "Cost is the whole issue." The result is that every faculty member annually gets a list of journals that are going to be discontinued. The guideline signatories assigned most blame in the situation to a handful of commercial publishers. Duane Webster, the Executive Director of the ARL, noted "The real call is for faculty to understand what is going on in the marketplace, what is going on in technology, and to be a part of the debate . . . And right now, they're not."[4] Several recommendations require faculty action.

When economists consider this ongoing problem, they inevitably comment that the marketplace will correct itself. One factor that has slowed that correction is a unique quality of scholarly journals—they do not easily substitute for one another. A *New York Times* letter writer noted that *Brain Research* costs more per pound than a Mercedes. Most people act in the marketplace by buying cheaper cars but the number of equivalent cheaper journals is quite small. Creating such journals is an important initiative. In the same way that generic drugs offer consumers a less expensive alternative to brand name drugs and operate as complete substitutes in the economic marketplace, generic-priced journals need to be created as alternatives.

The Solution: Nine Principles

As proposed by the AAU/ARL group, nine principles provide a useful construct for discussing the scholarly communications system and its interaction with the future of libraries. These principles expand a smaller set of initiatives outlined in "To Publish and Perish," a special issue of *Policy Perspectives*.[5]

1. *Cost to the academy of published research should be contained so that access to relevant research publications for faculty members and students can be maintained and even expanded.*

    Relentless journal price increases of 9 percent or more a year over the last fifteen years have greatly reduced the availability of on-campus subscriptions to journals for students and faculty. For instance, at its journal subscription high point

< 273 >

in 1991, Carnegie Mellon subscribed to 4,330 journals; today, only 2,935 journals are received. David Shulenburger, Provost of the University of Kansas, has summarized the problem: from 1986 to 1996, the consumer price index increased 44 percent while the price of health care went up 84 percent. Meanwhile, the cost of scholarly journals outpaced both by increasing 148 percent, more than three times the rate of inflation. The bottom line is that libraries would need budgets 2.5 times their current ones to stay even in resource purchases. Many faculty understand that these price increases are killing library collections and damaging the ability of faculty and students to do their research. If libraries are to have a future, this problem must be solved.

2. *Electronic capabilities should be used, among other things, to: provide wide access to scholarship, encourage interdisciplinary research, and enhance interoperability and searchability.*

Both faculty and students applaud the ease of access, convenience, and speed of electronic versions of paper journals, born-electronic journals, and Web resources. In the future, human attention will be the scarce commodity. Most material will be available electronically and individuals will use "knowbots" to alert them to new developments in their disciplines. Currently, only five to six percent of the material on the World Wide Web is scholarly in nature, even though students expect to be able to do all their research there. Disciplines must make active plans to communicate electronically in order to increase their efficiency and address future communication needs.

A Pew Roundtable idea that academia should decouple the credit that scholarly communications give faculty from print publication provides an alternative that will be affordable for even the poorest of disciplines. In a decoupled system, scholars could submit major papers to either leading journals or relevant scholarly society referees for certification and electronic publication—with the knowledge that promotion and tenure committees will value the two means of dissemination equally.[6] California Institute of Technology's Scholar's Forum illustrates how such a system might work (http://www.library.caltech.edu/publications/scholarsforum/). If scholarly societies refereed materials and mounted them on the web instead of putting all of them through print publication, costs could be reduced and access

< 274 >

could be augmented. However, to make this effective, such refereed Web articles would have to be counted equivalently for promotion and tenure.

3. *Scholarly publications must be archived in a secure manner so as to remain permanently available.*

At the last Coalition for Networked Information meeting in the 1990s, information technologists and librarians agreed that developing an archiving system was the number one priority for the future. Clifford Lynch, president of the coalition, is working with the Council on Library and Information Resources to effect a solution. Technical problems are nontrivial but can be addressed as long as the archive receives attention regularly. Unlike books, computer files will not last for centuries. Of all those who might do archiving—computer centers, commercial publishers, societies, the Online Computer Library Center—faculty trust academic libraries the most. An endowment to support an archive, so that no passing administration could neglect or abandon it, would provide a secure and trustworthy mechanism for assuring permanence.

4. *The system of scholarly publication must continue to include processes for evaluating the quality of scholarly work, and every publication should provide the reader with information about evaluation the work has undergone.*

Most participants, including administrators, faculty, discipline leaders, technologists and librarians, agree that this commitment is crucial to maintaining quality. The Caltech model shows that refereeing processes can easily be included in future methodologies. The Genome Database, a most successful example of how digital information supported rapid progress, featured the refereeing of information from its inception. Similarly, astrophysicists, who have nearly all of their discipline information online, provide refereed materials.

The exception to this commitment to formal evaluation has been the highly successful Ginsparg preprint server for particle physics. This service mounts papers that have not yet gone through the refereeing process; discipline members praise its speed in communicating new findings. Physicists say that they know the participants in their field and use their knowledge of reputations to guide their selections. The National Institutes of Health Harold Vargas initiative (now called PubMed Central) confronted this issue, with the result that

< 275 >

the public archive with its original, nonreviewed research has been slow in getting started.

Information on the Web grows at a rate of over a million pages a day. Already, information seekers are overloaded and seeking automated assistance to manage knowledge acquisition. In the future, quality assurance and provenance establishment will be important to faculty and students. Thus, scholarly societies that provide those marks of quality will flourish because libraries and faculty are bringing them to the attention of researchers and students.

5.   *The academic community embraces the concepts of copyright and fair use and seeks a balance in the interest of owners and users in the digital environment.*

Developments in this area are perhaps the most difficult to predict because they involve social and legal systems rather than technical ones. The purpose of copyright is to foster progress in the sciences and useful arts. Until 1976, US copyright protection was for 28 years; the author could then extend protection for another 28 years. Since then, length of copyright has been expanded to 75 years and, recently, to 95 years (because Disney Corporation's Mickey Mouse was about to pass into the public domain). The length of time that materials are likely to be out of print but in copyright creates a serious barrier for the creation of a digital library.

In 2000, music copyright issues were in the news quite frequently. Software that allowed students to download music from the Web became prevalent on college campuses, and even necessitated upgrading campus networks in some cases. The music industry sued software creators. Some musicians argued for free passage of their work to their fans while others sided with the recording industry in pushing for controls. At the same time, movie and print piracy in developing countries was and is widespread.

Also in 2000, at least six separate commercial ventures began to scan in copyright materials and make them available on the Web through subscription and purchase arrangements. University presses are moving ahead with pricing models and are signing non-exclusive agreements with a variety of commercial ventures. Many are finding that electronic versions with "Buy" buttons actually increase the sale of physical books. However, a study underway at Carnegie Mellon

< 276 >

indicates that most commercial presses are reluctant to grant permissions to digitize their materials.

The rights of authors to earn a livelihood and the rights of publishers to be recompensed for their risk war with the public need to have information freely available. In the Information Age, technology is going to facilitate access and change traditional profit margins. Innovative popular authors, such as Stephen King, are already serializing their works and selling them directly to readers over the Web with the idea of increasing their personal income. Desktop publishing allows authors to present their work professionally without the services of the publisher, and the Web as a mechanism for both advertising and dissemination obviates other publisher roles.

Enhancement of reputation is a more powerful motivator in the academy than sales because scholarly journals typically do not pay authors. Faculty are rewarded financially through institutional salary increases related to their international scholarly reputations. When academic institutions agree that decoupled, refereed Web publications are equivalent to those in paper, then faculty will prefer them because of their speed, convenience of use, and international accessibility. Faculty are typically more interested in the broad dissemination of their ideas than they are in jealously guarding their copyrights.

The next two decades will feature a seesaw back and forth between powerful business interests who want to maintain and expand existing long copyright periods and a variety of creators who want their ideas and expressions of them widely disseminated. Michael Shamos, a copyright attorney, computer science professor, and the head of Carnegie Mellon's Institute for eCommerce, notes that beyond the copyright law is the more powerful law of supply and demand. That will eventually determine the future of copyright. The more information that begins to flow on the Web without charge, the more students and faculty can work without having a library to pay fees for their access to information.

6. *In negotiating publisher agreements, faculty members should assign the rights to their work in a manner that promotes the ready use of their work, and should choose journals that support the goal of making scholarly publications available at reasonable cost.*

This principle might be moot in the future if copyright were to change radically. Under it, faculty are asked not to

< 277 >

sign away all the rights to their works, but rather to retain the right to use their own work in their teaching and future research, and to ask that the work be freely available to the remainder of the educational community. Association leaders, such as Educause, under the presidency of Brian Hawkins, have provided copyright statements that allow work to flow freely in the educational environment (http:// www.educause.edu/pub/eq/eq-pub-guide.html).

The second part of this principle asks faculty to choose judiciously where they submit their work. Many faculty colleagues have become sensitive to issues of cost and publish only in professional society journals. A recent study indicated that commercial journals tend to be 2.4 to 6.5 times more expensive for libraries than those of professional societies.[7] Faculty sensitivity to issues of cost and venue contributes to creating an environment in which prices can be contained and libraries can flourish.

7. *The time from submission to publication should be reduced in a manner consistent with the requirements of quality control.*

The future will be faster than the present, as argued in James Gleick's *Faster*.[8] The speedup that John Seely Brown and Paul Duguid say began with the telegraph now occurs every day for almost everyone through cellular telephone, email, and the Web.[9] This desire for speed in communicating information underlies preprint servers, PubMed Central, and initiatives in which publications are mounted directly on the web. Such initiatives also broaden access. Refereeing takes some time, but editorial boards should set themselves some reasonable limits and maintain them. Faculty and students want and deserve up to date information. Libraries of the future will have processes, practices, and policies to support that need.

8. *To assure quality and reduce proliferation of publications, the evaluation of faculty members should place a greater emphasis on quality of publications and a reduced emphasis on quantity.*

The information explosion has been just that—an explosion. During the period from 1970 to 1995, US academic research and development (R&D) spending increased by 250 percent, at the same time that the portion of university spending devoted to academic libraries was cut in half.[10] Faculty members are asked to contribute to cost and space control

< 278 >

by focusing their efforts on the quality of what they write and not on the volume of their publications.

The library's response to this 25-year period of rapidly increasing funding for research and attendant production of more information has been to move to a system of access, rather than one of ownership. Albert Henderson chastens the government for spending $15 billion on research and ignoring issues of knowledge dissemination. He also chastens libraries for "the parsimonious 'just in time, not just in case' rationale of the 'access, not ownership' gamble that has never paid off for researchers and their sponsors." He claims that interlibrary borrowing takes too long and fails 15 percent of the time.[11]

It seems unlikely that library funding will catch up with both the expansions in research funding and the journal price increases. The future must see both a movement of the disciplines to present their materials on the Web where they can be used immediately by researchers and students, and a more effective interlibrary loan system that takes advantage of digital technologies to offer same-day access to most materials. While some publishers are trying to persuade libraries to buy greater and greater bundles of their journals, others see the marketplace shifting into selling their product article by article. The latter strategy will quickly force an issue that many scholars are most reluctant to face—the number of times that a single article is actually read. And the acknowledgement of this truth will further the initiative for quality over quantity as an evaluation principle.

9. *In electronic as well as print environments, scholars and students should be assured privacy with regard to their use of materials.*

Privacy is an overwhelming issue in society today. Brown and Duguid note that in the US, individuals worry about the government having access to information about them, whereas in Europe the worry is about corporations having that access. Many scientists do not think privacy around scientific information is an issue worthy of comment; others are primarily concerned about the patent process and subsequent earnings. Nevertheless, privacy is considered a basic American entitlement. Library values require that circulation records and reference conferences be regarded as confidential. The details of these are not disclosed unless a legal request for the information is made. Maintaining this value in the

< 279 >

electronic environment will be more difficult, but librarians will strive to create systems that allow scholars and students to view information without fear that their preferences will be revealed.

TECHNOLOGY AND LIBRARIES

Technology will continue to transform libraries. Building and creating local repositories of resources; organizing and designing tools to access both local and remote information sources, regardless of format; and ensuring that users have the requisite tools, training and assistance to mine the exploding information and data available to them—these are some of the challenges. Begun 25 years ago as a means to mechanize and streamline circulation desks, library automation and computerization have expanded and fundamentally transformed the library. These changes have streamlined routine tasks and added information retrieval sophistication that once was only imagined by visionaries. Yet the effort to create this more powerful and robust system relies on individuals with increasing skills and knowledge to create and use systems more beneficial and helpful to users. Replacing card catalogs with online catalogs was a small step. Bigger and more profound changes will continue to transform the task of information seeking and evaluation.

VIGNETTES FROM THE FUTURE

The following vignettes suggest how in the future librarians will work with users and, aided by technology, make it possible to find and utilize resources of all types worldwide.

Librarian 24 x 7 Remote Assistance
On a Monday night, Manisha Patel, the librarian on call for the 4 p.m. to midnight shift, is at home or in her office with her computer opened to the library help channel. She's just told the unit to rerun the startup to be sure that all aspects of the system are up and running. The unit reports back that chat-room, Web, email, audio and video components are working fine and reminds Manisha to turn up the microphone volume a notch. Manisha begins her electronic survey of the system, on the alert for user queries and questions. Satisfied that there are no questions queued

< 280 >

and no failed automated assistance queries, she turns to examining system logs to evaluate the automated assistant responses to queries.

Student Support

It's 7 P.M. and Levon Bey is on a flight returning to Pittsburgh from a long mid-semester break in New York. He opens his e-device to recall the upcoming week's assignments. This e-device, a descendant of the e-book of 2000, is required of all students. At the time of course registration, he downloads course syllabi, course readings, supplementary material, and a research aid interface (RAI) specifically created for use with his course selections. The RAI, developed at the library, is designed to link the user directly not only to course materials but also to automated aids that assist users when searching. There are additional connections to library personnel who take up assistance where the automated aid leaves off. All of the RAI services are available when and where needed.

Levon realizes that he's forgotten an essay for his computing and society course. He turns to his RAI and begins investigating a topic that had interested him earlier—assessing the impact of Project Gutenberg on the development of electronic full text. Through his RAI, he quickly locates materials brought together for his course and integrates the full text with the notes he had already made. He wants some additional information and asks the automated aid to gather more information about the project. He closes his e-device and prepares for arrival in Pittsburgh, knowing that when he connects again, he'll find the needed sources grouped in a usable fashion.

Faculty Support

Professor Chu is working on a project on the history of science in the nineteenth century. Earlier this evening he read about some interesting and important diaries that seemed to be related to a specific event he was examining. Though Professor Chu doesn't have the e-device that student Bey does, Chu has an RAI customized for his courses and research. He initiates a search for those diaries and doesn't find them digitized anywhere. Though projects have existed to digitize older materials and much has been done, many of the earlier efforts to digitize all materials were set aside as the demand to manage currently released material took precedence. Much remains to be done with older material. Professor Chu does find the bound paper copies of diaries lo-

< 281 >

cated at several institutions. He initiates a request to have the materials scanned immediately. He looks at the clock and decides to call it a night, confident that the materials will be available in the morning. Because his library has established channels with institutions worldwide, users are able to obtain scanned documents quickly and on demand. Rather than send paper books and microfilmed archival papers to meet research needs, the owning library uses RAPID-Scan, a tool developed to scan and digitize materials needed for on-demand use rapidly. The scanned copies then become part of the libraries' digital universe.

Collection and Resource Management

On Tuesday morning at the library Ross Jones, a science librarian, opens up a file to see which courses for next term still need to have related materials identified and organized. A specially created automated information assistant—an intelligent aid that continually searches for full text resources relevant to upcoming courses—aids him. With the vast amounts of information available, librarians identify important resources useful for courses that are taught each term. Without an intelligent aid, Jones' work would be completely unmanageable. With time at a premium for everyone and the amount of possible information so vast, information pods are created to support coursework and research. Jones is in continual contact and dialog with faculty, students and researchers as he regularly updates the information pods for research and teaching. These information pods are a timesaver for faculty as well as for the students enrolled on campus and in distance education courses.

The librarian's role in the future library will focus on deploying current technology that best meets student and faculty needs for locating pertinent resources and creating a relevant information environment to support student learning and faculty teaching and research. With the wide array of resources and the deluge of information, robotics or artificial intelligence aides will help organize material. Highly trained and competent librarians will provide for students, faculty and researchers more skilled and precise retrieval. They will do this by teaching techniques that focus on formulating a research topic or question, evaluating information sources, locating the best information resource, and understanding the ethics of information and intellectual property.

< 282 >

The librarian's role in the digital library is varied. Michael Lesk, the Digital Initiatives Program Officer for the National Science Foundation, predicts that teaching will become more significant than buildings-related issues.[12] Teaching will have many guises. More and more, librarians will create online teaching modules to assist students at their convenience, as described in the vignettes. Nevertheless, the great forte of library teaching, the one-on-one interaction between a reference librarian and a student working on a project, will persist throughout the next 20 years, although it may occur remotely. Librarians will continue to assist in the overwhelming problem of locating the materials that individuals need through participation in browser, agent, and other device developments. Already browsers index only a fraction of the material on the Web. As the number of electronic records begins to double every 60 minutes, these browsers must become both more robust and more precise.

Building a local collection was one of the academic librarian's most important tasks. The nature of that task has changed and will continue to change as librarians decide what to contract for and what to borrow from other institutions. Contracting for electronic resources becomes increasingly important as publishers change their models for outright sale to leasing.

Three other roles connect librarians with the scholarly communications system that is the premier content provider. First, librarians can foster the creation of electronic alternatives to paper books and paper journals. Technologies now exist to create both of these in electronic form. The refereeing process and the author's subsequent revisions contribute to high quality in the academic world. Librarians can help manage the mechanics of these processes and be involved with the final editing and presentation of these all-electronic books and journals.

One reason for librarians to take on these roles is that we are the most trusted agents to preserve and archive electronic materials. Librarians have kept materials that were rarely used, they have explored digital alternatives for preservation, and they have collected unique manuscripts and papers. Librarians will be as scrupulous in their commitment to maintaining the electronic record as they have been to preserving the paper record.

Librarians also need to continue their commitment to the principles of fair use. New scholarship builds on existing scholarship, and the right to read existing intellectual property in or-

< 283 >

der to create new intellectual property must be championed. Librarians at Carnegie Mellon have already begun to function in this way. Most scholars believe in the free flow of their work to others in their fields. Librarians must work with them to sustain that effort. And as information becomes increasingly available worldwide, attention must be given to the needs of cultures whose understandings of knowledge as property may differ. As discussed above, the current tension between the technological possibilities of programs such as Napster and the legal arrangements between music publishers and music creators is enormously challenging.

While the future of the library is incontrovertibly digital, university administrators should not begin thinking about alternative uses for their library buildings. In *The Social Life of Information*, Brown and Duguid discuss how social forces shape the information environment. They stress the importance of the social network in overcoming the technical difficulties with machines and in creating a community of shared learning. They and others find that computer networked learning eventually leads to a demand for individuals to gather to share the learning experience.

The library as a place—with a traditional book collection, resources in a variety of media, and the infrastructure to support their use, librarians and student workers to provide help, other students to help students, an atmosphere of scholarship and collaboration, and gateways to the collections of other libraries—continues to be valuable for students and faculty. The library as a place is also a symbol for the aggregation of research, for the product of education, and for the atmosphere of study and individual inquiry. Libraries are quickly following the lead of chain bookstores in installing coffee shops and comfortable seating to foster an atmosphere of genteel intellectual life. Even a digitally engaged library like Carnegie Mellon works very hard to create and maintain that sense of place, including enhancement of existing reading areas and plans for the creation of new ones. For many students, the library place connotes a warm, supportive atmosphere in which they are encouraged to pursue learning. As a returning Carnegie Mellon graduate student remarked recently, "Coming to the library just makes me feel smarter."

CONCLUSION

As the authors have argued, the future of libraries is undeniably digital. In this digital future, the quantity of information will con-

< 284 >

tinue to increase rapidly. Academic libraries will help their students and faculty to navigate through this overwhelming quantity of material with an array of automated devices that direct attention to important items, present relevant materials on topics, assist with the creation of new documents, and manage payment and intellectual property issues.

The academy faces serious challenges as it brings its system of scholarly communications into the digital environment. High journal prices are currently destroying traditional libraries. The Association of American Universities' nine principles offer guidance to how faculty and academic administrators should act to create a bright and affordable future for the academy and its libraries. An improved scholarly communications system, the mechanism for disseminating information about new knowledge, is essential for the health of all disciplines and of the academy itself.

The library as a place will continue. Many traditional services will still be provided there, while most new services will be available at student and faculty desktops in their offices and homes. Libraries will actively develop the new tools that support the digital library. They will contract for the provision of proprietary information, support the creation of new content in book and journal form, and teach information seeking and selection skills in a variety of forms. Most importantly, as they have in the past, librarians will be those trusted with maintaining the scholarly record for the future. Academic libraries will serve as the official archives of digital scholarly communication.

The introductory quotes for this chapter reference overwhelming quantities of information, while the vignettes in the center of the article discuss strategies for sorting through and understanding those quantities. Although the librarian of the past was valued for the ability to locate and secure more and more pieces of information, the librarian of the future will be valued for linking students and faculty with precisely those pieces of information that meet current needs.

The paper library had an attractive and fostering ambiance that will be difficult to replicate in the online environment. Generations of library patrons have sung paeans to their experiences in it, their serendipitous encounters with unexpected sources, and their feeling of continuity with knowledge from the past as they make forays into the future. The authors think that human connections and relationships are crucial. The authors hope that while utilitarian needs will be met more efficiently through the digital

< 285 >

than the paper library, higher level social and cultural needs will also be met through an active engagement of the community of academic librarians and their faculty colleagues with the patrons of the library.

Notes

[1] Lysakowski, Rich. "Titanic 2020." *CENSA*. 1999. Hawkins, Brian. "The Unsustainability of Traditional Libraries." *Executive Strategies*. v. 2, no. 3, 3. Gordon Bell and James N. Gray, "The Revolution Yet to Happen," part 1, chapter 1 in Denning, Peter J. and Metcalfe, Robert M., *Beyond Calculation: The Next Fifty Years of Computing*. New York: Copernicus, 1997.

[2] CHE. "Principles for Emerging Systems of Scholarly Publishing," May 10, 2000, http://www.tulane.edu/~aau/Principles5.10.00.html (visited 8/10/00).

[3] English, Ray and Hardesty, Larry. "Create Change! Shaping the Future of Scholarly Journal Publishing," *C&RL News*. June 2000, pp. 515, 518.

[4] CHE. "Principles for Emerging Systems . . ."

[5] "To Publish and Perish," Policy Perspectives 7, no. 4, March 1998, p. 2. http://www.arl.org/scomm/pew/pewrept.html

The initiatives are: end the preoccupation with numbers; be smart shoppers; get a handle on property rights; invest in electronic forms of scholarly publication; and decouple publication and faculty evaluation for the purposes of promotion and tenure.

[6] *Ibid*. 5–10.

[7] Kiernan, Vincent. "Non-Profit Journals are Cheaper than Commercial Ones, Study Finds," *Chronicle of Higher Education [Today's News]*. September 20, 1999. http://www.chronicle.com/daily/99/99092002n.htm (visited 8/15/00).

[8] Gleick, James. *Faster: The Acceleration of Just About Everything*. New York: Pantheon Books, 1999.

[9] Brown, John Seely and Duguid, Paul. *The Social Life of Information*. Boston: Harvard Business School Press, 2000.

[10] Henderson, Albert. "Information Science versus Science Policy," *Science*. Volume 289, Number 5477, July 14, 2000, p. 243.

[11] *Ibid*.

[12] Lesk, Michael E., "The Organization of Digital Libraries," *Science & Technology Libraries*. Volume 17, Numbers 9-15, 1999, pp. 24–25.

< 286 >

CULTURE, SOCIETY, AND THE ARTS

Judith Modell and Patricia Maurides

Judith Modell is Professor of Anthropology, History, and Art at Carnegie Mellon. Her most recent studies of adoption and foster care focus on the social impact of federal and state laws and practices. A new project involves gathering photographs, stories and drawings from children who are in foster care in Pittsburgh. Professor Modell received her Ph.D. from the University of Minnesota in 1978, and has been teaching at Carnegie Mellon since 1984.

Patricia Maurides is the director of two interdisciplinary degree-granting programs at Carnegie Mellon: the Bachelor of Humanities and Arts (BHA) and the Bachelor of Science and Arts (BSA). She often works collaboratively on projects that intersect the biological sciences and the visual arts. She received her MFA from Carnegie Mellon University, and has been working at the University since 1999.

Carnegie Mellon University has a long history of interdisciplinary approaches to research, scholarship and practice. Colleges of Engineering, Science, Humanities and Social Sciences, and Fine Arts provide a springboard for interdisciplinary projects and exhibits. These efforts are enhanced by the alertness to public policy evident at the Heinz School and by the technological inventiveness of a renowned College of Computer Science. At Carnegie Mellon, interdisciplinary ventures grow out of the initiatives of

< 287 >

individual faculty and students, and help to redefine the nature of the disciplines and their relationship to changes in the larger society. Such redefinition is especially important in the new century, with its intensification of global movements of populations, ideologies, knowledge, and resources. Education becomes part of far-reaching cultural, political, and economic internationalization.

Interdisciplinary endeavors have been variably visible on the Carnegie Mellon campus; some endeavors gain widespread recognition, both on and off campus, especially those that represent dramatic breakthroughs in a field, innovations in a technological area, or contributions to the rewriting of public legislation. At the same time, other less visible sorts of interdisciplinary activities occur on a more individual level and far more directed toward refining a critical approach or expanding an imaginative vision or blending perspectives on a particular problem. The second kind of activity has been characteristic of the interdisciplinary efforts that link the College of Fine Arts (CFA) with the College of Humanities and Social Sciences (H&SS). At Carnegie Mellon, the College of Fine Arts houses the Schools of Art, Design, Drama, Architecture, and Music. Each one of these has high standards for professional performance and production. In the past decade, collaboration across the five schools has expanded professional standards with new insights, alternative forms of practice, and actual cooperative projects. While generally all schools in the College emphasize practice and production skills, revision of what those activities mean for students and for faculty has been underway, with consequent changes in the curriculum. The Schools of Art and of Design, for instance, have each introduced interdisciplinary programs that recognize the connections between creativity, context, and culture.

During the 1990s, the College of Fine Arts shifted its programs more substantially as students and faculty both advocated the importance to any artist of familiarity with the social and historical settings of artistic activity. The College as a whole has expanded curriculum and research projects to include humanistic approaches, social scientific methodology, and techniques developed in the hard sciences. Increasingly, too, the CFA curriculum includes a focus on the conditions under which art is produced, exhibited, argued about, and (sometimes) destroyed—anywhere they occur.

Another aspect of this change has been closer collaboration between the College of Fine Arts and the College of Humanities

< 288 >

and Social Sciences. Faculty and students in the Schools of Fine Arts have increasingly turned to their colleagues in the humanities whose work focuses on the cultural and social contexts of arts performance, creativity, and responses to art production. In counterpart, historians, anthropologists, and literary critics are turning to their colleagues in Fine Arts, who understand the "making" of art in a specialized and distinctive way. Whatever the direction the turn is made, the resulting collaboration often exploits the technological expertise available on campus—adding technology to "culture"(where it belongs). Collaborative work between the Colleges at its best accentuates an awareness of the political and social ramifications of research, writing, and production.

INTERDISCIPLINARY PROGRAMS AND CENTERS

In this chapter we describe two existing collaborative programs at Carnegie Mellon, one a degree program and the other a Center. First, we describe the Bachelor of Arts and Humanities (BHA) and the (newer) Bachelor of Arts and Sciences (BSA) degrees. Second, we outline the purposes and plans of the Center for the Arts in Society (CAS). The evolution in the form, content and administrative structures of both programs illustrates the potentials as well as the perils in greater collaboration between practicing artists, scientists and technicians, and scholars of culture and history. Third, we investigate the implications: the problems and obstacles that make the paths to collaborative work bumpy and, occasionally, impossible. Fourth, in conclusion, we reflect on the implications of collaborative programs for linking the University to wider communities, including those beyond our national borders. Interdisciplinary efforts, such as those we describe, bear directly on the widespread concern with ethnic diversity and conflict, commemoration of the past, the role of memory in the politics of the present, and the importance of artistic representation to the assertion of cultural identity, among other timely issues.

We bring to this chapter our own experiences in interdisciplinary work. Judith Modell, a cultural anthropologist, began to explore the various ways in which anthropologists and the people with whom they work visualize their worlds. Moving away from her earlier concentration on verbal testimony, Modell, in collaboration with photographer Charlee Brodsky, discovered ways of

< 289 >

using "pictures" to elicit alternative—often complementary and sometimes contradictory—interpretations by individuals. Combining "seeing" with "telling," these interpretations link the personal, and biographical details, with the public, and political events. Modell and Brodsky worked together in Homestead, the well-known steel town just outside of Pittsburgh. Together and separately, through words and pictures, they evoked the responses of a community to the downfall of its mill. That project has had numerous ramifications, in the courses in Visual Anthropology Modell teaches, in her use of visual material in every one of her anthropological inquiries, and in her view of the programs and projects springing up on a campus where the techniques of combining the visual with the verbal now go way beyond camera and tape recorder.

Patricia Maurides is a visual artist and director of two undergraduate interdisciplinary degree programs (BHA & BSA). Maurides' professional training is multidisciplinary and includes graduate studies in both molecular biology and visual arts. Maurides integrates her interests in molecular genetics and psychology to probe issues of identity and origins in her art practice. She frequently uses her body as subject, screen, or conduit for memory play. Maurides teaches Art and Biology, a studio & laboratory artmaking course that examines similarities, differences and interactions between art and biology. This course involves students from several Colleges within the Carnegie Mellon community. Maurides frequently works collaboratively on projects that intersect the biological sciences and the visual arts.

Maurides is interested in the visual processes of both artists and research scientists. There are numerous scientific research practices whose raw data are predominantly visual, such as light and electron microscopy. These practices share with artmaking the processes of careful observation, awareness, perception and interpretation of visual information. Central is the intent to make visible what was once either inexpressible or impenetrable. These "seekers" are involved in unmasking reality, in revealing the nature of a real world, and in translating discoveries into media that are useful, beautiful, and pleasing to all who contemplate the results.

THE BACHELOR OF HUMANITIES AND ARTS

The Bachelor of Humanities and Arts (BHA) program began in the fall of 1993. It is a unique degree program jointly offered by

< 290 >

the University's College of Fine Arts and the College of Humanities and Social Sciences. The degree itself was established in good part in response to student demands: a number of students wanted to cross boundaries, either placing their own artistic endeavors in historic and social context, or wanting to learn how to practice the "art" they were also analyzing in the critical vocabulary of a humanistic discipline.

The BHA enables a student to receive broader exposure to the humanities and liberal arts than is generally possible through a Bachelor of Fine Arts degree, while obtaining deeper and more substantial training in the fine arts than is generally possible through a Bachelor of Arts or Bachelor of Science degree in H&SS.

Students who are accepted into the degree program enroll in courses in both Colleges. In CFA, the BHA student receives extensive training in one or more of the fine arts disciplines (art, architecture, design, drama and music); in H&SS, the student will receive fundamental training in humanistic and social science approaches, as well as advanced training in research methods, writing skills, and critical thought. The BHA program encourages students to use their electives, as well as independently designed courses, to combine the major with other interests, for instance, in business or computer science.

Some BHA students cautiously treat the degree as a dual major; others branch out into unique curricular paths. In either case, a student with a BHA degree leaves the University with the ability to speak the language of more than one discipline and, importantly, to listen to those who speak yet other "disciplinary" languages. This interdisciplinary education encourages students to embrace non-traditional approaches to problem solving, art practice, and research.

The central tenet of the BHA Program is to integrate and blend the concentrations in CFA and H&SS. A few examples illustrate the possibilities: a student concentrating in creative writing in H&SS and drama in CFA may integrate the two disciplines for a career in playwriting. A student whose concentration is psychology in H&SS and design in CFA combines these disciplines for a contribution to the field of User Interface Design or of Human Computer Interaction. Finally, a student concentrating in history and visual art gains skills and background knowledge to pursue a career in art criticism or museum curation.

For his independent honors project, one BHA student produced a journal of BHA work. In the foreword, he outlined his goal for the journal and in the process provided insight into the

< 291 >

strengths of the BHA and into one participant's engagement with the program. His statement is both exemplary of student work and illustrative of interdisciplinary projects on campus.

This is a journal of the works of students from Carnegie Mellon's Bachelor of Humanities and the Arts program. Although it is a highly selective and growing program, most students and even some faculty are unaware of it, and are unfamiliar with the educational advantages that it can provide its students. By showing the individual creativity of its students and the new techniques that they develop through the mixture of their concentrations, this journal displays the strength and potential of the BHA program.

Of course, the idea that diverse sources of knowledge provide strength in all areas of understanding is far from a new concept; the classic idea of the Renaissance Man involves a familiarity with a wide variety of skills that, in today's society, might be considered scattered and unfocused. But until people grasp many fields of human knowledge, they aren't fully able to grasp any of them individually. It is exactly this sort of diversity that has led to some of the most fascinating intuitive leaps in knowledge, from DaVinci's notebooks to Einstein's theories.

However, many of today's educational practices have involved the specialization of fields to such exclusive levels that they are almost fully isolated from their intellectual origins, and are not geared for anything outside of their highly focused concentrations. Many of these specializations have put up artificial boundaries between disciplines as intellectual inquiries, separating (for example) Humanities into history, literature, philosophy and others. Unnecessary gulfs have grown between related disciplines, separating Social Sciences, such as statistics and psychology, from other studies of Humanities.

It was not until attempting to compile the work for this journal that I came to realize how diverse the studies of BHA students are. From relatively obvious combinations, such as Drama and Media Studies or my own Creative Writing and Fine Art to the less immediately intuitive mixtures, such as Social and Decision Science and Design or Philosophy and Music, no two students bear exactly the same viewpoints. Thus, to better recognize the combinations of techniques that are being employed by a student, it is vital to understand what

< 292 >

areas of study they have examined. All works in this journal are preceded by the creator's name, concentrations, and a brief description of the work in their own words.

The diversity of these studies allows for the strength of the new techniques to develop. In a world where people are required to possess an increasingly wide variety of information, these techniques may prove to be the beginning of a new Renaissance.*

THE BACHELOR OF SCIENCES AND ARTS

Similar in principle and in pedagogical goals to the BHA, a Bachelor of Sciences and Arts (BSA) degree program began in 1999. The BSA combines the strengths of the College of Fine Arts and the Mellon College of Science (MCS). BSA students are jointly admitted to both CFA and MCS and, like the BHA, are "citizens" of two colleges. BSA students have a curricular concentration in CFA and a curricular concentration in MCS (biology, chemistry, physics or mathematical sciences). These are exceptional and very accomplished students with talents and gifts in the arts and sciences who choose to pursue an education simultaneously in these areas. BSA students very wisely recognize that their "art" and their interests in the sciences are integrated into their lives and do not wish to stop the practice of one in order to pursue the other.

The BSA, similar to the BHA, indicates how much of the push towards interdisciplinarity originates from students—and how imaginative the combinations can be. A few examples of work in this program are illustrative: a student studying architecture and biology is interested in relationships between hospital design/architecture and the optimal healing environments for patients. A musician who studies biology hopes to one day attend medical school and specialize in understanding injuries incurred through playing specific musical instruments. An art and biology student is interested in exploring the biological concepts of identity in her art practice.

Students in the BSA program in general have the opportunity to explore interdisciplinary concepts both in a studio environment and in a science laboratory. Access to two specialized contexts provides an opportunity to combine sophisticated technology, such as video-probe microscopy, with the (presumed) "whims" and the (learned) conventions of artistic production.

< 293 >

The BSA and the BHA elicit a good deal of enthusiasm from students and from faculty members. The result has been a burst of collaborative projects between colleges and a substantial interchange across ranks and disciplines. With a common interdisciplinary spirit of invention, research and imagination, and common administrative space, participants in the BHA and the BSA programs create a lively community on the campus.

Overall, the notion of community—and its flexibility—is crucial to these programs and a lesson for the wider integration of studies of arts, culture, science and society at Carnegie Mellon. Community in the BHA and BSA programs is supported through student advisory council meetings, a yearly BHA-BSA bus trip to the Smithsonian Museums, and the freshman BHA-BSA Integrative Seminar. "Community" also refers to the area and region surrounding the University; so, for example, the Integrative Seminar features an ongoing community outreach project in cooperation with The Pittsburgh Children's Museum and sixth graders from Cardinal Wright Regional School. This collaborative team was one of only 14 partnerships funded by the American Association for the Advancement of Science.

In addition to the Integrative Seminar, there are opportunities for BHA and BSA students to meet with faculty and professionals through several primary collaborative centers that exist on campus. These include the Center for the Arts in Society (described below), the STUDIO for Creative Inquiry, and the Regina Gouger Miller Gallery. These venues support and feature the fine arts as translators of the concerns of science and, too, of culture and society.

Overall, the BHA and BSA programs direct attention to the campus as a whole, as well as to the participants (faculty and students) in the programs. At the end of every academic year, students mount an exhibition of the work produced during the year. Such exhibits include multimedia artworks, poetry readings, dramatic performance, documentation of architectural projects, and paintings and other artistic expressions. Not only do these demonstrate the range of activities and of collaborative work, they also allow the whole community a look at the many meanings "interdisciplinary" can have. For an interdisciplinary venture to succeed at all, it must talk to a wider community, must draw in the concerns of that wider community, and must absorb contemporary issues in a number of arenas. The BHA and the BSA constitute an inspiration for other programs on campus.

< 294 >

The STUDIO for Creative Inquiry

The College of Fine Arts' STUDIO for Creative Inquiry (founded in 1989) has a tradition of supporting collaborative projects between the fine arts and the humanities, sciences, and technology. The broad mission of the STUDIO is to support experimental and cross-disciplinary work in the arts and to facilitate work in two major areas: artistic creation and the development of educational tools.

Prime examples of the STUDIO's multidisciplinary projects are two multimedia interactive planetarium shows. The first, *Journey into the Living Cell* (1993), was a collaboration among the STUDIO, Carnegie Mellon's Science and Technology Center, and the Carnegie Science Center. The second, *Gray Matters-The Brain Movie* (1999), was a collaboration among the STUDIO, the Center for the Neural Basis of Cognition, and the Carnegie Science Center. Both shows were funded by the National Science Foundation and involved collaboration among artists, scientists, writers, educators, and museum professionals.

In addition, the STUDIO's current *Nine Mile Run Greenway Project* connects the expertise and concerns of artists, scientists, engineers, historians, ecologists and planners in a broad-ranging interdisciplinary effort to address the challenges and opportunities faced in transforming an urban, industrial waste site in Pittsburgh into a sustainable environment of private housing and public greenspace.

Regina Gouger Miller Gallery

The Regina Gouger Miller Gallery in the Purnell Center for the Arts opened in January 2000. This gallery is a University venue for inter/multidisciplinary collaborative and site-specific projects involving contemporary arts and other disciplines. It routinely provides a public forum for experiencing innovative projects in science, and visual and performing arts. The recent exhibition, Fusion! Artists in a Research Setting featured projects and panel discussion series about highly collaborative processes and multidisciplinary methods.

< 295 >

The Center for the Arts in Society (CAS)

The success of the BHA program encouraged efforts to implement further the ongoing collaborations between students and faculty in the College of Humanities and Social Sciences and the College of Fine Arts. While strong in their own right, the students in the BHA program also illustrated the need for expanding the kinds of projects, courses, and sensibilities they were developing independently as well as under the close tutelage of interested faculty in both Colleges. In the fall of 1998, Dean Martin Prekop of the College of Fine Arts and Dean Peter Stearns of the College of Humanities and Social Sciences drafted a proposal for a Center for the Arts in Society. The goal was to create a Center that would build on interests in merging arts and humanities that extend across all the colleges on the Carnegie Mellon campus.

In June 2000, with a generous grant from the A.W. Mellon Foundation (New York) and matching funds from Carnegie Mellon, the Center for the Arts in Society was established. The Center has four main thrusts: (1) developing a curriculum that not only merges arts and humanities but also recognizes the technological and scientific strengths on campus; (2) developing interdisciplinary research and performance projects; (3) sponsoring distinguished visiting faculty members, visiting fellows, lectures, and (every other year) large-scale conferences; (4) developing ways of intersecting more closely with the multiple arts, cultural, and historical institutions in Pittsburgh and the Western Pennsylvania region. The Center currently has a faculty membership of 30, representing all Schools in the College of Fine Arts, the Humanities Departments of History (with Anthropology), Modern Languages and Cultures, Philosophy, English (with Rhetoric and Creative Writing), and other units on campus, e.g., the STUDIO for Creative Inquiry.

A number of these faculty members have long been involved in collaborations between fine arts and humanities. Existing courses and projects form the foundation for the Center's move into the future. These include team-taught courses and independently taught courses that cross the boundaries between disciplines. A few examples include: Documenting the Visual, team taught by a photographer and a literary historian; Visual Anthropology, taught in the History Department; Language in Design, combining principles of rhetoric with principles of design; and Introduction to Interdisciplinary Studies in Music. The Center

< 296 >

will organize existing cross-disciplinary and multidisciplinary courses into a coherent curriculum that will be the basis for a university-wide minor. A Minor in Arts in Society allows students in any department or college to bring together an interest in "art" (however defined) with an inquiry into the contexts—historical, technological, cultural—of arts production and display; by its nature, a minor adds coherence to disparate interests and approaches, while drawing in a far wider range of students than a major. The minor will include a broad introductory course for freshmen and an intensely focused seminar for graduating seniors. The capstone and the culminating courses also provide students with experiences in common, with a vocabulary for considering the arts in a modern world, and an opportunity freely to talk within and against disciplinary boundaries. The introductory course and culminating seminars will be diversely designed, depending on faculty interest and student demand.

The Center also builds on existing research projects. With a long tradition at Carnegie Mellon, projects that merge disciplinary approaches and methods can now be directed toward assessing the role of the arts in solving social problems and in confronting cultural conflicts. Examples of existing projects include: a photographic and anthropological study of responses in Homestead, Pennsylvania to the shutdown and destruction of the once-famous United States Steel Homestead Works; a mural in Frankfurt, Germany, designed to represent a population's understandings of history and cultural change through their own drawings; a poetry project with a local high school, in which students from Carnegie Mellon work with high school students on writing, criticizing, and preparing poems for textual and oral presentation. Projects like these link the training and the skills present on a university campus to community needs and resources. Under the auspices of the Center, such projects draw on the long history and the cultural diversity of community-oriented projects in order both to develop critical analyses and to give voice to groups of people struggling with "self-representation" and with rapid modernization.

At the same time, an important part of the Center's goal is to problematize the meaning of "community." Together, participants in the Center question that, and other taken-for-granted concepts. The Frankfurt mural project exemplifies one approach to exploring the concept of community and, consequently, the process of collaboration: residents' input through drawings and interviews create both the form and the content of the piece. In the future,

< 297 >

the Center will continue to develop innovative ways of approaching community, eliciting interpretations of the concept from groups of people who share geographical boundaries or political interests or ethnic backgrounds and are simultaneously searching for ways to represent (and communicate) their commonalties. One reaction to internationalization has been an intense localism: in neighborhoods, cities, and regions, groups of people are engaged in recalling and commemorating their distinct identities, often through a work of art. Recently, America has seen an outburst of commemoration, and an accompanying controversy about the form, content, and placement of memorializing monuments. From the debate over the Vietnam War memorial to the arguments over the commemorative objects displayed after the Oklahoma City bombing and the Columbine massacre, it is clear that a view of "arts in society" occupies the "person in the street" as well as the scholar in her ivory tower.

On such issues of community art and public memorials, common to cultures over time and across space, the methods of the anthropologist and the historian enhance, and are enhanced by, those of the art historian as she contemplates the evolution of art forms and their meanings to creator and to spectator. In many ways, students are way ahead of faculty in contemplating these kinds of blends—as well as in adding technological expertise to the contemplation. During the fall of 2000, a group of students designed three new "art works" for the campus: one, a fountain which offered both aesthetic pleasure and a place to gather; two, a walking robot, prepared to answer questions or to provide a reassuring message at the press of a heart-shaped button; and an electronic "fence" housed in an aesthetically designed and highly interactive "booth" to provide information and a forum for debate in the center of campus. These are creative ideas, emerging from both the Center and from the initiatives of students working closely with faculty members. The Center for the Arts in Society will continue to foster and support curricular innovations that have this kind of applied impact on the University and on the wider community. Such innovations address the knotty issue of the meaning of the "arts in society," a phrase under continual debate.

Through these and other projects, the Center not only preserves the interdisciplinarity that marked its founding, but adds to that a deep engagement with "community," however and wherever that is defined. In fact, one of the goals is to consider the term "community" and the nature of representation within a community. Who is one addressing, as artist, scientist, or human-

< 298 >

ist, and how? What are the political implications of defining a community in one way and not another? How can researchers, scholars, and artists elicit the memories, stories, and interpretations of those whose interests and whose modes of expression are not their own? These are among the questions Center faculty and students will keep on the University's agenda.

New projects and future plans include: a centralized kiosk that will provide information about arts and culture on the Carnegie Mellon campus, in Pittsburgh, and perhaps ultimately in a broader area. The kiosk will utilize electronic media and thus the unique capabilities available at Carnegie Mellon; it will be interactive and accessible by students and faculty from all over campus. The design of the kiosk will result from a competition among selected entrants, so that the aesthetic dimension is given as much play as the technological and the informational dimensions.

Another project in the planning stages is the development of an archive. Under Center auspices, an Archive of Controversy will be created to house data on controversies surrounding the production and exhibiting of art works. Covering a broad range of issues, as well as spanning both space and time, the archive can be a valuable resource for scholars, for news media, for practicing artists, and for critics from a variety of disciplines. The project suits the University particularly well, since its creation draws on the technological skills as well as the academic strengths of the community. Construction of the archives—its form and content—may well yield a full-scale conference, as well as class work, small research projects, and other venues for ongoing discussions of art-in-context. An interactive dimension will permit informal discussions and debates to occur on a regular basis.

The idea prevalent in Center discussions, of breaking down the boundaries not only between disciplines but also between disciplines and the (so-called) outside world comes to fruition in this kind of project. Moreover, the project brings together students, faculty, and individuals with other skills in a collaborative undertaking.

REDRAWING BOUNDARIES AND BUILDING BRIDGES

The BHA and BSA degrees and the Center for the Arts in Society are prominent examples of the way in which Carnegie Mellon has utilized both its pedagogical traditions and its attention to contemporary events to develop new initiatives. They are not the

< 299 >

only examples. Changes in the teaching of arts histories and in the expectations for studio work already expand the concept of art and of the artist in the College of Fine Arts. Curricular development in the College of Humanities and Social Sciences, too, recognizes that "art" is a central cultural phenomenon, with political implications and with a role in the decisions governments make, in the ups and downs of a market, and in the "look" of a community. Thus the bridging goes on, albeit informally and often at the edges. Judging by the enrollments in courses that make such bridges, however, they attract the students who ordinarily are not exposed to "arts" and "humanities"—students in the Colleges of Science, Engineering, and Computer Science. Students ask for a rounded education, for an exposure to approaches to the world that are an alternative to "quantification," and that demonstrate the philosophical underpinnings to the ways in which the world is measured and mapped. As these students recognize, science belongs with humanities and arts, another (cultural) version of seeing, interpreting, and presenting insights to a surrounding society.

Do these and other changes at Carnegie Mellon simply represent one more turn in the prism of liberal arts? After all, liberal arts have been the subject of debate for decades in the United States and risks sounding "old hat." Combining the arts and the humanities in a degree (BHA) and through the Center for the Arts in Society certainly does suggest an old-fashioned liberal arts education. Expanding a liberal arts curriculum is not an unworthy goal. But given the distinctive features of Carnegie Mellon as an educational and a research-based institution, liberal arts could not simply sit in an old-fashioned mold. The rest of the campus impinges, for good and for bad: challenging the "uses" of a more rounded education, demanding reasons for turning away from one's "own" discipline, and questioning the worth of looking beyond the terms that are set by a profession. The challenges are fine; the responses are not so easy.

One response is to draw on the whole range of disciplines and approaches on the campus, and to make them part of "liberal arts." As the BSA exemplifies, "science" is no longer inevitably one side of a two-culture world—a trope that crops up too often in informal discussions of the University. It is a convenient and recognizable trope, shoring up the strengths of each side but also denying the blurring and the blending that currently characterize work on either side. The concepts in the title of this chapter, "society" and "culture," are encompassing, and a reminder that

< 300 >

human endeavors cannot be boxed in, in real life, and should not be boxed in a curriculum. While engineering and science projects and the applied nature of policy research push towards team work, the humanities and the arts are mistakenly relegated (by practitioners, often, as well as outsiders) to the category of "completely individualized" work. These are strong biases, not always detected, and they obscure the changes in "humanities" and "arts" which occur—perhaps mainly outside the academy walls, in street theater, say, or in "performance art," or in the collaborations between anthropologists and photographers, historians and musicians, and scientists and artists that reach a wide audience.

The obstacles to a merging of arts and humanities, then, have to do with engrained, ethnocentric expectations about scholarship, practice, and value. There are also obstacles of communication, related to expectations but also stemming from different "languages." To collaborate means to learn another's language. How, then, does the humanist *learn* to "speak" art? The artist *learn* the language of literary criticism? And, in each case, learn enough to argue, to grapple with, and to reject ideas the other expresses? Language is not narrowly defined here but refers broadly to ways of perceiving, interpreting, and describing the world. Ideally, what is translated is "sight" and "insight," not just words, styles, and methods. Obviously, patience and time are needed, and patience and time are not an abundant commodity at a highly competitive university. So they have to be scripted in, as we have suggested through courses, projects, and supporting programs and centers. They have to be scripted in through financial and institutional support, some of it pragmatic—an administrative framework, office space, and so on—and some of it philosophical—recognizing what was valuable in the old-fashioned notion of a "rounded" education.

And, last but not least, there is the problem of the "world out there." A merger of studies of arts, society, and culture faces the challenge of an increasingly global marketplace—of products, people, ideas, and innovations. Nothing really exists in separate spaces any more, as anthropologists who question even the concept of "society" itself recognize. Awareness of the collapse of boundaries does not, however, lighten the task of blending disciplines. Rather, such awareness compels educators and students, practitioners and scholars, to consider the political implications of combining modes of study. It obliges us to be especially alert to the possibly negative combinations that cross not only "fields" but also academic cultures, and fail to absorb the changing and

< 301 >

contradictory interests of the "ordinary" people of the world. With a long history of confidence in combining disciplinary approaches and a recognition of the importance of doing things "hands on," Carnegie Mellon is well positioned to move the study of society, culture, and the arts into an international arena.

Note

* Frederick Zeleny, Creative Writing and Fine Art.

References

Clifford, James. (1988) *The Predicament of Culture: Twentieth Century Ethnography, Literature, and Art.* Cambridge: Harvard University Press.

Geertz, Clifford. (1973) *The Interpretation of Cultures.* New York: Basic Books.

Gell, Alfred. (1998) *Art and Agency: An Anthropological Theory.* New York: Oxford University Press.

Gillis, John (ed.). (1994) *Commemorations: The Politics of National Identity.* Princeton, NJ: Princeton University Press.

Mitchell, W.J.T. (1994) *Picture Theory: Essays on Verbal and Visual Representation.* Chicago: The University of Chicago Press.

Modell, J. and C. Brodsky. (1998) *A Town Without Steel: Envisioning Homestead.* Pittsburgh: University of Pittsburgh Press.

Shlain, Leonard. (1991) *Art and Physics: Parallel Visions in Space, Time, and Light.* New York: William Morrow.

Web Resources

http://www.mitpress.mit.edu/e-journals/Leonardo/index.html
Leonardo Online International Journal for Arts and Sciences

http://www.exploratorium.com
The Exploratorium: The Museum of Science, Art, and Human Perception

http://www.umanitoba.ca/publications/mosaic/home/shtml
Mosaic: A Journal for the Interdisciplinary Study of Literature.

http://www.asci.org/
Arts and Sciences Collaborations, Inc.

http://www.janushead.org/JHSspg99/index.cfm
Janus-head: Journal of Interdisciplinary Studies in Literature and Continental Philosophy

< 302 >